Daily

GRADE 6

Fundamentals

Writing: Kathleen Jorgensen
Content Editing: Lisa Vitarisi Mathews
Copy Editing: Cathy Harber
Art Direction: Yuki Meyer
Design/Production: Jessica Onken
Susan Lovell
Paula Acojido

EMC 3246

Evan-Moor.
Helping Children Learn

Visit
teaching-standards.com
to view a correlation
of this book.
This is a free service.

Correlated to State and Common Core State Standards

Congratulations on your purchase of some of the finest teaching materials in the world.

Photocopying the pages in this book is permitted for single-classroom use only. Making photocopies for additional classes or schools is prohibited.

CONTENTS

What's Inside?

Daily Fundamentals has 30 weeks of cross-curricular skills practice. Each week provides targeted practice with language, math, and reading skills. The focused daily tasks progress in difficulty as students move from Day 1 tasks to Day 5 tasks. Item types range from multiple choice and matching to constructed response and open-ended questions.

Language items practice grammar, mechanics, spelling, and vocabulary.

Math items practice number and operations, algebraic thinking, geometry, measurement and data, and problem solving.

Reading items practice core reading comprehension skills such as inference, prediction, author's purpose, main idea and details, summary, fact and opinion, nonfiction text features, and literary analysis.

One language skill is practiced each week. A variety of item types provides rigorous practice and adds interest.

Math items focus on one concept or skill each week and provide opportunities for applying a variety of strategies.

Reading items target one reading comprehension or analysis skill each week and are based on nonfiction and fiction text selections. Questions elicit the use of multiple levels of thinking skills.

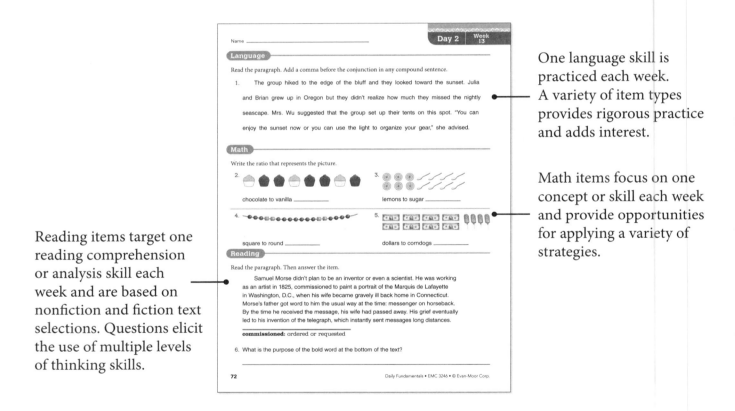

Answer Key

Correct or exemplar responses are shown on a reduced version of the actual page. An * is used to indicate an open-ended item or an item with many ways to word the answer. Accept any reasonable response.

How to Use This Book

Using *Daily Fundamentals* as morning work or bell ringers

Have the daily practice activity on students' desks when they arrive in the morning, after recess, or during a transitional period. Have students complete the assignment independently. Then have them share their answers and the strategy or approach they used. Encourage discussion about each item so students can share their thinking and provide support and insights to one another. These discussions may also provide you with teachable moments and information to guide your instruction.

Using *Daily Fundamentals* for homework

Assign one weekly unit at the beginning of each week. Students will have the autonomy to manage their time to complete the assignment, and they will benefit from the focused practice of language, math, and reading comprehension skills. At the end of the week, display the answer key and allow students to correct their own work. Facilitate a class discussion about the items and allow students to share their answers. Encourage students to model how to solve problems or answer items that their classmates may have struggled with.

Using *Daily Fundamentals* as an informal assessment

You may wish to use the weekly lessons as an informal assessment of students' competencies. Because each week's practice focuses on a particular skill or concept, the tasks provide you with a detailed view of each student's level of mastery.

Skills Scope and Sequence

Use the scope and sequence chart to identify the specific skills that students are practicing.

Student Progress Chart

Students can monitor their own progress by recording their daily scores and thinking about their success with different skills. Reproduce and distribute the progress chart to students at the beginning of each week. For older students, you may wish to have them write the number correct out of the total number of items.

Student Record Sheet

Record students' scores on the record sheet. This form will provide you with a snapshot of each student's skills mastery in language, math, and reading and serve as a resource to track students' progress throughout the year.

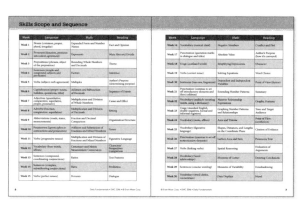

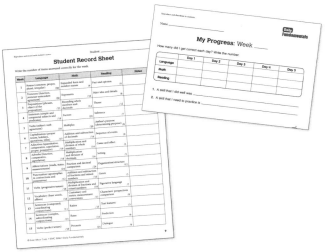

Skills Scope and Sequence

Week	Language	Math	Reading
Week 1	Nouns (common, proper, plural, irregular)	Expanded Form and Number Names	Fact and Opinion
Week 2	Pronouns (function, pronoun-antecedent agreement)	Exponents	Main Idea and Details
Week 3	Prepositions (phrases, object of the preposition)	Rounding Whole Numbers and Decimals	Theme
Week 4	Sentences (simple and compound subjects and predicates)	Factors	Inference
Week 5	Verbs (subject-verb agreement)	Multiples	Author's Purpose (determining purpose)
Week 6	Capitalization (proper nouns, holidays, quotations, titles)	Addition and Subtraction of Decimals	Sequence of Events
Week 7	Adjectives (quantitative, comparative, superlative, proper, possessive)	Multiplication and Division of Whole Numbers	Cause and Effect
Week 8	Adverbs (function, comparative, superlative)	Multiplication and Division of Decimals	Setting
Week 9	Abbreviations (roads, states, measurements)	Fraction and Decimal Comparison	Organization/Structure
Week 10	Punctuation (apostrophes in contractions and possessives)	Addition and Subtraction of Fractions and Mixed Numbers	Genre
Week 11	Verbs (progressive tenses)	Multiplication and Division of Fractions and Mixed Numbers	Figurative Language
Week 12	Vocabulary (base words, affixes)	Customary and Metric Measurement Conversions	Characters' Perspectives Comparison
Week 13	Sentences (compound, coordinating conjunctions)	Ratios	Text Features
Week 14	Sentences (complex, subordinating conjunctions)	Rates	Prediction
Week 15	Verbs (perfect tenses)	Percents	Dialogue

Daily Fundamentals • EMC 3246 • © Evan-Moor Corp.

Week	Language	Math	Reading
Week 16	Vocabulary (context clues)	Negative Numbers	Conflict and Plot
Week 17	Punctuation (quotation marks in dialogue and titles)	Absolute Value	Author's Purpose (how it's conveyed)
Week 18	Usage (confused words)	Simplifying Expressions	Character
Week 19	Verbs (correct tense)	Solving Equations	Word Choice
Week 20	Sentences (run-ons, fragments)	Dependent and Independent Variables	Point of View (fiction)
Week 21	Punctuation (commas to set off introductory elements and direct address)	Extending Number Patterns	Summary
Week 22	Vocabulary (multiple-meaning words, using a dictionary)	Number Relationship Expressions	Graphic Features
Week 23	Usage (standard English, double negatives, formal and informal registers)	Graphing Number Patterns and Relationships	Tone and Target Audience
Week 24	Vocabulary (roots, affixes)	Area and Volume	Point of View (nonfiction)
Week 25	Vocabulary (figurative language)	Shapes, Distances, and Lengths on the Coordinate Plane	Citation of Evidence
Week 26	Punctuation (commas to set off nonrestrictive elements)	Surface Area and Nets	Persuasive Text
Week 27	Verbs (linking verbs)	Spatial Reasoning	Evaluation of Arguments
Week 28	Vocabulary (word relationships)	Measures of Center	Drawing Conclusions
Week 29	Sentences (concise wording)	Measures of Variability	Foreshadowing
Week 30	Vocabulary (word choice, connotation)	Data Displays	Mood

Name _____

My Progress: Week _____

How many did I get correct each day? Write the number.

	Day 1	**Day 2**	**Day 3**	**Day 4**	**Day 5**
Language					
Math					
Reading					

1. A skill that I did well was _____.

2. A skill that I need to practice is _____.

Name _____

My Progress: Week _____

How many did I get correct each day? Write the number.

	Day 1	**Day 2**	**Day 3**	**Day 4**	**Day 5**
Language					
Math					
Reading					

1. A skill that I did well was _____.

2. A skill that I need to practice is _____.

Student: _____

Student Record Sheet

Write the number of items answered correctly for the week.

Week	Language	Math	Reading	Notes
1	Nouns (common, proper, plural, irregular) /28	Expanded form and number names /9	Fact and opinion /8	
2	Pronouns (function, pronoun-antecedent agreement) /20	Exponents /16	Main idea and details /8	
3	Prepositions (phrases, object of the preposition) /23	Rounding whole numbers and decimals /14	Theme /12	
4	Sentences (simple and compound subjects and predicates) /18	Factors /29	Inference /7	
5	Verbs (subject-verb agreement) /16	Multiples /20	Author's purpose (determining purpose) /8	
6	Capitalization (proper nouns, holidays, quotations, titles) /15	Addition and subtraction of decimals /14	Sequence of events /9	
7	Adjectives (quantitative, comparative, superlative, proper, possessive) /19	Multiplication and division of whole numbers /16	Cause and effect /5	
8	Adverbs (function, comparative, superlative) /18	Multiplication and division of decimals /16	Setting /5	
9	Abbreviations (roads, states, measurements) /24	Fraction and decimal comparison /24	Organization/structure /12	
10	Punctuation (apostrophes in contractions and possessives) /12	Addition and subtraction of fractions and mixed numbers /16	Genre /5	
11	Verbs (progressive tenses) /16	Multiplication and division of fractions and mixed numbers /18	Figurative language /7	
12	Vocabulary (base words, affixes) /18	Customary and metric measurement conversions /11	Characters' perspectives comparison /8	
13	Sentences (compound, coordinating conjunctions) /11	Ratios /15	Text features /5	
14	Sentences (complex, subordinating conjunctions) /13	Rates /14	Prediction /6	
15	Verbs (perfect tenses) /19	Percents /24	Dialogue /6	

Student Record Sheet, *continued*

Week	Language	Math	Reading	Notes
16	Vocabulary (context clues) /12	Negative numbers /24	Conflict and plot /5	
17	Punctuation (quotation marks in dialogue and titles) /17	Absolute value /22	Author's purpose (how it's conveyed) /5	
18	Usage (confused words) /20	Simplifying expressions /21	Character /6	
19	Verbs (correct tense) /11	Solving equations /17	Word choice /6	
20	Sentences (run-ons, fragments) /9	Dependent and independent variables /10	Point of view (fiction) /5	
21	Punctuation (commas to set off introductory elements and direct address) /24	Extending number patterns /5	Summary /6	
22	Vocabulary (multiple-meaning words, using a dictionary) /9	Number relationship expressions /10	Graphic features /7	
23	Usage (standard English, double negatives, formal and informal registers) /10	Graphing number patterns and relationships /12	Tone and target audience /6	
24	Vocabulary (roots, affixes) /16	Area and volume /11	Point of view (nonfiction) /10	
25	Vocabulary (figurative language) /9	Shapes, distances, and lengths on the coordinate plane /9	Citation of evidence /6	
26	Punctuation (commas to set off nonrestrictive elements) /14	Surface area and nets /6	Persuasive text /5	
27	Verbs (linking verbs) /20	Spatial reasoning /5	Evaluation of arguments /6	
28	Vocabulary (word relationships) /14	Measures of center /12	Drawing conclusions /5	
29	Sentences (concise wording) /13	Measures of variability /16	Foreshadowing /5	
30	Vocabulary (word choice, connotation) /9	Data displays /5	Mood /5	

Daily Fundamentals • EMC 3246 • © Evan-Moor Corp.

Language

Read the sentence. Complete it with the correct pronoun(s) to match the underlined antecedent(s).

1. After Paolo showed <u>Kim and me</u> the problem, he showed _____ how to fix it.

2. When <u>Pam</u> or <u>I</u> call you, bring up your project and give it to _____ or _____.

3. Even though <u>they</u> had good directions, our house was difficult for _____ to find.

4. Pointing to <u>Juan</u>, I said, "If it weren't for _____, my dog would still be missing."

Math

Write the term as an expression.

5. 16^4

6. $\left(\frac{2}{7}\right)^3$

7. 12.5^2

_____   _____   _____

Circle the expression that is equivalent to $\left(\frac{1}{8}\right)^5$. Then explain your choice.

8. $\frac{1}{8} \times 5$ $\frac{1}{8} \times \frac{1}{5}$ $\frac{1}{8} \times \frac{1}{8} \times \frac{1}{8} \times \frac{1}{8} \times \frac{1}{8}$

_____

Reading

Read the paragraph. Then answer the items.

      Koa Halpern was raised as a vegetarian, so he hadn't given much thought to fast food or the problems associated with it. That changed when his family hosted a foreign exchange student. Their guest's first goal was to eat at a fast-food restaurant. Halpern wondered what the appeal was. After a lot of research, his website was born.

9. Write what the text is mostly about in your own words.

_____

10. Write one supporting detail from the text in your own words.

_____

Language

Read the sentences. Write a possessive pronoun to match the underlined antecedent.

1. That's not <u>my notebook</u>. _____ has a green cover.

2. Our seats are better than <u>the Asadas' seats</u>. _____ are in row 23.

3. <u>Your camera</u> takes better pictures than my camera. May I borrow _____?

4. <u>Carla's apartment</u> is at the end of the building. My apartment is right next to _____.

Math

Simplify the expression.

5. 4.3×10^7

6. 9.9×10^{11}

7. 3.6×10^8

_____   _____   _____

What is an advantage of writing very big numbers as an expression with a power of 10?

8. _____

_____

Reading

Read the paragraph. Then answer the items.

It seemed that 17-year-old Liu Wu's purpose in life was to play pranks on the gentle artisans who lived in the city. He spent his days stealing or damaging their goods or playing tricks on them. His father was a well-respected merchant and a strict father. But most of the year he was away from the city, trading with other merchants.

9. How did Liu Wu treat the townspeople where he lived? Give an example.

_____

10. Why didn't Liu Wu's father discipline him better?

_____

Language

Read the sentence. Underline the prepositional phrase(s). Then circle the object of the preposition(s).

1. Give a permission slip to each student.

2. You'll find the stairs just beyond the kitchen.

3. Please buy some fruit for our guests.

4. We bought Dad a new camera to take on our vacation.

5. The store where we usually shop is right around the corner.

6. Look at the stars falling across the sky!

Math

Complete the sentence with a rounded number.

7. School Stuff sells color markers for about

   $_____ per set.

$4.98

93.8

8. I weigh about _____ pounds.

Reading

Read the paragraph. Then answer the items.

Once upon a time, a farmer, a cabinet maker, and a street sweeper visited King Kalil with a complaint. "Why should we work so hard, day after day, to support your army? They may be ready to defend the land, but so far, they have done nothing but enjoy the food, materials, and services we provide. They produce nothing," the trio protested.

9. What is a theme of this text? _____

10. What issue in the text illustrates this theme?

    _____

    _____

11. Describe a situation in your life or someone else's life that illustrates the same theme.

    _____

    _____

Language

Read the sentence. Underline the prepositional phrase(s). Then circle the object of the preposition(s).

1. Please send the package to us soon.

2. Tate's favorite teacher is right next to me in the photo.

3. Our grandparents always hide little gifts for my sister and me to find.

4. The Goldfarbs found a park near them after they moved.

5. The student beside you is my math tutor.

6. Make your bed and clean beneath it.

Math

Complete the paragraph with rounded numbers. Then answer the item.

7.   Khalid was trying to decide where to vacation in March. In Coalville, the average March rainfall is 2.31 inches. In Stagway, it is 8.14 inches. Khalid said, "I'd rather go to Coalville because it rains only about

_____ inches that month. I'd need

an umbrella to deal with the _____ inches of rain we might get in Stagway!"

8. Why are rounded measurements more appropriate in this situation?

_____

_____

Reading

Read the paragraph. Then answer the items.

On a shelf inside the barn were bricks of aging cheese. Crow pranced around the cheeses, stopping to peck at each brick, until he finally found the perfect flavor. Crow boldly pulled off such a large piece of the cheese that he had trouble flying back to his nest. The farmer heard the crow flapping his wings madly and gave chase. The bird narrowly missed the farmer's grasp and almost dropped his treasure! When the rest of the flock returned from eating bugs and worms in the farmer's freshly plowed field, Crow would show off the cheese and devour it in front of them.

9. Explain how the theme of greed relates to the action in the text.

_____

_____

10. Would the theme be the same if Crow had found a large bug in the field? Explain your answer.

_____

Language

Read the sentence. Underline the prepositional phrase(s). Read the sentence again without the prepositional phrase. Then explain the phrase's function.

1. Passengers on the Denver flight have arrived at Gate 15.

   _____

   _____

2. A colony of bees includes a queen, workers, scouts, and drones.

   _____

   _____

Math

Circle any of the situations in which rounding a number would make sense.

3. a) deciding how much money to bring to a store

   b) measuring ingredients in a recipe

   c) timing a race

   d) measuring lumber to construct a desk

   e) determining whether it's cold enough to wear a wool sweater

   f) figuring out the fastest route to school

   g) weighing vegetables at the cash register

Reading

Read the paragraph. Then answer the items.

Traveling to Alta California with mules and cattle proved to be a challenge for our families. After the hot summer days had passed, it was windy and barren, and the desert provided little water and grass for our animals. After a month, we reached the banks of the Colorado River. The cold, bitter winter had made fording the river impossible. We had never seen such a wide river and such rushing water. Finally, a narrow flow was found to the north, where thick brush scratched our arms and legs and icy winds tossed dust at us.

4. Write one theme that you think is explored in this text. Explain how you identified the theme.

   _____

   _____

5. Write a sentence that could be added to the text that supports the theme.

   _____

   _____

Language

Read the sentence. Draw a line to separate the complete subject from the complete predicate.

1. The family of field mice ran when they heard the foreign noise.

2. The loud buzzing sound from the forest whined on and on.

3. Suddenly, the mice in their hideout heard a tremendous crashing sound!

4. The largest spruce tree in the woods landed with a huge thud that echoed.

Math

Write all the factors of the given number.

5. **64** _____

6. **120** _____

7. **79** _____

8. **51** _____

9. **143** _____

Reading

Read the paragraphs. Then answer the items.

"I can't just *not* go," Christine said exasperated. Tamara was not even trying to understand. "My parents are going!"

Tamara's fingers pushed through the cool grass. "Actually," she said, "you could stay with us. My parents would take care of you if you didn't want to go. I know they would."

10. What is most likely Christine and Tamara's relationship?

_____

11. What is Tamara probably unhappy about?

_____

Language

Read the sentence. Circle the simple subject and underline the simple predicate.

1. The old house on the hill creaked when the door was pushed open.

2. Its weary and sagging floors groaned at the sudden movement.

3. Abandoned spiderwebs hung like curtains in the corners.

4. Finally someone was coming to give the lonely house some love.

Math

Write the number as an expression using prime factors.

5. **20** _____

6. **63** _____

7. **54** _____

8. **66** _____

9. **39** _____

10. **150** _____

11. **32** _____

12. **105** _____

13. **210** _____

14. **231** _____

Reading

Read the paragraph. Then answer the items.

"Great joke," Beth said to Mary as she pointed to a motionless iguana stretched out on top of the TV. Mary laughed as she watched her misplaced pet climb down the front of the TV and crawl toward her. Beth exclaimed, "It's even got batteries!"

15. What did Beth think was sitting on her TV?

_____

16. Why did she think the iguana had batteries?

_____

Language

Read the sentence with a compound subject. Circle all of the simple subjects.

1. J.K. Rowling and S.E. Hinton are my favorite authors.

2. The little scruffy dog and the large black bear stared at each other tensely.

3. Jaime's brother, Katie's cousin, and George went to Reshma's party.

4. State parks across the country and California's beaches have been photographed many times.

Math

Find the greatest common factor (GCF) of the number pair.

5. 15, 25 _____   10. 36, 20 _____

6. 16, 26 _____   11. 44, 66 _____

7. 21, 28 _____   12. 19, 57 _____

8. 20, 30 _____   13. 24, 60 _____

9. 32, 40 _____   14. 45, 75 _____

Reading

Read the paragraph. Then answer the item.

Daniel Inouye represented Hawaii in Congress for 53 years. As an American born to Japanese parents, he was forbidden from serving in the military. He appealed to the White House and was eventually allowed to join the army in a Japanese American unit. After being seriously injured during World War II, he studied government, law, and economics. In Congress, he helped pass laws on behalf of minorities and the disabled.

15. Write a description of how Daniel Inouye may have felt after the war.

_____

_____

Language

Read the sentence with a compound predicate. Circle all of the simple predicates.

1. During summer vacation, Janine visited her grandparents and read five books.

2. I have been to the zoo and know all about giraffes.

3. At the county fair, Micah will ride the Zipper or look at the 4-H animal displays first.

4. Last night, Eliana called me and asked me to help her study.

Math

Read the problem. Then answer the items.

David is organizing magazines into boxes at the school library. He has 18 issues of *Cobblestone* and 12 issues of *National Geographic Kids*. He wants to put the same number of issues in each box. Each box will have only one type of magazine.

5. What is the greatest number of issues he can put in each box? _____

6. How many boxes of each magazine will there be?

_____ boxes of *Cobblestone* and _____ boxes of *National Geographic Kids*

Reading

Read the paragraph. Then answer the item.

Seven-year-old Helen Keller was trapped inside a dark and quiet world. A fever she had as an infant had left her blind and deaf. She used simple signs to let her family know her most basic needs, but she did not understand language. She did not know why the people around her moved their lips. She did not know that things had names. She frequently hurled fragile objects across the room and threw wild temper tantrums.

7. Why did Helen probably act so violently at this age?

_____

_____

Language

Write one sentence with a compound subject and another sentence with a compound predicate. Circle the simple subject(s) and underline the simple predicate(s) in each sentence.

1. _____

_____

2. _____

_____

Math

Read the problem. Then answer the items.

Makela is filling grocery bags at a food pantry. Each bag's contents will be identical, and there will be no food left over. Makela has 27 boxes of oatmeal and 18 boxes of raisins.

3. What is the greatest number of bags can she fill? _____

4. How many boxes of each food will go in each bag?

_____ boxes of oatmeal and _____ boxes of raisins

Reading

Read the proclamation. Then answer the item.

In accordance with a proclamation from the Executive of the United States, all slaves are free. This involves an absolute equality of personal rights and rights of property between former masters and slaves, and the connection … between them becomes that between employer and hired labor. The freedmen are advised to remain quietly at their present homes and work for wages. They … will not be supported in idleness either there or elsewhere.

5. How do you think life changed for the freedmen who stayed with their employers?

_____

_____

Daily Fundamentals • EMC 3246 • © Evan-Moor Corp.

Language

Write the present tense form of the verb in parentheses that agrees with its subject.

1. There _____ many reasons to learn how to dance. **(be)**

2. Because of the drought, you now _____ to ask for water at a restaurant. **(have)**

3. Contrary to popular belief, Ida _____ know how to cook. **(do)**

4. Pierre _____ beautiful wood cabinets and bookcases. **(make)**

Math

Answer the item.

5. Write the first eight multiples of **8**. _____

6. Write the first six multiples of **12**. _____

7. Write the first seven multiples of **9**. _____

8. Write the first seven multiples of **13**. _____

9. Write the first eight multiples of **15**. _____

Reading

Read the stanza from the poem *Tuen Ng—The Dragon Boat Races* by Judith Nicholls.
Then answer the item.

> Fish scatter in dismay
> as dragon-racers slice the surface.
> Wings dip, whip water into waves;
> waves rise like flames,
> set light by sun.

10. Which does the author probably want to do: provide details or help the reader visualize? Explain.

_____

_____

Language

Read the sentence and underline the modal auxiliary and verb. If the verb is correct, write *correct* on the line. If not, write the correct verb form.

1. You can parks anywhere on the street after 6:00.   _____

2. Rick should goes to the doctor if he doesn't feel better by tomorrow.   _____

3. If the law passes, it would affects the whole town.   _____

4. Mei Li might arrive early if traffic is light.   _____

Math

Answer the item.

5. Are all multiples of 5 also multiples of 25? Explain. _____

_____

6. Are all multiples of 25 also multiples of 5? Explain. _____

_____

Reading

Read the paragraph. Then answer the items.

Abby, Oliver, Chanel, and Bruce had walked to Tea and Letters Café after school almost every single day for the last two years, after working on a social studies project together. Tea and Letters had become almost like a second home. The friends dropped their backpacks onto "their" sofa and went to the café counter to order a tea from their favorite barista. Little did they know that today their ritual was about to come to an end.

7. Does the author probably want to teach, explain, persuade, or entertain? _____

8. Explain your answer. _____

_____

       Daily Fundamentals • EMC 3246 • © Evan-Moor Corp.

Language

Read the sentence. Complete it with the infinitive form of the given verb or with a form that agrees with the subject.

1. After Rob _____ the lawn, he likes _____ lemonade.
   mow   **drink**

2. If you want _____ a movie, you need _____ your chores.
   see   **finish**

3. Kami _____ asleep easily after she _____ a hot bath.
   fall   **take**

Math

Find the least common multiple (LCM) of the number pair.

4. 5, 9 _____   9. 11, 33 _____

5. 6, 9 _____   10. 8, 18 _____

6. 14, 21 _____   11. 12, 16 _____

7. 12, 18 _____   12. 9, 15 _____

8. 7, 6 _____   13. 21, 28 _____

Reading

Read the paragraph. Then answer the items.

     Are you looking for a fun pastime? Do you like to watch things grow? If so, you'll love gardening. You can grow vegetables, flowers, cacti, and small trees. You don't even need a yard if you use container gardening. You can move plants indoors or outside, depending on the weather. And a container garden takes up much less space.

14. Is the purpose of this text to explain, persuade, teach, or express? _____

15. Explain your answer, using examples from the text. _____

_____

_____

Language

Read the sentence. Circle each verb and draw an arrow to the noun it agrees with.

1. The student who wins the contest receives a cash prize.

2. The best project from all the entries demonstrates the effects of sun exposure.

3. The parents of the winner say that their child is fascinated by science.

4. The judge who awards the ribbons hopes other students are inspired.

Math

Read the problem. Then answer the items.

Ms. Barko bought paper plates and napkins for a school dance. The paper plates came in packs of 60, and the napkins were sold in packs of 140.

5. What is the minimum number of packs of each that will she need to buy in order to have the same number of both?

   _____

6. How many of each will she have? _____

Reading

Read the paragraph. Then answer the items.

Why on earth are engineers studying birds? Designers of a high-speed train were trying to eliminate the loud noise the train made while passing through a tunnel. They saw similarities in how kingfisher birds dive into water and how the train exits a tunnel. They designed the train's nose cone to operate in a manner similar to the kingfisher's pointed beak.

7. What is the purpose of this text?

   _____

8. Why did the author mention kingfishers?

   _____

Language

Read the paragraph. Complete it with verbs that make sense and agree with their subjects.

1.   One of the best places I _____ to visit _____ Juneau, Alaska.

Everywhere you _____, there _____ rugged mountains, even on the

coast! You can _____ totem poles that _____ tall and _____

stories of local clans. One of the prettiest glaciers that are receding quickly _____

Mendenhall Glacier.

Math

Solve the problem.

2. Jamal walks once around the track in 5 minutes. Keisha jogs once around the track in 3 minutes. If they start from the same place on the track at the same time, how long will it take them to arrive together at the start again?

_____

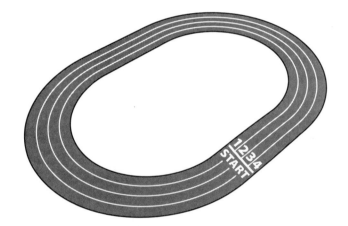

Reading

Read the paragraph. Then answer the item.

      Have you noticed changes in your skin? Oil + dead skin cells + bacteria is the equation for acne! Keeping your skin and hair clean is a start, but you're going to need a little more help. PowDerm is a new powder that treats acne. It dries up excess oil while killing bacteria. Use PowDerm after every wash. Sprinkle it on damp skin, let it sit, and wash it off—your skin will never feel smoother! It'll be your new best friend in no time.

3. What is the purpose of this text? Explain how you know.

_____

_____

Language

Read the sentence. Draw three lines (☰) under any letter that should be capitalized.

1. In mary's first issue of *national geographic,* she read an article on the great wall of china.

2. The magazine said that emperor qin shi huang ordered the wall built to keep out invaders.

3. In the mid-1600s, the manchus broke through the wall and ended the ming dynasty.

Math

Add.

4. 651.73 + 41.88

_____

5. 3.125 + 11.894

_____

6. 17.29 + 24.504

_____

7. 32.1857 + 687.43

_____

Reading

Read the paragraph from a fiction story. Then look at the plot diagram and answer the items.

After I moved in with my grandparents in northern Maine, I realized how much I missed Florida, playing beach volleyball in the warm sand after school and waterskiing in the sultry Gulf of Mexico. I first realized how much my new surroundings were affecting me when I skipped two morning cheerleading practices. Callie asked if I had the flu, and my coach asked if something was bothering me—before giving me a warning. All I knew is that I was tired for no reason.

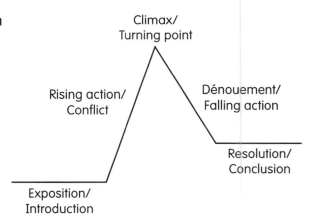

Climax/
Turning point

Rising action/
Conflict

Dénouement/
Falling action

Resolution/
Conclusion

Exposition/
Introduction

8. Make an X on the plot diagram to show where in the story this paragraph most likely appears.

9. Explain why you placed the X where you did.

_____

_____

Language

Write three sentences that include the name of a holiday. Capitalize the holidays.

1. _____

_____

2. _____

_____

3. _____

_____

Math

Read the problem. Then answer the items.

Nigel is making butterscotch pudding. The recipe requires 0.473 liter of milk. He is also making oatmeal that calls for 0.237 liter of milk.

4. How much milk should Nigel have on hand before he starts cooking?

_____

5. Nigel has 0.059 liter milk more than he needs. How much milk does he have when he starts?

_____

Reading

Read the paragraph from a fiction story. Then answer the items.

When I returned to the dining room, my ordinary Saturday turned really strange. Mickey's mom was combing her hair with a fork. Mickey's dad jumped up from his chair and ran to a nearby wall. He pressed his body against the wall, making himself as flat as he could. Mickey himself was acting bizarre, squeezing all the food between his fingers— even his soup and salad! I felt confused and sweaty. Can I help, or should I escape? Suddenly, I remembered something my mom had said this morning, and I knew the problem was with *me,* not with Mickey's family.

6. Which part of the plot is this paragraph most likely from?

Ⓐ introduction

Ⓑ conflict

Ⓒ falling action

Ⓓ resolution

7. Which of these will probably happen next?

Ⓐ The problem will get worse.

Ⓑ The problem will be solved.

Ⓒ We'll learn more about the characters.

Ⓓ We'll learn more about the setting.

Name _____

Language

Read the sentence. Draw three lines (≡) under any letter that should be capitalized.

1. The store clerk said, "your cat will really like this brand of cat food."

2. "as I was saying," Mrs. Palacios continued, "your assignments are due tomorrow."

3. "where can I find tarpey road?" Terry asked the gas station attendant.

4. Just as the race started, he heard shouts of "go adelberto!" and "you can do it!"

Math

Subtract.

5. 95.34 − 94.36

.98

6. 213.476 − 11.680

201.796

7. 57.29 − 35.355

21.935

8. 157.6 − 42.89

113.71

Reading

These notes were taken from a story to write a plot outline, but they are not in plot order. Read each note. On the line, write the part of the plot it belongs to, using the terms from the word box.

> 1 introduction   2 rising action   3 climax   4 falling action   5 resolution

9. _____3_____ The mice come up with a way to always know where the cat is.

_____2_____ The mice meet to discuss what to do about the cat.

_____5_____ The mice see how their plan is working.

_____1_____ The household cat has hurt several mice.

_____4_____ The mice vote on the plan.

Language

Rewrite the title using correct capitalization.

1. *the lion king*

   The Lion King

2. *a wrinkle in time*

   A Wrinkle in time

3. *how to train your dragon*

   How to Train your Dragon

4. "*the key to good soil*"

   The Key to Good Soil

Math

Read the problem. Then answer the items.

A cup of white beans provides 0.0211 gram of iron. A cup of kidney beans provides 0.0172 gram of iron.

5. How much more iron does a cup of white beans have?

   0.0039

6. Laila needs to consume 0.015 gram of iron daily. She prefers to eat pinto beans, which provide 0.0036 gram of iron per cup. If she eats one cup of pinto beans per day, how much more iron will she need to get from another source?

   0.0114

Reading

Read the text. Then answer the items.

Here are the steps for creating a crossword puzzle:

1) Get a sheet of graph paper, two sheets of plain paper, and a pencil with an eraser.

2) Make a list of 10 to 15 words. You might choose words about a topic or theme.

3) Write one of your longer words on the graph paper, one letter per square.

4) Add other words, each crossing another word where they share a letter in common.

5) Number the words going across starting with 1 at the top left corner. Work in order until all have a number. Repeat with the words going down, starting over with 1.

6) Write and number a clue for each word. Group the clues for words going across in one column and the clues for the words going down in another.

7. What could happen if you numbered the words as you added each one to the puzzle?

_____

8. Why should you write the clues last?

_____

Language

Read the dialogue. Draw three lines (☰) under any letter that should be capitalized.

1.   "Excuse me. Can you tell me how to get to the seaview bridge?" asked zach. "I thought it was near the cranston art gallery on second avenue."

"The gallery is on bloomfield road," replied the woman at the gas station. "Take a right on halstead lane, drive past matt's meat market, and turn left at that new thai food place. follow the signs to hartsfield, and you'll find the bridge."

Math

Read the problem. Then answer the items.

Cara is shopping for school supplies. She has a $20 bill. She found a calculator for $17.75, a notebook for $3.49, and a dictionary for $15.98.

2. Which two supplies can she buy, and what is the total cost?

_____

_____

3. How much change will she receive?

_____

Reading

Read the text. Then answer the items.

How to Hold a Garage Sale

1) Have your parents advertise the garage sale in the newspaper or online. Make signs for your neighborhood announcing the sale and put them up.
2) Collect usable items that you want to sell.
3) Sort the items into categories: books, clothes, toys, gadgets, furniture, etc.
4) Get at least one table for each category of items.
5) Decide how much to charge for each item. Make price tags.
6) Have plenty of cash the day of the sale to make change. Be ready to make deals!

4. Ashok researched how much other people sold certain items for. During which step did he probably do this?

_____

5. Hardly anyone came to the Shahs' garage sale. Which step did they probably do out of order?

_____

Language

Read the sentence. Circle the descriptive and quantitative adjectives. Then draw an arrow to the noun each adjective describes.

1. I think some days are more memorable than other days.

2. When she was young, Ms. Turner lived in a minuscule cottage for five years.

3. The astonishing finish of the game followed several rounds of overtime play.

4. After continual reminders, Aliya finally returned the overdue library books.

Math

Multiply.

5. 825 × 67 = _____

7. 184 × 901 = _____

6. 1,528 × 56 = _____

8. 2,269 × 380 = _____

Reading

Read the paragraph. Then answer the item.

Colin Powell, a four-star general in the U.S. Army and a U.S. secretary of state, was born in 1937 to parents who had emigrated from Jamaica. While he was growing up, his parents stressed the importance of working hard and doing one's best. Powell attended City College of New York, where he joined the Reserve Officers' Training Corps (ROTC). He felt a sense of purpose in ROTC and eventually earned the rank of unit commander. He graduated from the corps as a cadet colonel, the highest rank. He entered the army after college.

9. What part of Colin Powell's background probably led to his army career?

_____

_____

Language

Read the sentence. Write the appropriate adjective.

1. Joy's cheesecake was the _____ of the whole competition.
   creamier   creamiest

2. Windy Pine Lane is more _____ than Haverhill Avenue.
   narrow   narrower

3. My second performance was the _____ of the two shows.
   better   best

Math

Divide.

4. $513 \div 27 =$ _____

6. $43,360 \div 542 =$ _____

5. $8,132 \div 38 =$ _____

7. $80,997 \div 3,857 =$ _____

Reading

Read the paragraph. Then answer the item.

In the 1840s, passengers traveling on sailing ships from Ireland to the United States lived in the hold of the ship, where products were usually carried. The number of passengers on the ships varied. Often there were 400 to 1,000 passengers crowded into the hold, where they each had only two to three square feet of space throughout the long voyage. The ships' captains received part of the money the passengers paid for their voyage, so they did not limit the number of passengers.

8. Why did the captains give passengers so little room?

_____

_____

 Daily Fundamentals • EMC 3246 • © Evan-Moor Corp.

Language

Read the sentence. Write the proper adjective of the proper noun in parentheses.

1. The bouzouki is a _____ musical stringed instrument. **(Greece)**

2. Did you know that bagels are a _____ food that originated in Poland? **(Jew)**

3. The _____ savanna has a five-month-long rainy season. **(Africa)**

4. _____ architecture represents many historical building styles. **(Paris)**

Math

Multiply or divide.

5. 1,008 × 56 = _____

7. 37,380 ÷ 35 = _____

6. 5,790 ÷ 965 = _____

8. 48,568 × 13 = _____

Reading

Read the paragraph. Then answer the item.

  Lisa's cousin Elena was coming from Mexico to live with her for the rest of the school year. Mom had insisted that Lisa give up her activities after school. "I can't drive back and forth all day," Mom had said. "I have to pick you both up right after school. It wouldn't be fair to have Elena wait an hour for you to finish play practice." Lisa had a big part in the school play. She hadn't yet told Mr. Blake, the drama teacher, that she couldn't come to rehearsals. She was hoping Mom would change her mind.

9. Why was Lisa going to have to drop out of the school play?

_____

_____

Language

Read the sentence. Write *this, that, these,* or *those* on the line. Then circle the word it refers to.

1. I much prefer _____ fresh berries to the berries you bought last week.

2. Please check on _____ customer at the corner table.

3. My grandparents had one of _____ old phones with a round dial.

4. I'm almost finished with _____ chapter, and then I'll eat lunch.

Math

Solve the problem.

5. Max will haul 1,235 cubic feet of gravel to a construction site. His truck can carry 95 cubic feet of gravel at a time. How many trips will he have to make to deliver all the gravel?

_____

6. A sled dog running in the Iditarod race needs 2,750 calories from beef per day. There are 16 dogs on a racing team. The race usually lasts 9 days. How many calories from beef will the team of dogs consume over 9 days of the race?

_____

Reading

Read the paragraphs. Then answer the item.

Mrs. Griffin explained that the class was a melting pot of its own. To demonstrate how they all meshed together to create one unique class, she asked her students to bring in things that represented their heritages. "If you have nothing that represents your heritage, draw a picture of something that does," she said. "If you don't know where your ancestors are from, bring in something from a culture that has influenced you."

At lunch, Tom, who was adopted, sullenly complained to classmate Carlos. "I don't want to choose a culture that has influenced me. I wish I knew where my ancestors were from."

7. What effect did the assignment have on Tom? _____

_____

Language

Read the sentence. Complete it with the possessive adjective that matches the underlined antecedent.

1. <u>My aunt and uncle</u> sold _____ house and moved next door to me.

2. They planted a <u>garden</u>, and _____ flowers smell quite fragrant.

3. They said, "If <u>you</u> plant certain flowers, _____ garden will smell good, too."

4. When the <u>flowers</u> bloom, _____ scent will attract butterflies and bees.

Math

Solve the problems.

5. Simone's company sells custom T-shirts for $35 each. Last year, she sold 1,857 T-shirts. How much money did she receive?

_____

6. The income from the T-shirts is split evenly between Simone, the artist, the marketer, the order processor, and the materials supplier. How much does Simone get to keep?

_____

Reading

Read the paragraph. Then answer the item.

On a shoe-shopping trip, a salesman refused service because Martin Luther King, Jr.'s father, a civil rights leader, would not sit in the "black section" of the store. While the younger King was angry, he saw that anger would not defeat injustice. After King finished his schooling in the North, he became the pastor of a church in Montgomery, Alabama. When an African American named Rosa Parks was arrested for not giving up her bus seat to a white rider, King organized the community with a plan of nonviolent boycotts, marches, and sit-ins.

7. What effect did Martin Luther King, Jr.'s childhood experiences have on his adult life?

_____

_____

Language

Read the sentence. Circle the word that correctly completes the sentence.

1. Marco sang _____ in the talent show.   **amazing**   **amazingly**

2. Ms. Sharma bought a new car that is very _____.   **safe**   **safely**

3. I'll get to the hospital as _____ as I can.   **quick**   **quickly**

4. You did an _____ job on your science fair project!   **awesome**   **awesomely**

Math

Multiply.

5. $6.92 \times 4 =$ _____   7. $37.22 \times 0.6 =$ _____

6. $55.2 \times 3.1 =$ _____   8. $804.3 \times 0.08 =$ _____

Reading

Read the paragraphs. Then answer the item.

Sam set his books on the table and looked for Gramps. Gramps was in charge of the house while Sam's mom and dad were at work. The patio door was open. Gramps was sitting on a garden bench. He didn't look at Sam or say hello.

"He's probably tired of waiting for me," Sam thought. "I'm late, but Gramps shouldn't be mad. I was working on my science project. He's always telling me to study."

9. Is the setting for this story a school, a home, or a place of work? Explain your answer.

_____

_____

Language

Read the sentence. Complete it with an adverb from the word box that matches the given type.

up	now	never	away	then	often	next	usually	indoors

1. **place:** The family will go _____ if the hurricane comes closer.

2. **time:** Add the flour, and _____ add the eggs.

3. **frequency:** I have _____ wondered what my future holds.

Math

Divide.

4. $16.25 \div 13 =$ _____

5. $9.86 \div 0.17 =$ _____

6. $0.648 \div 7.2 =$ _____

7. $38.962 \div 1.15 =$ _____

Reading

Read the paragraph. Then answer the item.

I remember my mother telling me the importance of cleanliness. As a young child, our village bathed in the Nile River. Now, my family uses a stone bathtub. The water goes cold between bathers, but we add hot stones to the water to make it warmer. I add other things to my bath water, too, such as scented oils or salt from the Dead Sea. It is said that the salt is healing and calming.

8. Does this story take place in the past, present, or future? Explain your answer.

_____

_____

Language

Read the sentence. Complete it with an adverb from the word box. Then underline the word it modifies.

> too   not   very   also   once   really   again   already   enough

1. The music is definitely loud _____!

2. Let's practice that dance step _____.

3. You finished your assignment _____ fast.

Math

Multiply or divide.

4. $110.2 \div 14.5 =$ _____

6. $18.567 \div 0.09 =$ _____

5. $21.26 \times 7.4 =$ _____

7. $3.03 \times 218.4 =$ _____

Reading

Read the paragraphs. Then answer the item.

      Mabel found the factory's parching heat distracting. She tried to swallow as she looked over at Elianet's loom to see how far she'd gotten on her cloth. "Oh dear! If I don't find a way to catch up in the next ten hours, I will surely be dismissed!" she said under her breath.

      "No talking! No wonder you are so slow!" warned Mrs. Severson, the floor supervisor. "And if you are even a minute late from your lunch break, we will lock you out permanently."

8. How does the setting probably influence Mabel's feelings?

_____

_____

Language

Read the end of the sentence. Write the beginning, including *more, less, the most,* or *the least* and an adverb.

1. _____ than I can.

2. _____ of all of us.

3. _____ of the whole class.

4. _____ than you do.

Math

Solve the problems.

5. A 770-gram box of frozen ravioli makes 3.5 servings. How many grams are in each serving?

   _____

6. A different brand of frozen ravioli contains 8 servings that are 4.23 ounces each. If a family of 3 cooks the entire bag and shares it equally, how big will each serving be?

   _____

Reading

Read the paragraphs. Then answer the item.

Ned entered the classroom, pig in tow. Quincy waddled through the neat rows of wooden desks, right on Ned's heels. When Ned took his seat, Quincy rested his chin on Ned's knee.

"Well, that's the oddest-looking dog I ever did see!" Ms. McCann remarked, breaking the silence. "I guess 'best friend' can mean different things to different people," she said as the students resumed their chatter.

7. Compare how this scene might affect the story if the setting is a big city versus a country farm town.

_____

_____

Language

Read the sentence starter. Complete it, including *better, best, worse,* or *worst.*

1. My cousin writes _____.

2. Ms. Arnold listened _____.

3. Chef Kwan cooks _____.

4. The golf team played _____.

Math

Solve the problems.

5. Nijat makes $12.72 per hour at his job. Last week, he earned $359.34. How much time did Nijat work last week?

   _____

6. Nijat is saving money to buy a new bike. He will have just enough money when he has worked 35.75 hours. How much does the bike cost?

   _____

Reading

Read the paragraph. Then answer the item.

Diego cleared his throat and shifted uncomfortably in his seat. He glanced at the walls of the room. In 15 minutes, the Bedford city council meeting would begin, and he would have to speak in front of almost 200 people. Even though he was apprehensive, Diego knew he was making the right decision to speak to the crowd. What had started out as a school project was now going to be broadcast on the 6 o'clock news.

7. How does knowing the setting of this story help you understand the character's feelings?

   _____

   _____

Language

Answer the questions using abbreviations for the street names.

1. What street do you live on?

   _____

2. What street is your school on?

   _____

3. On what street does your best friend live?

   _____

4. What is the busiest street in your neighborhood?

   _____

Math

Circle the fraction that is closest to the benchmark fraction.

5. benchmark: $\frac{1}{2}$ $\frac{5}{8}$ $\frac{2}{8}$

6. benchmark: $\frac{1}{4}$ $\frac{1}{8}$ $\frac{3}{4}$

7. benchmark: $\frac{1}{3}$ $\frac{5}{9}$ $\frac{3}{6}$

8. benchmark: $\frac{3}{4}$ $\frac{7}{16}$ $\frac{10}{12}$

9. benchmark: $\frac{2}{3}$ $\frac{6}{10}$ $\frac{1}{4}$

10. benchmark: $\frac{1}{5}$ $\frac{3}{9}$ $\frac{3}{10}$

Reading

Read the paragraph. Then answer the items.

     Jennifer Rodríguez was born in 1976. She discovered a talent for roller-skating while very young and began taking lessons at the age of four. Only a year later, Jennifer started to compete in figure roller-skating and speed skating. By the time she graduated from high school, she was the only woman to have won medals in both types of skating. She moved her speed-skating skills to the ice in time to compete in the 1998 Olympic Games.

11. The structure of this text is _____.

   Ⓐ cause and effect

   Ⓑ time sequence

   Ⓒ main idea and details

   Ⓓ steps in a procedure

12. The text's structure helps us _____.

   Ⓐ understand how to skate

   Ⓑ find out how athletes train

   Ⓒ know when events happened

   Ⓓ learn about the late 20th century

13. Why does this structure make sense for this text?

   _____

   _____

Language

Read the sentence. Write the two-letter abbreviation of each state's name above it.

1. The Gulf states are Texas, Louisiana, Mississippi, Alabama, and Florida.

2. Michigan, Wisconsin, and Minnesota are three states that touch the Great Lakes.

3. The Mason-Dixon Line runs between Maryland, Delaware, and Pennsylvania.

4. Four Corners is where Utah, Colorado, Arizona, and New Mexico all meet.

Math

Compare. Write $>$, $<$, or $=$ in the $\bigcirc$.

5. $\frac{3}{15}$ $\bigcirc$ $\frac{9}{45}$

6. $\frac{4}{10}$ $\bigcirc$ $\frac{7}{35}$

7. $\frac{23}{50}$ $\bigcirc$ $\frac{7}{8}$

8. $\frac{6}{9}$ $\bigcirc$ $\frac{40}{70}$

9. $\frac{2}{3}$ $\bigcirc$ $\frac{5}{6}$

Reading

Read the paragraphs. Then complete each sentence.

Rights and responsibilities are shared by citizens of every country, although they vary from country to country. A right is anything that a citizen may do. For instance, U.S. citizens have the right to follow any religion they want or to not follow any religion at all. Neither the government nor their families can force them to do one or the other.

In contrast, a responsibility is something a citizen must do. For instance, in Norway, all citizens must register to serve in the military when they reach 18 years old. There are often legal consequences for those who do not meet their responsibilities.

10. To organize this text, the author _____ rights and responsibilities.

11. The author describes one way they are _____ and one way they are

_____.

12. The phrase _____ is a clue to the structure of the text.

Language

Rewrite the measurement conversions using abbreviations for the underlined words.

1. 2 cups = 1 pint   _____

2. 16 tablespoons = 1 cup   _____

3. 1 gallon = 128 ounces   _____

4. 1 liter = 1.06 quarts   _____

5. 2.2 pounds = 1 kilogram   _____

6. 1 ounce = 28.35 grams   _____

7. 1 ton = 2,000 pounds   _____

8. 1 pound = 16 ounces   _____

Math

Circle the decimal that is closest to the benchmark decimal.

9. benchmark: 0.25   0.37   0.84

10. benchmark: 0.5   0.59   0.46

11. benchmark: 0.33   0.21   0.4

12. benchmark: 0.67   0.7   0.5

13. benchmark: 0.1   0.3   0.04

14. benchmark: 0.75   0.57   0.8

Reading

Read the interview of a meteorologist. Then answer the items.

What do you do with all the information that the weather balloon and radar provide?
We input all the data into a supercomputer, which uses equations to model weather patterns likely to occur in our area. Then comes the hardest part of my job: predicting the weather.

Doesn't the supercomputer predict it for you?
Actually, the computer gives us calculations that we use to make predictions. As the weather happens, it can affect its own patterns. Also, a fire or a volcano erupting can affect the weather.

15. What is the organizational structure of the text? Explain your answer.

_____

_____

16. What other structure might the author have used? Would it have been as effective?

_____

_____

Language

Read the sentence. Then write the abbreviation of each underlined word above it.

1. Send the package to 485 Eastlake Road,

   Cheyenne, Wyoming.

2. Mix 5 grams of salt into 10 milliliters of water.

3. In Iowa, I lived at the corner of First Avenue

   and Elm Lane.

4. The Quinns' new baby weighed 7 pounds

   9 ounces at birth.

Math

Compare. Write **>**, **<**, or **=** in the ◯.

5. 0.456 ◯ 0.546

6. 0.7 ◯ 0.023

7. 0.140 ◯ 0.14

8. 0.09 ◯ 0.2

9. 0.888 ◯ 0.88

Reading

Read the paragraph. Then answer the items.

   Air pollution has been a problem for over a hundred years. Factories that burn coal or oil emit toxic smoke. Pollutants also come from cars and planes and even household cleaners. These poisons in the air can cause health problems, such as asthma and cancer. When the substances settle in water, they have the effect of making fish sick or unsafe to eat. Polluted rain results in damage to the precious plants that produce oxygen for us to breathe. For this reason, clean-air technologies are more important than ever.

10. What is the organizational structure of the text? What signal words help you know?

   _____

   _____

11. What types of topics work well using this organizational structure?

   _____

   _____

Language

Read the sentence. Then write the word that the underlined abbreviation stands for above it.

1. Mom bought 13 gal. of gas at the station

   on Forest Blvd.

2. A small TX pecan orchard can produce

   5 T of nuts per year.

3. Add 2 tsp of food coloring to 1 L of water.

4. The store on Hitch Dr. sells chicken feed

   in 20-kg bags.

Math

Answer the item.

5. Jenna got the following scores on her last four quizzes: 6/10, 7/9, 6/8, 5/6. Explain whether or not she is generally improving.

   _____

   _____

   _____

6. Write the following weights in order from lowest to highest:

   0.49, 0.38, 0.6, 0.474

   _____

Reading

Read the paragraph. Then answer the items.

   The tongue of a giraffe is about 18 inches (46 cm) long. The giraffe uses its tongue not only to eat but also to keep clean. Giraffes do not bathe. They lick their bodies clean. A giraffe even cleans its nose and ears with its long tongue! Oxpecker birds usually help giraffes with their grooming. The birds walk up and down a giraffe's back, eating insects and getting rid of dry skin and loose hair.

7. Is the organizational structure of the text problem/solution or description? Explain your answer.

   _____

   _____

8. Rewrite the beginning of the paragraph using a main idea/details structure.

   _____

   _____

Language

Read the sentence. Circle the word or words that need an apostrophe.

1. The Collins farm has organic eggs for sale.   **Collins   eggs**

2. Could you put some cat treats in my cats bowl?   **treats   cats**

3. They are serving tamales in the schools cafeteria.   **tamales   schools**

4. My aunts house is across the road from the malls parking lot.   **aunts   malls**

Math

Add. Show your work.

5. $\frac{7}{16} + \frac{7}{8} =$ _____

6. $\frac{11}{27} + \frac{1}{9} =$ _____

7. $\frac{6}{12} + \frac{3}{15} =$ _____

8. $\frac{14}{17} + \frac{3}{5} =$ _____

Reading

Read the paragraph. Then answer the item.

Phillis Wheatley was born in West Africa around 1753. At nine years old, she was torn from her home and sold into slavery in the United States. She grew up with the Wheatley family in Boston, Massachusetts. The Wheatley family discovered that Phillis was very intelligent and allowed her to learn to read. She learned English, Greek, and Latin. She began writing poetry as a teenager and published a book of poems in 1773.

9. Which genres describe this text? Choose all that are true.

Ⓐ science fiction

Ⓑ biography

Ⓒ nonfiction

Ⓓ poetry

Language

Read the sentence. Rewrite it, correcting any errors in apostrophe use.

1. Look at the color's of the rainforest's deciduous trees' leave's!

_____

2. Chinas and Germanys famous walls were created for different purposes.

_____

_____

Math

Subtract. Show your work.

3. $\frac{9}{18} - \frac{2}{6} =$ _____

4. $\frac{34}{52} - \frac{6}{13} =$ _____

5. $\frac{4}{14} - \frac{1}{4} =$ _____

6. $\frac{11}{13} - \frac{5}{7} =$ _____

Reading

Read the paragraph. Then answer the item.

Once upon a time, there were three smart pigs. No, these aren't the ones you may have heard about whose houses were blown down, but their younger cousins. These pigs had learned from the misfortunes of their relatives and had constructed houses that were sturdy, secure, and comfortable. And while an earthquake or flood might cause damage, a wolf certainly would not.

7. Is this probably the beginning of a myth, a fable, or a legend? Explain your answer.

_____

_____

Language

Read the dialogue. Rewrite word pairs as contractions wherever possible.

1.   "Please do not tell anyone my secret," Kirti begged her little sister, "or you will be sorry!"

   "You can not threaten me," Reshma replied. "You could have hurt me. It is time I spoke up."

   "If only I had told Dad when it happened, I would not be in this mess," Kirti muttered to

   herself. "When Reshma spills the beans, Dad is going to say, 'You are grounded for life!'"

Math

Add or subtract. Write the answer as a mixed number and as an improper fraction. Show your work.

2. $10\frac{5}{8} + 4\frac{7}{8} =$ _____ _____

3. $11\frac{2}{14} + 8\frac{6}{7} =$ _____ _____

4. $11\frac{1}{5} + 23\frac{3}{16} =$ _____ _____

5. $5\frac{1}{72} + 32\frac{19}{24} =$ _____ _____

Reading

Read the paragraph. Then answer the item.

   The junior firefighter program at the Polk County Fire Department is a great program for kids. Currently, the minimum age is 14 years, but you should lower it to 11 years old. Many kids as young as 11 years old are excited about firefighting. Plus, 11-year-olds can perform most of the tasks that the 14-year-olds in the program can. They can also help clean the station and learn about safety and first aid. So please give more kids the chance to serve the community by lowering the minimum age to 11 for junior firefighters.

6. What genre of writing is the text? How can you tell?

_____

_____

Language

Read the sentence. Circle the word that completes the sentence.

1. If _____ going to the store, please buy me some gum.   **your**   **you're**

2. Next month, _____ try out for the play together.   **lets**   **let's**

3. The opossum seems to have hurt _____ paw.   **its**   **it's**

4. Oh no, my brand-new _____ been stolen!   **bikes**   **bike's**

Math

Read the problem. Then answer the items.

Roger is in a clam-collecting contest. He has collected two buckets of clams weighing $31\frac{5}{8}$ pounds and $33\frac{3}{16}$ pounds. The first person to collect 80 pounds wins.

5. How many pounds of clams has he collected so far?   _____

6. How many pounds of clams does he still need to find?   _____

Reading

Read the text. Then answer the item.

Jerome: I have a personal favor to ask. I heard that you speak Italian.
Lee: Well, I've heard enough at home to fake it pretty well.
Jerome: Yeah? Well, I'm going to Italy this summer. Do you think you could teach me?
Lee: I could probably teach you some phrases. Do you think you could show me the secret of your long-distance football pass?

7. Is the text from a play or an interview? Explain your answer.

_____

_____

Language

Read the paragraph. Add apostrophes where needed.

1.   Kevins got the next two months planned out. Now that hes finished his school projects, he

and his brother are driving to their cousins cabin. Theyre going to borrow Valeries train passes

and head east through the Rockies. "Im hoping its not too hot," he thought while turning on the

cars radio. "Were expecting a freak snowstorm in the Rockies foothills," the announcer began.

Math

Read the problem. Then answer the items.

Mrs. Norris is using a 30-foot roll of green paper to cover her bulletin boards. So far, she has cut lengths measuring $10\frac{7}{12}$ feet, $10\frac{7}{12}$ feet, and $6\frac{1}{3}$ feet. She will need $4\frac{5}{6}$ feet for the last bulletin board.

2. How much paper has she used so far? _____

3. Will there be enough left on the roll for the last bulletin board? Explain your answer.

_____

Reading

Read the paragraph. Then answer the item.

     Alfred Bullfrog Stormalong was the tallest and strongest sailor that ever lived. No ordinary sailing ship was big enough for him. Every time he stepped from the port to the starboard side of a ship, it rocked around like it was hit by a hurricane. Stormalong had to sleep on the deck because of his size. Several times he almost tipped over a ship when he rolled about in his sleep. The sailors complained about the splashing, but Stormalong always turned the ship right-side up before they fell into the water.

4. Underline one sentence from the text that shows it is a tall tale. Explain your choice.

_____

_____

Language

Write a helping verb to complete the progressive tense in the sentence.

1. I _____ having a bad dream when my alarm clock went off.

2. Melissa _____ working on her social studies project right now.

3. The twins _____ celebrating their twelfth birthday this weekend.

4. The squirrels _____ gathering nuts when they noticed the snarling dog.

Math

Multiply. Then answer the item.

5. $\frac{5}{9} \times 15 =$ _____

7. $\frac{10}{23} \times \frac{3}{8} =$ _____

6. $\frac{9}{11} \times \frac{5}{6} =$ _____

8. $\frac{15}{4} \times \frac{17}{32} =$ _____

9. Write a math problem that can be solved using $\frac{3}{4} \times \frac{1}{2}$. _____

_____

Reading

Read the paragraph. Then answer the item.

> Homesickness hit David's *abuela* like a tidal wave. He could see how much his grandmother missed Mexico as they walked slowly along the quiet beach. She talked about the green hills that spread out like a wrinkled blanket. She talked about the friends she had left behind. David rattled the seashells in his pockets and listened.

10. Circle the two similes in the text. What is being compared in each?

a. _____

b. _____

Language

Write the correct form of the verb in parentheses to complete the sentence.

1. I am _____ late this morning. **(run)**

2. Who will be _____ the extra-credit assignment this week? **(do)**

3. The pollen has been _____ my eyes, so I went to the doctor. **(irritate)**

4. Diego is _____ a famous poem in the talent show. **(recite)**

Math

Divide. Then answer the item.

5. $\frac{2}{13} \div 5 =$ _____

7. $\frac{24}{55} \div \frac{6}{7} =$ _____

6. $\frac{8}{31} \div \frac{3}{12} =$ _____

8. $\frac{20}{9} \div \frac{11}{12} =$ _____

9. Write a math problem that can be solved using $\frac{7}{10} \div \frac{1}{4}$. _____

_____

Reading

Read the paragraph. Then answer the items.

You've probably heard about Pecos Bill, the Texas wrangler who was as tall as a two-story house and as strong as an ox. When it was time to round up the cattle and drive 'em to Abilene, Bill would just point his nose toward the sky and let out a coyote howl that echoed all across Texas.

10. Underline all the uses of hyperbole in the text.

11. Choose one hyperbole from the text. Explain its meaning.

_____

_____

Language

Circle the best verb to complete the sentence.

1. Shawn _____ when her phone rang. **shopped** **was shopping** **has shopped**

2. Everyone _____ a mistake before. **made** **was making** **has made**

3. Yesterday I _____ some milk. **bought** **was buying** **have bought**

4. We _____ in a play next weekend. **perform** **are performing** **have performed**

Math

Multiply or divide. Write the answer as a mixed number.

5. $25 \div 2\frac{6}{15} =$ _____

7. $4\frac{3}{8} \div 6\frac{7}{8} =$ _____

6. $14\frac{1}{4} \times 5\frac{3}{16} =$ _____

8. $9\frac{5}{22} \times 10\frac{10}{17} =$ _____

Reading

Read the paragraph. Then answer the items.

Jodie had been trying to solve the riddle all day. No way was her big brother going to hold this over her head! He never failed to remind her that he was the smartest student in his grade, and he made it look easy. As hard as Jodie persevered, she just didn't seem to have his talent for problem solving. "Why can't I figure this out?" she muttered to a caterpillar as she watched it climb a wall. And instantly the solution popped into her head! "I guess relaxing my brain is the key to creativity!"

9. What is the metaphor in the underlined sentence? _____

10. What is the metaphor being compared to?

_____

Language

Write a sentence using the given verb and tense.

1. **wonder** (past progressive): _____

   _____

2. **save** (present progressive): _____

   _____

Math

Read the problem. Then answer the items.

Nancy jogs every day. She covers a mile every $\frac{1}{6}$ hour. Yesterday she jogged for $1\frac{1}{4}$ hours.

3. How many miles did she jog yesterday? _____

4. Nancy wants to jog on a park path that is $12\frac{3}{4}$ miles long. How many hours will it take?

   _____

Reading

Read the paragraph. Then answer the item.

Her fascination with bicycle racing began with that book Aunt Linda had given her. It transformed her love of riding into a personal challenge and a new set of goals. Now, though, Marisol realized that the book had given her a little bit of tunnel vision, as well. When she mounted a bike now, fun was not part of the ride; it was all about building strength, technique, speed, and control. Today she was just a little weary.

5. Explain what the idiom *tunnel vision* means.

   _____

   _____

Language

Read the sentence. Write another sentence using a different verb in the same tense as the bold verb.

1. The baseball game **will be starting** at 7:00.

_____

2. Aaron **has been volunteering** at the food bank for two years.

_____

Math

Read the problem. Then answer the items.

Uncle Saul's car goes $42\frac{3}{10}$ miles on a gallon of gas. There are $2\frac{1}{2}$ gallons of gas remaining in his gas tank.

3. How many miles can he drive before running out of gas? _____

4. Saul drives a total of $19\frac{9}{10}$ miles each day during his 5-day workweek. Will he need to buy more gas for the upcoming week? Explain your answer.

_____

Reading

Read the paragraph. Then answer the item.

One soft fall night, Grandma and I sat on the porch swing, gazing out at the twinkling sky. A breeze suddenly tagged a small pile of leaves, calling upon them to dance pirouettes and then fall back to the ground just as quickly. That's when I saw the first star of the evening, and I squeezed Grandma's arm and made a silent wish. Grandma looked up and smiled slowly, but there was sadness behind her smile.

5. Underline the sentence that uses personification. Explain how you know.

_____

_____

Language

Read the sentence. Circle the base of the bold word.

1. I **misinterpreted** the instructions for the history report.

2. Ms. Scopelitis works for a **nonprofit** agency.

3. Pythons don't **frighten** me, but wasps do.

4. The **heroic** passerby pulled the driver out of the burning car.

5. The main road was **impassable** after the snowstorm.

6. My neighbor's cat is the **unfriendliest** creature I have ever met.

Math

Complete the conversions.

7. There are 16 ounces in a pound.

   24 ounces = _____ pounds

8. There are 1,000 grams in a kilogram.

   1,250 grams = _____ kilograms

9. There are 4 tablespoons in $\frac{1}{4}$ cup.

   2 cups = _____ tablespoons

10. There are 10 millimeters in a centimeter.

    98 centimeters = _____ millimeters

Reading

Read the text. Then answer the items.

Coletta dug her cellphone out of her purse, opened the GPS app, gave it an address, and took off. Her passenger, Sachi, started unfolding the map she had brought. "Oh, we won't need that," Coletta assured her friend. "My phone knows where we're going."

"I know it will get us to the new stadium, but don't you want to see where we're going?" Sachi asked, nose buried in the pastel colors of the map's terrains.

"I can see that we're approaching Xavier Expressway," Coletta retorted.

"No, you're heading for a barricaded road. There must be an accident," Sachi warned, consulting her map again. "Take a right here, then another right. The road around the lake will be less crowded." Coletta sighed, waiting for her phone to recalculate the directions.

11. What is Coletta's perspective on navigating? _____

_____

12. What is Sachi's perspective on navigating? _____

_____

Language

Underline the prefix in the word. Then explain what the **whole** word means.

1. illegible

   _____

2. international

   _____

3. multitalented

   _____

4. prepackaged

   _____

Math

Solve the problem.

5. A golfer hit the ball 280 meters toward the hole. There are 1,000 meters in a kilometer. How far did she hit the ball in kilometers?

   _____

6. A recipe for 20 servings of punch calls for 1 gallon of grape juice. There are 16 cups in a gallon. Armin wants to make only 5 servings. How much grape juice will he use?

   _____

Reading

Read the paragraphs. Then answer the items.

     Idris is trying to decide which electives to take next year. "In my 'Games Galore' class, you'll use basic computer programming skills to bring a computer game to life!" Ms. Maru told him. "You'll learn how to debug, too. It's the coolest problem-solving skill that you can use in any area!"

     Mr. Otoski's "News and Views" class sounds interesting as well. "Communication is the most important skill you use. From the time you wake up in the morning, throughout all your classes and while talking with and texting your friends, you are communicating. Come see how the professionals do it, and contribute to your school paper."

7. Which skill does each teacher think is most valuable?

   Ms. Maru: _____   Mr. Otoski: _____

8. Why do the teachers have differing opinions on the value of each skill?

   _____

Language

Read the pair of related words. Write their base. Then write each word's part of speech.

1. **glorious, glorify**

   base: _____

   glorious: _____

   glorify: _____

2. **attraction, attractive**

   base: _____

   attraction: _____

   attractive: _____

Math

Solve the problem.

3. Wallpaper is sold on rolls that are 27 inches wide. Tazio needs to cover a wall that is 80 square feet. To figure out how many feet of wallpaper to buy, she will divide 80 by the width of the wallpaper roll in feet. How wide is the roll in feet?

   _____

4. Tonnie divides a 2-liter bottle of iced tea equally among 8 people. How many milliliters does each person get?

   _____

Reading

Read the two accounts. Then answer the items.

Susie, to her family: It was the worst thing I've ever tasted! Gross! Richard was bragging about the great chocolate malt he got at that new hamburger place. I swear I saw him take a swig before he put the rest in the refrigerator. I only wanted to try a little sip. I think that cup was filled with cold gravy! I'm never touching my brother's drinks again!

Richard, to his friends: You should have seen the look on Susie's face when she took a sip of my "chocolate malt"! It was priceless! I've never had so much fun watching someone steal something of mine. That should put an end to her constant "accidentally" grabbing the wrong drink!

5. What does Susie think happened? _____

_____

6. What does Richard think happened? _____

_____

Language

Read the sentence. Write a prefix from the word box to complete the sentence.

| en   inter   re   trans |

1. I _____act very quickly whenever I see a spider!

2. The school board plans to _____act a new dress code next year.

3. Banks _____act a lot of business with their customers.

4. It's interesting to watch the zookeeper and the chimpanzees _____act.

Math

Solve the problems.

5. Jula's pet snail usually travels 39 inches per hour. How many yards can her snail travel during the 6 hours Jula is at school?

_____

6. The snail left a slime trail 208 inches long one night. How many minutes did it take the snail to leave the trail?

_____

Reading

Read the notice and the letter. Then answer the item.

Notice to Pronto Pasta customers:

As of January 1, we will start charging 10 cents for a cup of water. We regret that we can no longer provide water for free, but we have to pay for the cups, too.

Dear Pronto Pasta management:

As of January 1, I will be a customer of Caffey's Coffee. For two years, I have stopped by Pronto Pasta every morning after I jog with my dog. I buy a hot chocolate for myself and get a cup of water for Ginger. Is the cup charge really worth losing a customer?

7. Compare the perspectives of the two writers.

_____

_____

_____

_____

Language

Circle the base of the given word. Then use the same base with a different prefix or suffix to make another word. Use your word in a sentence. Circle the base in your word.

1. **discover**

_____

_____

2. **joyous**

_____

_____

Math

Answer the item.

3. Groups in Ms. Shiotsu's math class each measured an amount of liquid. However, each group used a different unit. Ms. Shiotsu wrote their results on the whiteboard. List the measurements in order from smallest to largest amount.

5 cups	1.2 quarts
2.75 pints	0.33 gallon

_____

_____

_____

_____

Reading

Read the secondhand account of the California goldrush of 1849. Then answer the item.

    The people found that panning for gold was hard, backbreaking work. Many of these people turned back toward home. Some moved on to new gold and silver strikes. Some of these miners found gold, but most were disappointed. Instead of gold, they found rough mining camps full of crime and wild behavior. The "shanty towns" attracted people ready to take the miners' money. Gunfights started over gold claims. There were few laws, and the people in the camps carried out their own kind of justice.

4. Imagine you are a gold miner in 1849. Write an account of this event from your perspective.

_____

_____

_____

_____

_____

Language

Read the sentence. Determine whether it is a compound sentence.
Write *yes* if it is a compound sentence. Write *no* if it is not.

1. The driver honked his horn, and the stray dog jumped out of the way. _____

2. Wanda brushed her long, dark hair and put it in a ponytail. _____

3. The girl I met while I was in Boston, Massachusetts, just texted me. _____

4. First you add the flour, and then you measure the milk. _____

Math

Read the phrase. Match it to its corresponding ratio.

5. 2 staples for every 10 pages •

6. 3 teaspoons of cocoa for every 8 ounces of milk •

7. 10 dollars spent on ads for every new customer •

8. 1 egg for every 3 pancakes •

• 1 : 3

• 1 : 10

• 2 : 10

• 3 : 1

• 3 : 8

• 10 : 1

Reading

Read the chart on being safe. Then answer the item.

Emergency Situation	Action Plan	Supplies
Downed Power Line	Call the power company and emergency (911); do not approach the power line.	power company's phone number; cellphone or corded landline phone
Tornado	Seek shelter in a basement, a room without windows, or a bathtub.	radio with batteries, water, flashlights
Earthquake	Go outside into an open area or take shelter under a desk or table, or against an inside wall.	radio with batteries, water, flashlights, food and supplies for three days

9. If a power line is down, what should you do, and what will you use to do it? _____

_____

Name _____

Language

Read the paragraph. Add a comma before the conjunction in any compound sentence.

1.   The group hiked to the edge of the bluff and they looked toward the sunset. Julia

and Brian grew up in Oregon but they didn't realize how much they missed the nightly

seascape. Mrs. Wu suggested that the group set up their tents on this spot. "You can

enjoy the sunset now or you can use the light to organize your gear," she advised.

Math

Write the ratio that represents the picture.

2.

chocolate to vanilla _____

3.

lemons to sugar _____

4.

square to round _____

5.

dollars to corndogs _____

Reading

Read the paragraph. Then answer the item.

Samuel Morse didn't plan to be an inventor or even a scientist. He was working as an artist in 1825, commissioned to paint a portrait of the Marquis de Lafayette in Washington, D.C., when his wife became gravely ill back home in Connecticut. Morse's father got word to him the usual way at the time: messenger on horseback. By the time he received the message, his wife had passed away. His grief eventually led to his invention of the telegraph, which instantly sent messages long distances.

commissioned: ordered or requested

6. What is the purpose of the bold word at the bottom of the text?

_____

Language

Read the sentences. Rewrite them as a single compound sentence, adding a coordinating conjunction.

1. Guillermo tried to be careful. He lost his key anyway.

_____

2. Tanika had never been to Argentina. The terrain seemed very familiar.

_____

_____

Math

A map key shows a scale of 2 inches = 30 miles. Use the graph to answer the items.

3. Two cities are 3 inches apart on the map. How far apart are they in real life?

_____

4. Cindy knows that Dawes is 90 miles from her hometown. How many inches from her hometown is Dawes on the map?

_____

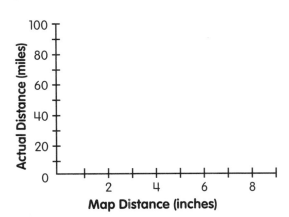

Reading

Read the page from an index in a book on weaving. Then answer the item.

shuttle, 13, 15, 22, 33, 54–56	warp, 5–9, 12, 22, 34, 55–61
spinning jenny, 13	weft, 5–8, 12, 22, 55–60
tapestry needle, 15–18	yarn
twill weave fabrics	cotton, 28
denim, 32	linen (flax), 28
gabardine, 34	silk, 17, 27
wool twill, 33	wool, 18, 29

5. On what pages would you find information about wool?

_____

Language

Read the sentence. Rewrite it as a compound sentence, making two independent clauses.

1. The festival is held every May and attracts lots of visitors.

   _____

2. We guarantee your carpets will be clean or give you your money back.

   _____

   _____

Math

Read the problem. Then answer the items.

   A 50-pound sack of chicken scratch feeds Kim's 30 chickens for a week.

3. What is the ratio of pounds of scratch to chickens? _____

4. How many pounds of scratch will 15 chickens eat in a week? _____

5. Kim's 15 hens lay 84 eggs in a week. What is the ratio of pounds of scratch to eggs laid?

   _____

Reading

Look at the photo and its caption. Then answer the item.

A horse-drawn fire engine is on its way to a fire in 1911.

6. What information does the caption add?

   _____

   _____

   _____

   _____

   _____

Language

Write two compound sentences about your favorite hobby.

1. _____

_____

2. _____

_____

Math

Solve the problem.

3. A recipe that makes 4 servings uses 10 ounces of chicken. Kenichi needs to make 6 servings. How much chicken will he need?

_____

4. Sarah wants to build a doghouse, but first she builds a smaller model to practice. The biggest piece of wood she will need for the full-size doghouse is 39 inches wide and 24 inches tall. If she uses a piece for the model that is 8 inches tall, how wide should it be?

_____

Reading

Read the text and the sidebar. Then answer the item.

Many people use the Internet for research. Since anyone can post information, it's important to make sure you use worthy sources. Find out the sponsor, the author's sources, and the posting date.

Look at the URL ending for the sponsor:
• edu = a college
• org = an organization
• com = a business
• gov = government

5. Who is the likely sponsor of a website at www.MiceAreUs.com?

_____

_____

_____

_____

_____

Language

Read the dependent clause. Write an independent clause to complete the complex sentence.

1. When the phone rang, _____.

2. After Pierre fed the dog, _____.

3. _____ if you like science fiction.

4. _____ unless that's too early.

Math

Read the statement and write the unit rate as a ratio.

5. Dad's car gets 33 miles per gallon.   _____

6. Rachel reads 124 words per minute.   _____

7. The speed limit is 75 kilometers per hour.   _____

8. Salmon costs 22 dollars per pound.   _____

Reading

Read the paragraph. Then answer the item.

In the shower that evening, Deb thought about her science project. She had to create a concept for a new kind of energy. She tried to conjure up images of magnets, windmills, and falling marbles as she enjoyed the warm water beating on her tired leg muscles. It reminded her of the electric massage chair at the mall. Deb was sore from riding her muddy bike home in the rain through soggy piles of leaves. As she rinsed the soap off and watched the suds swirl through the drain, an idea finally hit her!

9. What kind of idea do you think Deb had? Why do you think so?

_____

_____

Daily Fundamentals • EMC 3246 • © Evan-Moor Corp.

Language

Read the independent clause. Write a dependent clause to complete the complex sentence.

1. _____, you get good grades.

2. _____, I still miss my old school.

3. While it is snowing, _____.

4. When Phoebe goes hiking, _____.

Math

A parking lot in Hamilton City charges $2.50 per hour. Figure out how much drivers with these parking stubs would owe.

5.
| Time In: 11:30 a.m. | Time Out: 12:30 p.m. |
| Rate: $2.50 per hour | 1 hour of parking |

Total Due: _____

6.
| Time In: 1:15 p.m. | Time Out: 6:15 p.m. |
| Rate: $2.50 per hour | 5 hours of parking |

Total Due: _____

7.
| Time In: 8:42 a.m. | Time Out: 11:42 a.m. |
| Rate: $2.50 per hour | 3 hours of parking |

Total Due: _____

8.
| Time In: 7:05 a.m. | Time Out: 6:05 p.m. |
| Rate: $2.50 per hour | 11 hours of parking |

Total Due: _____

Reading

Read this introduction to an article. Then answer the item.

When you walk through your yard or a park, do you want to see weeds? They are often the tallest plants, hiding prettier flowers or competing with vegetables for water and nutrients. Many weeds have sharp stickers that hurt skin if grasped or stepped on. Weeds are the uninvited guests of the plant world. They sprout up in yards, gardens, forests, pastures, and even in the cracks of streets and sidewalks. They can put down roots in places where other plants can't grow at all. You may not like to see weeds, but they are important in many ways.

9. What kind of information would you probably read in the rest of this article?

_____

Language

Read the sentences. Rewrite them as a single complex sentence, adding a transition word.

1. Mayra scores another goal. The Kangaroos win the game!

_____

2. The traffic has been much worse. The new mall opened last month.

_____

_____

Math

A cheerleading squad holds a car wash to raise money. Use the graph to answer the items.

The graph shows how many cars they wash in a given time.

3. What is the cheerleaders' car-washing rate?

_____

4. At this rate, how long would it take the cheerleading squad to wash 45 cars?

_____

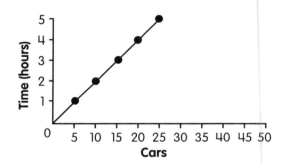

Reading

Read the paragraph. Then answer the item.

Groundhog Day was only a week away, so Punxsutawney Phil was busy doing research. The local citizens relied on Phil to tell them when to expect spring. Phil reviewed old folk wisdom descriptions of animal behaviors and the kind of weather they indicate, such as, "When squirrels bury nuts early on, winter will be both hard and long." Then he scooted over to his computer, activated his webcam, and called each of his animal friends, starting with Amy Squirrel.

5. What kind of conversations do you think the animals had?

_____

_____

Language

Read the paragraph. Add a comma after the dependent clause if needed.

1.   Seahorses are very unusual fish. While most fish swim parallel to the ocean floor seahorses swim upright. If you compare swimming fish to human swimmers seahorses look like they are treading water. Since they can't swim very fast they mostly hang on to seaweed. They snap up any brine shrimp that swim too close.

Math

Solve the problems.

2. Sergio read the first 18 pages of a novel in 2 hours. What is the unit rate at which he is reading?

_____

3. The novel is 216 pages long. If Sergio continues to read at the same rate, how long will it take him to finish reading the entire novel?

_____

Reading

Read the paragraph. Then answer the item.

    Landfills contribute to Earth's environmental problems by generating gases, such as methane, that cause air pollution. Methane remains in Earth's atmosphere for years. It traps the sun's heat and leads to an increase in atmospheric temperatures. In addition, trash pollutes oceans, which traps or suffocates some aquatic animals. It can also poison them or block their digestive systems, causing them to starve. However, we can improve our air and oceans by reusing items.

4. What do you think the rest of the article will be about?

_____

_____

Language

Write two complex sentences about a sport.

1. _____

_____

2. _____

_____

Math

Solve the problems.

3. Between 2001 and 2016, the Columbia glacier in Prince William Sound has retreated, or shrunk, a total of 165 km. What is its rate of retreat?

_____

4. In 2016, the glacier was 51 km long. If the glacier continues to retreat at the same rate, about how long will it take before it disappears from the Sound?

_____

Reading

Read the text titles. Then answer the items.

a. Genes for Survival (nonfiction)   **b. A Winter to Forget (fiction)**

5. What do you think each text will be about?

a. _____

b. _____

6. Write a question that can be answered by making predictions based on the title of a text.

_____

Language

Read the sentence. Use the present perfect tense of the verb in parentheses to complete it.

1. Cecilia _____ in trouble before. **(be)**

2. Marti _____ Mexico five times now. **(visit)**

3. The sixth graders _____ lunch already. **(eat)**

4. We _____ for a table long enough; let's try a different restaurant. **(wait)**

Math

Write the percent as both a fraction and a decimal.

5. 19% _____ _____

6. 2% _____ _____

7. 80% _____ _____

Write the fraction or decimal as a percent.

8. $\frac{53}{100}$ _____

9. $\frac{9}{36}$ _____

10. 0.47 _____

11. 0.82 _____

Reading

Read the paragraphs. Then answer the item.

"What's inside?" I asked as Grandpa handed me the dusty box. I opened the lid and took out an old shoe. It looked like an ordinary shoe, but it was pretty lightweight.

"They're cardboard shoes," Grandpa answered, as Daniel and I exchanged quizzical looks. "They were called imitation leather," Grandpa continued, "but they're actually cardboard. In 1945, the United States was at war. There were an awful lot of soldiers needing shoes. The government told families here at home that they could buy only so many leather shoes each year. When a boy outgrew his leather shoes, he got shoes made of something else like canvas or cardboard."

12. In which way does dialogue contribute to this story?
    Ⓐ It shows the speaker's personality.
    Ⓑ It helps the reader visualize the action.
    Ⓒ It lets a character tell a story within a story.
    Ⓓ It establishes the relationship of the speaking characters.

Language

Read the sentence. Use the past perfect tense of the verb in parentheses to complete it.

1. We _____ on our project for three days when Al joined the group. **(work)**

2. Terry _____ of that book before Saleh mentioned it. **(hear)**

3. There _____ four accidents by the time the city finally installed a stoplight. **(be)**

4. I _____ the street when I heard someone call out my name. **(cross)**

Math

Find the part of the whole.

5. 5% of 200 is _____.

6. 25% of 496 is _____.

7. 75% of 12 is _____.

8. 56% of 5,550 is _____.

Solve the problem.

9. Johan buys a backpack for $41. He has to pay 8% sales tax. How much is the tax?

   _____

Reading

Read the paragraphs. Then answer the item.

Suddenly, Jordan made his move, crossing the finish line just ahead of Zach. Wiping his face with a damp towel, Zach headed for the bleachers.

"Whoa," said a voice behind Zach. "Great race, buddy. Thanks for tiring out the other runners with that fast start. It made winning a lot easier for me."

Zach turned to see Jordan grinning at him. "Save a little speed for the last half," Jordan continued. "Then, next time, maybe you'll finish ahead of me—if I'm not so far out in front that you can't catch me, that is."

"Yeah, thanks," Zach said to Jordan once he had his breath and his temper under control. "I'll keep that in mind."

10. What can you tell about Jordan from the dialogue?

_____

_____

_____

Language

Read the sentence. Use the future perfect tense of the verb in parentheses to complete it.

1. They _____ a new TV before you fix the old one. (buy)

2. If Vivian can go to Juneau, Alaska, she

   _____ to all 50 state capitals. (travel)

3. I _____ dinner by the time you arrive. (finish)

4. You _____ fencing lessons for two years in June. (take)

Math

Find the whole.

5. **8** is 20% of _____.

6. **1** is 4% of _____.

7. **169** is 65% of _____.

8. **9** is 18% of _____.

Solve the problem.

9. Taryn's puzzle book has 15 crosswords in it. If the crosswords make up 12% of all the puzzles in the book, what is the total number of puzzles?

   _____

Reading

Read the paragraphs. Then answer the item.

They stopped near a berry patch in the woods and took two pails out of the cart. Jebediah couldn't tell his six-year-old sister the real reason they were in the woods. If the authorities stopped them, it was better she didn't know.

"Rebeccah, let's pick some berries for Aunt Sarah. Thee shall have berries and cream for thy dinner," Jebediah said. "Thee can start on this side of the berry patch. I'll go to another."

Jebediah hurried down to the cave by the riverbank, where runaway enslaved Africans often hid. "This is the road!" Jebediah called into the cave. "Hurry! There is danger."

10. Compare the dialogue and narrative sections. What effect does each style have on the story?

_____

_____

_____

_____

Language

Read the sentence. Circle the verb in the best tense to complete it.

1. I _____ this book twice so far.

   read   **have read**

2. Ricardo cleaned his room but still _____ his glasses.

   has not found   **did not find**

3. When the laundry was done, Naomi _____ the clothes.

   hung up   **has hung up**

4. After the movie ends, the parking lot _____ empty.

   will have been   **will be**

Math

Find the percent.

5. 18 out of 90 is _____%.

6. 4 out of 25 is _____%.

7. 13 out of 52 is _____%.

8. 21 out of 300 is _____%.

Solve the problem.

9. There were 55 words on the spelling test. Edyta spelled 44 words correctly. What percent of the words did she spell correctly?

   _____

Reading

Read the paragraphs. Then answer the items.

Two sisters inherited orchards from their father. Over time, Etta's carefully tended trees produced cartloads of produce, while Gretta's wild trees had few blossoms and even less fruit. "Soon, dear pear tree," cooed Etta sweetly, "you will grow tall and strong, and your magic blossoms will turn to fruit. Then I will take your juicy pears to the marketplace for all to admire."

Gretta confronted her sister. "Aha! It *is* magic!" she accused. "I knew it! It would be impossible to grow fruit or vegetables on your worthless land without magic."

That night, Gretta dug up Etta's pear tree and planted it in her own orchard. "Now I have the magic tree," she proclaimed. "Its juicy pears will grow for me; my sister will have none at all."

10. List any words or phrases in the text that describe or tell how characters spoke.

_____

11. Explain why knowing **how** something was said can help you understand a story better.

_____

_____

Language

Write three sentences about an accomplishment. Use a different perfect tense verb in each sentence.

1. _____

_____

2. _____

_____

_____

3. _____

_____

_____

Math

Solve the problems.

4. Mr. Caan has a coupon for a discount of 15% off his next purchase. What does "15% off" mean?

_____

_____

_____

5. Mr. Caan buys a $130 microwave oven. How much will he pay if he uses the coupon?

_____

Reading

Read the paragraphs. Then answer the item.

"Let's land our spaceship on that planet right there," said officer Elshta. "Apparently, this 'Earth' planet has all of the delicious goodies we seek."

"Magnificent!" exclaimed their leader, Sphigm. "So, it must have broccoli, cauliflower, celery, spinach, lettuce, and asparagus. How I long to eat asparagus again," he murmured wistfully. "I have not eaten any since our own planet ran out of it," remarked Sphigm, rubbing his belly.

"We must arrange to trade with the inhabitants," Elshta said. "Perhaps we can get rid of all of this unsavory food we've been carting all over the galaxy. I only hope that the Earthlings will want things like chocolate, peppermint, caramel, taffy, and jelly beans, although I cannot imagine who would find this disgusting stuff tasty."

6. How does the dialogue build suspense and further the plot?

_____

_____

_____

Language

Read the sentence. Use context to figure out the meaning of the underlined word.
Then match the sentence to the word's meaning.

1. My mother, <u>livid</u> about my lie, grounded me for a month. •   • very angry

2. Mr. Rime <u>endeavored</u> for a week to explain the difficult concept. •   • something in the way

3. The mattress <u>conforms</u> to your body. •   • to try hard

4. The view was blocked by an <u>obstruction</u>. •   • to be similar to

Math

Plot the numbers on the number line.

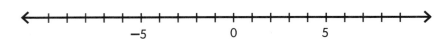

5. **4**   6. **−2**   7. **−10**   8. **7**   9. **−4**

Write **>**, **<**, or **=** in the ◯ to compare the numbers.

10. 4 ◯ −10   11. −2 ◯ 7   12. −2 ◯ −10   13. −4 ◯ 4

Reading

Read the paragraph. Then answer the item.

When Anna returned home, her mother asked her, "Did you take my ring? I set it on the dresser so it wouldn't catch on the threads while I was sewing. It's not there."

"I did put it on my finger, but I didn't take it," Anna replied. "I put it back on the dresser where I found it." The ring had been in the family for a hundred years, maybe longer.

"Anna, are you sure?" her mother pleaded. "It couldn't just fly away."

"Really I didn't. I'll go look for it." Anna checked every inch of the room; the ring was gone.

14. What is the conflict in the story?

_____

_____

Language

Read the sentence. Use context to figure out what the underlined word means.
Write the meaning on the line.

1. At the start of the race, Carlos <u>accelerated</u> quickly to a faster pace than the other runners.

_____

2. Mariska left only a <u>morsel</u> on her plate; her cat helped himself to the small crumbs.

_____

Math

Read the weather report. Graph each temperature on a Fahrenheit thermometer. Then answer the item.

Today was a cold day in North Dakota. Bismarck got up to 8 below zero, and Minot reached a high of 12 below. Meanwhile, Carrington was a balmy 3 degrees.

3. **Bismarck**
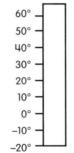

4. **Minot**

5. **Carrington**
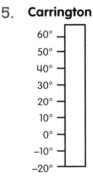

6. Which city had the lowest temperature? _____

Reading

Read the paragraph. Then answer the item.

     The king disbanded his army and called on every soldier to provide goods or services to others. Some former soldiers found they had a talent for growing crops. This created a problem for the kingdom's farmers. As former customers, the ex-soldiers knew the farmers' prices, and they undercut them. Furthermore, the ex-soldiers were no longer buying produce from the farmers, who were growing poorer by the day.

7. Which characters is the conflict between? Explain their concerns.

_____

_____

Language

Read the sentence. Use context to figure out what the underlined word means.
Write the meaning on the line.

1. The imposter ran off when the real magician arrived.

   _____

2. The little fish was caught in the net, but it liberated itself and swam freely away from the boat.

   _____

Math

Read the statement and write the positive or negative number described.

3. In the U.S., drones may not fly higher than 400 feet.   _____

4. The city of Jericho sits at least 233 meters below sea level.   _____

5. The Cave of the Crystals in Mexico is located 951 feet underground.   _____

6. The zip line starts at 450 meters up in the forest's trees.   _____

Reading

Read the paragraphs. Then answer the item.

   "I could live here," thought Charmaine, "for the rest of my life." On the last day of vacation, Charmaine rowed her canoe out to the tiny mound in Lake Paz. It was like a private treehouse.
   As she stroked toward the shore, she fantasized behind closed eyelids about buying a little cabin and working as a writer someday. The water seemed thicker with her eyes shut. When she opened them, she saw water seeping through a crack just as she felt her shoes getting wet.

7. Is the main conflict in the story internal or external? Explain your answer.

   _____

   _____

Language

Read the sentence. Use context to figure out what the underlined word means.
Write the meaning on the line.

1. <u>Ungulates</u>, such as deer, zebras, and moose, have hooves and eat grass.

_____

2. Dilip met the <u>criteria</u> for joining the group by paying dues and attending three meetings.

_____

Math

Read the situation and write a positive or negative number to represent it.

3. earning $15 for weeding   _____

4. donating $5 to charity   _____

5. lending a friend $1.50   _____

6. selling a guitar for $60   _____

7. spending $25 at the movies   _____

Reading

Read the paragraphs. Then answer the item.

John heard the crack of the bat. He spotted the ball and took a few steps toward it as it dropped five feet away. Rob yelled, "You didn't even reach for it. Where is your head?"

Until recently, John's world was baseball. Lately, he'd been more concerned with his grades. Was he growing up? Caring about your future sounds mature, but not at the expense of losing your joy. Well, he'd have to figure it out later, because another ball was on its way toward the infield.

8. Is the main conflict in the story internal or external? Explain your answer.

_____

_____

Language

Read the sentence. Use context to figure out what the underlined word means.
Write the meaning on the line.

1. The map showed rivers, mountains, and other <u>topography</u> of the region.

_____

2. Ms. Takei managed the <u>supply chain</u>, including the manufacturer, store, and transportation.

_____

Math

Use the coordinate grid to complete the items.

3. Plot these points. Then connect them.

   A (−3, 2)   B (5, 2)   C (−3, −1)

4. Find the distances.

   $\overline{AB}$ _____

   $\overline{AC}$ _____

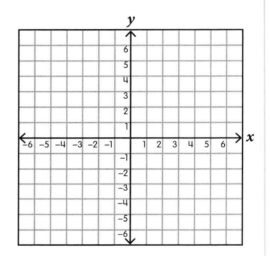

Reading

Read the paragraphs. Then answer the item.

> The protesters stood hand in hand around five Douglas firs. Nearby, the group's leader explained: "We won't leave until the town council calls off their plan to cut down these trees. An outdoor community stage is a good idea, but not in place of these beautiful, healthy trees."
>
> The lumberjack foreman impatiently poked buttons on his cellphone. In ten minutes, the town council president's car screeched onto the scene.

5. How do you think the conflict might be resolved?

_____

_____

Language

Read the sentence. Then add quotation marks where they are needed.

1. Aisha yelled, Don't forget to call me after tennis practice today.

2. I can't call you then, Larissa responded, because I have a dentist appointment afterward.

3. Well, give me a call after your appointment, Aisha said while running to class.

4. Larissa agreed, Okay, unless my mouth is numb, and she turned to go.

Math

Write the absolute value of the number.

5. |5| _____

6. |−11| _____

7. |−34| _____

8. |2| _____

9. |168| _____

10. |−2| _____

11. |43| _____

12. |−3,859| _____

13. |707| _____

14. |−6.45| _____

Reading

Read the paragraph. Then answer the item.

   I have heard that the United States is considering discontinuing the penny. I am not happy about this idea. First, charities and other organizations rely on people contributing loose change. Pennies may seem more annoying than they are worth, but when donated and added together, they go a long way toward helping fund nonprofit organizations. Secondly, all prices will have to be rounded up to the nearest five cents. Prices go up too quickly as it is! Let's keep the penny.

15. How does the author make the persuasive purpose of the text clear?

_____

_____

Language

Read the sentence. Then edit to add quotation marks where they are needed or cross them out if they are not needed.

1. The ticket-taker told us "to have our tickets ready."

2. Keiran gasped, "Oh no! Where did I put mine? as he checked his pockets.

3. Alex said "that he would buy him another ticket."

4. No, that's okay," Keiran muttered as he promised to "be more careful.

Math

Write **>**, **<**, or **=** in the ◯ to compare the values.

5. −16 ◯ |16|

6. |72| ◯ 72

7. |83| ◯ 91

8. |−22| ◯ −3

9. |−42| ◯ |42|

10. 0.78 ◯ |−17.8|

Reading

Read the paragraph. Then answer the item.

The first thing we kids did at our grandparents' house was devour a large lunch. Then we slammed our way outside through Grandma's backdoor. We chased barn cats, stomped in cow pies, and threw each other into haystacks. We explored every nook and cranny of Grandpa's old barn. Sometimes we snatched up our little cousins and took them for rides in wheelbarrows or into the barn to kiss the cows, who mooed their complaints when we entered their domain.

11. How does the author help the reader know the descriptive purpose of the text?

_____

_____

Language

Write a dialogue of at least four sentences telling someone how to do something.

1. _____

_____

_____

_____

_____

Math

Read the situation. Match it to the number that represents it.

2. Rita collected 5 fresh eggs from her chickens. •   • 5

3. Henny is sitting on 5 more eggs than Penny has. •   • −5

4. Rita used 5 eggs to make a custard. •   • |5|

Reading

Read the paragraph. Then answer the item.

   The United Nations is an international alliance that works to prevent war. It was formed after World War II, in which roughly 60 million people died and many faced poverty or were forced to move to new lands. The nearly 200 member countries agree to these principles:

- cooperate in solving problems
- maintain international peace and security
- promote respect for human rights
- assist refugees fleeing war, famine, and persecution

5. How does the author make the informational purpose of the text clear?

_____

_____

Language

Read the sentence. Then add quotation marks around the title.

1. The poem The Road Not Taken is about making decisions for your future.

2. We read the article The Two Carolinas, and it really made me think.

3. Australians voted in 1984 to make Advance Australia Fair their national anthem.

4. Turn to the story Star in the Storm in your reading book.

Math

Solve the problem.

5. A hot-air balloon is flying at an altitude of 1,240 feet. A bristlemouth fish is swimming at a depth of −3,362 feet. Which is closer to sea level?

   _____

6. The daytime temperature on the moon reaches 107°C. The nighttime temperature reaches −183°C. Is it closer to freezing (0°C) during the day or night?

   _____

Reading

Read the paragraph. Then answer the item.

This bookcase is easy to assemble. First, fill the holes on one shelf with glue. Then fill a pair of holes on a side board with glue. Next, place two pegs in the glued holes on the side board and attach the shelf. Repeat with the remaining shelves. Tap each shelf with a hammer and wipe off the excess glue. After the glue sets, repeat the gluing, tapping, and wiping with the other side board and let set. Finally, attach the back of the bookcase with the screws provided.

7. How can the reader tell that the text's purpose is instructional?

   _____

   _____

Language

Read the sentence. Then underline the title.

1. My grandmother's favorite movie is called West Side Story.

2. Ranger Rick magazine has a great article about anteaters.

3. Do you think they'll ever make the book Walk Two Moons into a movie?

4. The cartoon The Simpsons has been on TV since 1989.

Math

Read the problem and look at the diagram. Then answer the item.

The Mauna Kea volcano may not look like it, but it is the tallest mountain on Earth. Its visible summit stands at 13,796 feet, while the base of the volcano is at −19,685 feet, hidden under the sea.

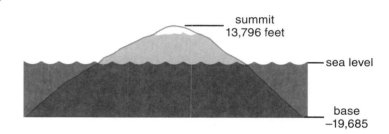
summit
13,796 feet
sea level
base
−19,685

5. How tall is Mauna Kea, from base to summit? _____

Reading

Read the ad. Then answer the item.

Fluffy is a winner. She has a room filled with trophies and blue ribbons to prove it. She's been named "Top Cat" at shows all over the country. To keep her prize-winning form, Fluffy eats top-quality Super Cat cat food. The ingredients in Super Cat keep Fluffy healthy and content. Feed your cat Super Cat, and watch your feline friend develop winning ways!

6. What techniques or words does the writer use to encourage readers to buy this product?

_____

_____

_____

Language

Read the sentence. Complete it with the correct word from the word box.

lie   lay   laid

1. When I was in kindergarten, we _____ on mats at nap time.

2. The doctor tells Mom to _____ still when she gets a headache.

3. Please _____ your pencils on the desk now.

4. The hen _____ two eggs yesterday!

Math

Write the expression using exponents.

5. $9 \times 9 \times 9 \times 9$ _____

6. 78×78 _____

7. $\frac{5}{8} \times \frac{5}{8} \times \frac{5}{8}$ _____

8. 6.01×6.01 _____

Write the expression using operational symbols.

9. 14^5 _____

10. $(2\frac{1}{2})^3$ _____

11. 81.99^2 _____

Reading

Read the paragraphs. Then answer the items.

"I'll be helping my parents run a medical clinic in Africa," said Christine.

"Are you afraid," whispered Tamara, "of being in a place where everything is different?"

It was a little scary, and Christine was timid about trying new things. She didn't worry about snakes and lions too much, and her parents had assured her they would cook familiar foods. "I don't know what will happen," she shrugged.

"But why do you *want* to leave, Christine?" Tamara asked, but what Christine heard in her friend's question was, "Why do you want to leave *me*?"

Selfishly, she was glad that Tamara felt sad about her going. "My parents and my brother are going," she explained gently. "I want to be where they are. And I want to do some good. I think this is what I'm supposed to be doing."

12. Which word best describes Christine?
    Ⓐ giving
    Ⓑ greedy
    Ⓒ scared
    Ⓓ shy

13. Which story phrase supports your answer?
    Ⓐ worry about snakes and lions
    Ⓑ timid about trying new things
    Ⓒ glad that Tamara felt sad
    Ⓓ want to do some good

 Daily Fundamentals • EMC 3246 • © Evan-Moor Corp.

Language

Read the sentence. Complete it with the correct word from the word box.

> whose   who's

1. _____ cellphone is ringing?

2. _____ going to the game tonight?

3. I know _____ going to be surprised tomorrow!

4. I apologize to the person _____ sandwich I accidentally ate.

Math

Write an expression to represent the situation.

5. Rhoda got 114 more votes than Petro.

_____

6. Matt took 10 minutes longer than twice as long as Bryce took to do his assignment.

_____

7. A hamburger costs 29¢ less than half as much as a full meal.

_____

Reading

Read the paragraphs. Then answer the item.

Margaret ran errands to earn money for a bike. "Here's my little Miss Sunshine, right on time!" Mrs. Perry greeted her. "I put the grocery money envelope on the table, I think."

"Be back soon, Mrs. Perry." Margaret put the envelope in her jacket pocket and walked quickly to the supermarket. When Margaret went to pay for the groceries, the envelope was empty. "I, I must have lost the money," Margaret stammered. There was only one thing to do. Margaret got the money she was saving for a bike from her house and went back to the market.

"How did you manage to get the groceries?" Mrs. Perry asked when Margaret finally returned. "I found the grocery money in another envelope."

"I used the money I'd saved," Margaret explained. "I didn't want you to think I had taken it."

"Never!" said Mrs. Perry, giving Margaret a hug. "I don't know what I'd do without you!"

8. Write three words that describe Margaret. Cite details in the text that support your description.

_____

_____

Name _____

Simplify the expression by combining like terms.

Read the sentence. Complete it with the correct word from the word box.

> fewer   less

1. We're trying to use _____ water during the drought.

2. There are _____ reasons to stay home than to take the trip.

3. This shirt costs _____ money than the blue one.

4. Nadia has two _____ hobbies than I do.

Math

Simplify the expression by combining like terms.

5. $x^2 + 3a + 7 + a =$ _____

6. $y^3 + 5b - 1 - 3b =$ _____

7. $c \times c - 4c + 3c - 12 =$ _____

8. $k^2 \times k - 8k - 6k^2 + 48 =$

   _____

Reading

Read the paragraphs. Then answer the item.

    The crow cocked his head to show off the prized piece of cheese he had just stolen from the preoccupied farmer. "You are as handsome as you are clever, friend crow," the fox began. "Your feathers glisten in the sunlight. I see iridescent shades of green and a rainbow of colors dancing on your wings, and your eyes sparkle like jewels. How I would love to replace my feet with yours so I could perch on a tree branch and watch the world below me. There is no creature in the forest that can compare to you." The crow nodded in agreement.

    "I don't wish to interrupt your dinner," said the fox, "but as a favor to this poor fox who will never be able to imitate your soothing, melodious tones, please sing a few notes."

    The crow was pleased to hear the fox's flattering remarks. "How can I refuse such a great admirer as the fox?" thought the crow.

    As the crow opened his beak to sing, his piece of cheese fell into the fox's ready mouth.

9. How are the personalities of the crow and the fox alike? How are they different?

_____

_____

Day 3   Week 18

98   Daily Fundamentals • EMC 3246 • © Evan-Moor Corp.

Language

Read the sentence. Complete it with the correct word from the word box.

    imply   infer

1. Did you mean to _____ that Glynnis is wrong?

2. Seeing his frown, I will _____ that you told Leon the bad news.

3. The fact that I'm in a wheelchair does not

   _____ that I don't play sports.

4. We can _____ which flavor is the most popular by looking at which has sold out.

Math

Use the distributive property to write an equivalent expression.

5. $10(7 + 22) =$ _____

6. $3(p + 2q) =$ _____

Use the greatest common factor (GCF) to write an equivalent expression.

7. $4t - 20 =$ _____

8. $6 + 18r =$ _____

Reading

Read the paragraphs. Then answer the item.

The tribesman called everyone to the meal. He smiled at Devin as he handed the boy a huge leaf, which apparently would be his plate. But when Devin saw what was on the menu, he did not want to fill his plate. One bowl contained raw meat. Another bowl contained a green slimy paste that looked like rotten leaves. A third bowl contained large cooked slugs, and the final bowl had shaved coconut. Devin just took a little coconut and sat down.

Suddenly, the tribe stopped eating and started dissecting him with their eyes. The tribe leader stood and held his bamboo knife firmly as he slowly approached Devin, who sat frozen. Had he offended them? The leader lifted the weapon above Devin's head as Devin cowered. After hearing a *thud,* Devin opened his eyes and saw a huge, squirming snake on the ground.

9. Does the tribesman do something you would expect or not? Explain your answer.

_____

_____

_____

Language

Read the sentence. Complete it with the correct word from the word box.

> that   which

1. Sandeep wants a career _____ allows him to work outside.

2. A forest ranger career, _____ requires a college degree, would be fun.

3. Shauna's apartment, _____ is downtown, was built in 1907.

4. Will I ever find an apartment _____ I can afford?

Math

Solve the problems.

5. A pet store gives away 3 dog treats with every food bowl sold. Write an expression to represent this situation.

_____

6. If the store sells 9 bowls, how many treats are given away?

_____

7. A clerk gave away 57 treats one day. How many bowls did he sell?

_____

Reading

Read the paragraphs. Then answer the item.

A boy went to pick fresh blackberries for his mother, who was baking a pie. Off he went with his pail. In the berry patch, he came upon a sleeping giant. The boy looked into the giant's pockets. "No berries here," he said. Then he peered into the giant's ears. "Nothing in there." The boy walked into the giant's nose.

"Aaah-choo!" the giant sneezed. The boy flew out of the giant's nose and landed on top of a tall pine tree. "People make me sneeze!" bellowed the giant.

"Your sneeze blew me up into the tree," said the boy. "I'm looking for berries."

"Berries?" the giant roared. "Not in my berry patch!" The giant pulled the boy's tree out of the ground and sent it sailing through the air.

"Whee! I'm flying over the forest like a bird!" shouted the boy. "I can see farms and villages."

8. How is the boy's personality shown in the action?

_____

_____

Language

Read the sentence. Write the correct tense of the verb. Then underline the tense signal word or phrase.

1. Yesterday, a bird _____ right into our classroom. **(fly)**

2. The Santanas _____ us when they leave their house. **(call)**

3. Takeshi _____ dinner when the phone rang. **(make)**

4. Now Frieda _____ to go to school every day. **(like)**

Math

Read the equation. Circle the bar diagram that represents it.

5. $81 + a = 175$

81	175
a	

81	a
175	

7. $3g = 39$

39		
g	g	g

g		
39	39	39

6. $d - 364 = 198$

d	
198	364

364	
198	d

8. $20 \div m = 4$

20			
m	m	m	m

20			
4	4	4	4

Reading

Read the paragraph. Then answer the items.

"Something must be done," said Percy, collapsing on the floor of his mouse house after _____ through the hole in the wall, exhausted. His tail had a nasty gash in it, and his body shook uncontrollably. That cat was on the prowl again!

9. Which word best completes the sentence, matching the tone of the scene?

Ⓐ passing

Ⓑ charging

Ⓒ stepping

10. Explain your answer. _____

_____

Language

Read the sentence. Write its verb tense. Then write a sentence in the same tense using a different verb.

1. Ms. Edson was preparing a math lesson during the show. _____

_____

2. Kylie has volunteered for two months at the animal shelter. _____

_____

Math

Draw a bar model to represent the equation. Then solve the equation.

3. $13 + r = 486$ $r =$ _____

5. $w - 611 = 40$ $w =$ _____

4. $f + 184 = 201$ $f =$ _____

6. $7,624 - h = 887$ $h =$ _____

Reading

Read the paragraph. Then answer the item.

We expected to find a town and lodging in Monterey, but because the settlement was new, there weren't enough buildings to shelter us. We had to huddle inside our tents during the storms. Even so, we gave thanks that we did not have to endure a longer journey. Some of our party would go farther north to a larger bay, but our family stayed in Monterey. We looked for land and began the construction of our adobe house.

7. Why do you think the author wrote *endure* instead of *experience* or *go through*?

_____

_____

Daily Fundamentals • EMC 3246 • © Evan-Moor Corp.

Language

Read the paragraph. Cross out any verb that is in the wrong tense and write it correctly above.

1.   Archana set up the tent in her backyard. She is really looking forward to her first

camping experience. She borrowed her brother's sleeping bag. Her father was giving her some

snacks. After looking up at the stars for a while, Archana crawls into her tent and will zip it up.

She had just fallen asleep when a snorting sound outside the tent wakes her up.

Math

Draw a bar model to represent the equation. Then solve the equation.

2. $5y = 95$ $y =$ _____

4. $168 \div c = 8$ $c =$ _____

3. $6b = 72$ $b =$ _____

5. $v \div 7 = 5$ $v =$ _____

Reading

Read the paragraph. Then answer the item.

Before the day was done, everyone knew that the milkmaid had challenged the magician to a contest to see who was the smarter of the two. Insulted that he had to compete with a mere milkmaid, the magician acknowledged his strong ambition to become governor and accepted the conditions.

6. Circle the word that helps you visualize how the magician felt about the challenge. Explain how a word with a different shade of meaning would change what you visualize.

_____

_____

Language

Write a sentence about something happening in the given tense.

1. **present:** _____.

2. **past:** _____.

3. **future:** _____.

Math

Write an inverse operation equation. Then use inverse operations to solve the equation.

4. $18 + k = 60$ $18 + k - 18 = 60 - 18$ $k =$ _____

5. $e - 225 = 392$ $e - 225$ _____ $= 392$ _____ $e =$ _____

6. $72 \times w = 936$ $72 \times w$ _____ $= 936$ _____ $w =$ _____

7. $j \div 26 = 11$ $j \div 26$ _____ $= 11$ _____ $j =$ _____

Reading

Read the report card comments from two of Jerry's teachers. Then answer the item.

from Ms. Kodaly: Jerry's confident participation in class persuades his classmates to agree with his point of view. He perseveres in problem solving, using his own ideas.

from Ms. Grieg: Jerry's cocky attitude dominates class discussions, intimidating other students to agree with him. He stubbornly resists learning new ways of doing things.

8. The teachers have different opinions. Write a more neutral description of Jerry's performance.

_____

_____

Language

Write a paragraph to convey a sequence of events.

1. _____

_____

_____

_____

_____

_____

Math

Read the problem. Use any strategy to solve it. Show your work.

2. A craft fair sold $1,485 of Erynne's necklaces. Before the fair, Erynne had spent 198 hours making the necklaces.

How much money did Erynne earn per hour? _____

Reading

Read the paragraph. Then answer the item.

"Amy," the woman scolded, "I thought you had more sense than to go swimming this time of year. What would your mother say if she could see you playing in the water on a cold day like this? How careless of you! Some children just think of themselves."

3. How did *scolded* prepare you for the rest of the dialogue? Rewrite the first sentence, changing *scolded* to a word with another shade of meaning and making what follows match.

_____

_____

_____

Language

Read the sentence. Rewrite it to correct the run-on.

1. That's the biggest dog I've ever seen it's as tall as a horse.

_____

2. Let's see the movie on Sunday instead of Saturday, I'm going shopping on Saturday.

_____

_____

Math

Read the situation and identify the variables. Complete the sentence to explain how the variables are related.

3. Every package of paper contains 250 sheets.

   The number of _____ affects the number of _____.

4. Every 15 minutes of jumping rope burns off 195 calories.

   The number of _____ depends on the number of _____.

Reading

Read the paragraph. Then answer the item.

Uncle James, Mother's brother, sailed to America two years ago. He wrote to tell Mother what a fine place Boston was. He sent some money with a sailor who was returning to Ireland. There wasn't enough for all of us to go to America. When Mother's friend, Mary, was leaving to join her husband in Boston, Mother decided it would be better for us two boys there.

5. Who is the narrator in this story? How can you tell?

_____

_____

Language

Read the sentence. Then explain why it is a run-on sentence or correct.

1. The planes took off one after another, they flew in a tight formation.

_____

2. The Thunderbirds, a team of Air Force pilots, are performing at the air show.

_____

Math

Read the situation and identify the independent and dependent variables.

3. A box of cereal makes 18 servings.

   independent variable: _____   dependent variable: _____

4. Wrapping paper costs $4 for 108 inches.

   independent variable: _____   dependent variable: _____

Reading

Read the paragraphs. Then answer the item.

   Sam picked up a letter off the floor and read the envelope. He took the letter to Gramps. "You got a letter from the president?" he asked.
   Gramps nodded. "And twenty thousand dollars."
   "How come?" Sam asked. "Is the president hiring you to write his speeches or something?"

5. From what point of view is the story told? Explain how you know.

_____

_____

Language

Read the sentence. Rewrite it to correct the fragment.

1. The jacket on the left side of the closet in the hallway.

_____

2. The science experiment that we did last Friday.

_____

Math

Read the situation. Write a variable in each table heading. Then complete the table with data that represent the situation.

3. Carnival tickets cost $4 each.

1	
	8
3	

4. Rides last 8 minutes each.

	16
4	
	48

5. Win a prize for every 3 bottles knocked down.

1	
	9
6	

Reading

Read the paragraph. Then answer the item.

It was about 105 degrees at Camp Clear Creek the day Hoa's parents dropped him off. Then he saw the cabin where he'd be staying for two weeks. There was no air conditioning, nor was there electricity. "The brochure said it was 'rustic,'" Hoa muttered, "but 'primitive' is more like it." Just then, his roommate appeared.

6. Is the narrator's knowledge limited or unlimited? Explain how you know.

_____

_____

Language

Read the sentence. Then explain why it is a complete sentence or a fragment.

1. The old Chinese restaurant near the downtown train station.

   _____

2. The new restaurant did not impress me very much.

   _____

Math

Read the situation. Then answer the items.

In American football, a touchdown scores 6 points.

3. What is the independent variable? _____ Explain your thinking. _____

   _____

4. What is the dependent variable? _____ Explain your thinking. _____

   _____

   _____

Reading

Read two versions of a paragraph. Then answer the item.

Third person: As Susan recovered from having fainted, she wondered how she could see both the ceiling light fixtures and her feet at the same time. Then her doctor spoke.

First person: As my eyes opened, I saw only the light and my feet. "How did I get... wherever I am?" I wondered. "Am I in danger? Think quickly!" Then my doctor spoke.

5. Compare the effect of the different points of view.

   _____

   _____

Language

Read the paragraph. Then rewrite it, correcting the fragments and run-ons.

1. When Tamara went to the doctor. A twisted ankle and a bruised hip. Her doctor thought she'd run into another soccer player. Actually, she tripped on the curb then she fell on the sidewalk.

_____

_____

_____

Math

Read the situation. Complete the table and answer the item.

2. Janelle's pancake recipe requires 2 eggs for every batch of 11 pancakes. Write the independent variable in the first column and the dependent variable in the second column of the table. Then complete the table for 2, 4, and 6 eggs.

   How many pancakes will 6 eggs make?

   _____

Reading

Read the paragraph. Then answer the item.

Billiken jumped up on Kaitlin's chair. His front paws kneaded her stomach while his back legs balanced delicately on the armrest. He blocked her view of both the TV and the computer on the table next to her. "Why don't you sit here next to me?" Kaitlin suggested as she patted the empty cat-sized spot next to her leg. He just purred and kept kneading.

3. Rewrite the paragraph with Billiken, the cat, as the narrator.

_____

_____

_____

Daily Fundamentals • EMC 3246 • © Evan-Moor Corp.

Language

Read the sentence. Add commas where needed.

1. Emi please hand me that shovel.

2. Dad is Mom working late today?

3. I don't mind the hours Ms. Minnes as long as the job is interesting.

4. Please come visit us soon Grandpa.

5. The food is hot everyone so dig in!

6. Excuse me ma'am can I help you find something?

7. My stomach is bothering me doctor.

Math

Read the situation. Then complete the table.

8. There are 3 minutes of commercial ads after every 14 minutes of TV show.

Ads	Show
3	14
6	
9	
12	
15	
18	

Reading

Read the paragraph. Then answer the item.

   Chocolate comes from cacao trees grown on large tropical plantations. Although native to Mexico, cacao trees now grow all over the world in the tropical zones near the equator. Blossoms form throughout the year, and football-shaped pods develop from the flowers. The pods hang from the trunk and branches of the tree, full of cocoa beans. It takes five to six months for a pod to ripen. Once the pod is ripe, the white almond-sized cocoa beans inside can be harvested.

9. Which of these would be the best title for this text?
   Ⓐ Tropical Plantations
   Ⓑ From Cacao to Candy
   Ⓒ How to Make Chocolate
   Ⓓ Where Chocolate Comes From

Language

Read the sentence. Add a comma where needed.

1. No I don't think that answer is right.

2. Yes your plan sounds good to me.

3. This is that song you like no?

4. You recommended this magazine didn't you?

5. He doesn't give bad advice does he?

6. Yes please tell us more about Laos.

7. The twins will be in different classes won't they?

Math

Read the situation. Then complete the table.

8. Lupita and Sheebah are 5 years apart in age.

Lupita	Sheebah
9	4
11	
15	
18	
21	
26	

Reading

Read the paragraphs. Then answer the item.

"When I was your age, 80 years ago," Luke's great-grandmother began, "a wagon pulled by horses picked me up outside our house to take me to school. There wasn't room for us in the schoolhouse, so all of us West End kids went to school in the basement of the library."

Luke was surprised. "That sounds like a fun way to get to school! I ride the school bus. I hope we don't ever have too many kids to fit in my school, because our town library doesn't have a basement!"

9. Paraphrase the dialogue.

_____

_____

_____

Language

Read the sentence. Add a comma where needed.

1. Hey why can't I stay up that late?

2. Sorry I thought you were someone else.

3. Well I can understand your point.

4. Okay now the microwave is working.

5. Oh that soup is way too hot for me!

6. Gee rowing is much harder than we thought it would be.

7. Aw your new puppy is adorable!

Math

Read the situation. Then complete the table.

8. Marni burns a candle half of its length every day that she uses it.

Day	End Length (cm)
1	18
2	
3	
4	
5	

Reading

Read the paragraph. Then answer the item.

Native American paintings and jewelry are often made of natural materials such as sand, plant dyes, stones, seeds, and shells. They also include many bright colors and distinct symbols. The colors and symbols used in Native American art often tell a story. Many of the stories show a deep respect for animal and plant life and for the beauty of the natural world. You can sometimes find Native American crafts and art for sale at craft fairs.

9. Summarize the paragraph.

_____

_____

_____

Language

Read the sentence. Then explain why it is punctuated correctly or incorrectly.

1. Joe has gone to summer camp three years in a row.

   _____

   _____

   _____

2. Joe has the food at camp improved at all?

   _____

   _____

   _____

Math

Read the situation. Then complete the table.

3. Mrs. Jindal ordered 12 cans of tennis balls for her P.E. class. The cans cost $2.50 each. The shipping and handling fee is $5.60 for every order.

Cans per Order	Cost
12	$35.60
24	
48	
60	
120	

Reading

Read the table. Then answer the item.

Topic: Teaching self-defense in public schools	
Pro	**Con**
Self-defense classes are good exercise.	Schools shouldn't teach kids how to fight.
They teach discipline, responsibility, and concentration.	Self-defense classes are not the best use of school resources.
They also help kids protect themselves.	Kids can get hurt too easily.

4. Summarize each side of the argument.

   Pro: _____

   _____

   Con: _____

   _____

Language

Read the text. Add commas where needed.

1.   "Yuri do you still want to play baseball when you grow up?" Mariah asked.

    "No I'm not a great player," Yuri replied. "I'm thinking about being a historian."

    "Wow that's quite a switch," Mariah remarked. "It's hard to get a job as a historian isn't it?"

    "Well it depends on where you look," Yuri explained. "Historians are often hired by museums and libraries."

    "Hey I guess you could teach history as well couldn't you?" Mariah suggested.

    "Yes Mariah but teaching is harder than baseball!" Yuri responded.

Math

Read the situation. Then complete the table.

2. Thor has 60 apples to give away at the grand opening of his new grocery store.

Customers	Apples for Each
5	12
6	
10	
12	
15	
20	

Reading

Read the paragraph. Then answer the items.

    Giraffes' towering height is the key to their ability to survive in their often-dry habitat. It allows them to reach the tender leaves at the top of acacia trees. Because these leaves are about three-quarters water, they also provide moisture when there are no watering places nearby. Giraffes didn't just decide to grow longer necks to reach these leaves! Over hundreds of generations, the tallest giraffes, who could reach more leaves, became healthier, lived longer, and had more offspring. Gradually, the average height increased.

3. Paraphrase the first two sentences of the text.

_____

4. Summarize the paragraph.

_____

_____

_____

Language

Read the dictionary entry. Use it to answer the items.

> **minute** (MIHN-it)   *Noun*   1. a short amount of time; 60 seconds
> **minute** (my-NOOT)   *Adj*   1. very tiny

1. How many meanings does *minute* have? _____

2. What parts of speech can *minute* be? _____

3. Which syllable of *minute* is accented here? "I made a *minute* change." _____

Math

Read the problem. Then answer the items.

An elephant's heart beats an average of 30 beats every minute.
How many times will it beat in 60 minutes?

4. Describe the relationship between the heart beating and minutes passing. _____

_____

5. Circle the correct expression to represent the problem.

   a. $30 \div 60$ **b.** 30×60 **c.** $60 \div 30$

Reading

Read the timeline. Then answer the items.

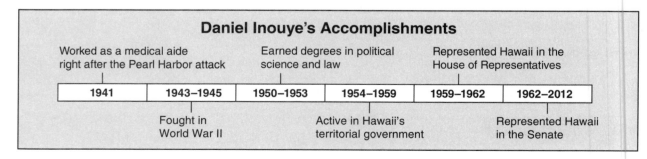

Daniel Inouye's Accomplishments

Worked as a medical aide right after the Pearl Harbor attack		Earned degrees in political science and law		Represented Hawaii in the House of Representatives	
1941	1943–1945	1950–1953	1954–1959	1959–1962	1962–2012
	Fought in World War II		Active in Hawaii's territorial government		Represented Hawaii in the Senate

6. When did Inouye serve in Hawaii's territorial government? _____

7. During what years did Inouye serve as a government representative after Hawaii became a state? _____

Language

Read the dictionary entry and the sentence. Use them to answer the items.

> **sole** (SOHL) *Noun* 1. the bottom of a foot or shoe
> *Adj* 1. only

The *sole* reason I joined the choir was that my best friends had joined.

1. Which meaning is used in the sentence? _____

2. What part of speech is it? _____

Math

Read the problem. Then answer the items.

> Erica is reading a 224-page book. If she reads *r* pages per day,
> how many days will it take her to finish the book?

3. Describe the relationship between the book length and Erica's reading rate. _____

_____

4. Circle the correct expression to represent the problem.

   a. $r \times 224$ **b.** $224 \times r$ **c.** $224 \div r$

Reading

Look at the map and key. Then answer the items.

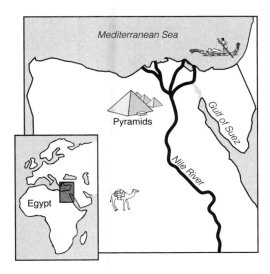

5. In what part of Africa are the Egyptian pyramids located?

_____

6. What water sources does Egypt have access to?

_____

_____

Language

Read the dictionary entry and the sentence. Use them to answer the items.

> **interest** (IN-trest) *Noun* 1. a desire to learn about or be involved in something
> 2. money paid for a loan or earned on a bank account

Ishmael has an *interest* in the finance industry and hopes to work on Wall Street someday.

1. Which meaning is used in the sentence? _____

2. How can you tell? _____

Math

Read the problem. Then write and simplify an expression for the problem.

3. In a school fundraiser, students earn 15 points for every calendar they sell and 8 points for every T-shirt they sell. Camille sold 23 calendars and 41 T-shirts. How many points did she earn?

   expression: _____   answer: _____

4. Oak Knoll Vista School requires one chaperone for every 12 students on a field trip. If 192 students are visiting a museum, how many tickets will the school buy?

   expression: _____   answer: _____

Reading

Read the weather forecast diagram. Then answer the item.

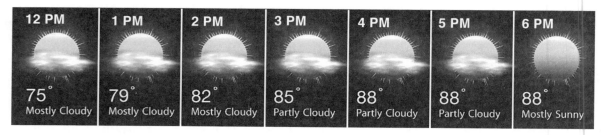

12 PM	1 PM	2 PM	3 PM	4 PM	5 PM	6 PM
75° Mostly Cloudy	79° Mostly Cloudy	82° Mostly Cloudy	85° Partly Cloudy	88° Partly Cloudy	88° Partly Cloudy	88° Mostly Sunny

5. How would this forecast affect how you prepare for this day?

_____

_____

_____

Language

Read the dictionary entry. Then write a sentence using one of the definitions. Circle the definition.

film (FIHLM)	*Verb*	1. to make a movie
	Noun	1. material sometimes used to shoot photos or movies
		2. a thin layer over the surface of something

1. _____

_____

Math

Read the problem. Then write an expression to represent the situation.

2. A frozen yogurt shop charges $2 per ounce of yogurt. Toppings cost $0.25 each. How much did Craig's yogurt cost if he got *y* ounces and *t* toppings?

expression: _____

3. A movie theater has 302 seats. Tickets cost $8.75. How much did the theater make if there were *u* unsold seats during the last show?

expression: _____

Reading

Look at the diagram. Then answer the item.

A food chain in an ecosystem

4. What is the function of the arrows in the diagram?

_____

_____

_____

_____

_____

_____

Language

Read the dictionary entry. Use it to answer the items.

> **learned** (LURND)   *Verb*   1. past tense of *learn,* to gain knowledge or facts
>
> **learned** (LUR-ned) *Adj*   1. well educated

1. If you heard the phrase "my learned colleague," how would this entry help you find its meaning?

_____

_____

Math

Read the problem. Write an expression to represent the situation. Then simplify the expression using the given values.

2. The animal shelter orders 14 pounds of dog food for every big dog (*b*) and 11 pounds of dog food for every small dog (*s*).

   expression: _____

3. There are 15 big dogs and 6 small dogs at the shelter. How many pounds of food will the shelter order?

   expression: _____   answer: _____

Reading

Look at the photo and its caption. Then answer the item.

Farm schoolhouse, Great Depression (1935)

4. Make an inference about what a farm schoolhouse was like during the Great Depression.

   _____

   _____

   _____

   _____

   _____

Language

Read the sentence. Rewrite it using standard English.

1. Ms. Henderson didn't give us no homework today.

   _____

2. Cece never does nothing wrong in the hockey rink.

   _____

Math

Graph the equation on the number line.

3. $b = -3$

4. $2 \times 15 = w$

5. $d = 2.5$

6. $46 \times f = 23$

Reading

Read the paragraph. Then answer the items.

   Whenever you hop on a plane, think about Orville and Wilbur Wright. In 1903, the Wright brothers made history with the first for real airplane flights. They first got to thinking about flying when their dad gave them some toy helicopter thing. First, they had to learn stuff. Wilbur and Orville were totally into reading library books.

7. Is the tone formal or informal? Underline the words or phrases that support your answer.

   _____

8. For what audience might this text be appropriate?

   _____

Language

Read the sentence. Complete it with a word from the word box.

> a   have   of

1. You should _____ heard Samji laugh when he read your text!

2. Is Hoda that strong _____ swimmer that she can miss a week of practice?

3. There are lots _____ options for our science projects.

Math

Graph the inequality on the number line.

4. $g > -2$

5. $18 + 22 \geq k$

6. $n \leq 0$

7. $y \div 2 > 15$

Reading

Read the letter. Then answer the item.

     I am afraid that I must miss an art class next week. On April 14, I have an appointment with my orthodontist at 2:15. My mother attempted to schedule it for after school, but the doctor did not have any time available then. I will find out the homework assignment ahead of time and turn it in along with the rest of the students in class.

8. Who do you think this letter is intended for? How do you know?

_____

_____

_____

Language

Read the sentence. Rewrite it using standard English.

1. I can't hardly wait til y'all come visit us next summer!

   _____

2. If it ain't fixing to rain soon, let's all of us go dig for clams.

   _____

Math

Read the situation. Then graph it on the number line.

3. There were at least 100 people in the parade.

   <-->

4. An ad for a clothing store says, "All T-shirts are under $10, some as low as $3!"

   <-->

Reading

Read the paragraph. Then answer the item.

   Graphic novels are vastly superior to regular books because the pictures are sick, plus, if kids don't comprehend a story, they can look at the pictures and enhance their understanding. Bug your school for more graphic novels!

5. Rewrite the paragraph to be appropriately formal for a newspaper's letter to the editor.

   _____

   _____

   _____

   _____

Language

Read the sentence. Rewrite it using standard English.

1. That's what I hope is that we'll all get a part in the play.

_____

2. It's the worst possible decision is to lend Scott more money.

_____

Math

Read the situation. Then complete the table and graph the data.

3. Erino walks her dog 35 minutes every day. The equation below shows this relationship.

$m = 35d$

Day	Min.
1	
2	
3	
4	

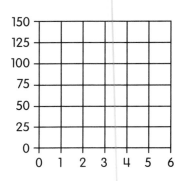

Reading

Read the paragraph. Then answer the item.

Have you ever heard of the Westwind Science Club Pumpkin Toss? Believe it or not, this crazy contest is all about seeing who can fling a ten-pound pumpkin the farthest. But it's not about muscles. It's about brains, which gives wimps like me a fighting chance!

4. Is the tone of the paragraph informative, humorous, or insulting? What effect do you think this tone is likely to have on readers?

_____

_____

_____

Language

Read the letter to a school principal. Make the formality appropriate by crossing out and rewriting words as needed.

1.   So, I was chilling at lunch the other day, and this substitute dude is like, "Your hair is

too long according to school policy." I'm all, "What's up with rules about our hairstyles?"

I think students oughta be able to wear their hair any way they wanna. My hair is not like

trashy or anything. It's like, clean. This rule is messed up.

Math

Read the situation. Then answer the item, complete the table, and graph the data.

2. Dimitri's basic cellphone plan costs $28 per month. If he exceeds his data limit, he is charged an extra $12 per gigabyte. Write an equation to represent this situation.

_____

Extra GB	Cost
0	
1	
2	
3	

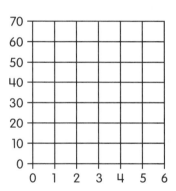

Reading

Read the paragraph. Then answer the item.

     The North Street railroad crossing has been a problem for years. Why on earth did
they build a new ball field next to it? What a lame idea! This crossing has no barriers
to prevent someone from being on the track when a train is coming. What were they
thinking? The city is just asking for trouble. Either close the ball field or put up a barrier.

3. How would you describe the tone of this text? What kind of tone might be more effective?

_____

_____

_____

Language

Read the roots and definitions in the word box. Use them to write a definition of each word.

> **flex** = bend   **schola** = school

1. **flexible:** _____

_____

_____

2. **scholar:** _____

_____

_____

Math

Find the area of the quadrilateral using the formula $A = bh$.

3.

2.4 in.

4.9 in.

_____

4.

4.1 m

3.9 m

1.3 m

_____

Reading

Read the paragraph from a student newspaper. Then answer the items.

Fall Dance a Success

On the last Friday in September, Mt. Peary Middle School held its annual Fall Breezes Dance. Students in grades 6, 7, and 8 were able to dance, eat great munchies, and hang out with friends while listening to great music. Ming Xie, a seventh grader, said, "This was my first dance, and it was really fun."

5. From what point of view is the text written? Explain how you know.

_____

_____

6. Why is this point of view typically used for newspaper articles?

_____

_____

Language

Read the roots and definitions in the word box. Use them to write a definition of each word.

> **multi** = many   **logy** = study of

1. **multilegged:** _____

_____

2. **volcanology:** _____

_____

_____

Math

Find the area of the triangle using the formula $A = \frac{1}{2}bh$.

3.

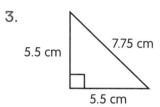

5.5 cm

7.75 cm

5.5 cm

_____

4.

4.6 ft

5.9 ft   3.7 ft

_____

Reading

Read the paragraphs from a science lab report. Then answer the items.

It is already known that plants need water, light, and nutrients to grow. Different types of plants need different nutrients. Plants growing in the wild get what they need from the soil. Indoor plants grown in pots need nutrients provided by people.

My hypothesis is that sugar helps plants grow. I did an experiment with two healthy potted sunflower plants, both four inches tall. I added sugar to the water for one plant to see if it would affect the plant's growth. I took measurements every day for two weeks.

5. From what point of view is each paragraph written?

first paragraph: _____   second paragraph: _____

6. Why are two different points of view used?

_____

_____

Language

Draw a line to match a prefix with a root to make a word. Then define two of the words.

Prefixes	Roots
1. micro •	• cycle
2. kilo •	• scope
3. bi •	• meter

4. _____

_____

5. _____

_____

Math

Find the volume of the figure.

6.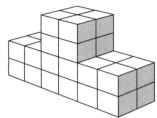

_____ cubic units

7.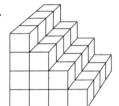

_____ cubic units

Reading

Read the paragraph. Then answer the items.

   If your last flight was horrible, you should have flown Aero Air. Then your luggage would have arrived at the same time as you—and on time! Even better, you could have enjoyed plenty of legroom and a free movie. So book your next flight on Aero Air, where all passengers fly first class.

8. In what point of view is the text written? Explain how you know.

_____

_____

9. What other types of nonfiction writing use the same point of view?

_____

_____

_____

Language

Read the words in the word box, which all have the same root. Circle the root. Then figure out the meaning of the root and write it on the line.

> dictation   predict   dictionary

1. _____

> spectator   inspect   spectacle

2. _____

> uniform   unique   unison

3. _____

Math

Find the volume of the figure using the formula $V = lwh$.

4.

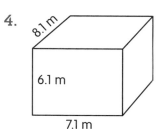

8.1 m
6.1 m
7.1 m

_____

5.

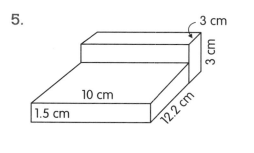

3 cm
3 cm
10 cm
1.5 cm
12.2 cm

_____

Reading

Read the paragraph. Then answer the items.

   Author Laurence Yep's parents felt that a good education was very important. They read to their children and had their children read to them. Laurence's favorite stories took place in the Land of Oz. He searched for the books in the library and read them all. Next, he read every science fiction book he could find. He understood how the characters felt. They were thrust into strange worlds where they didn't belong. That was how he felt about being Chinese and American.

6. Is the paragraph from a biography or an autobiography? How can you tell?

_____

7. Imagine that this paragraph were written from a different point of view. What effect would it have?

_____

_____

_____

Language

Read the sentence. Underline the base of the bold word. Then write another word with the same base.

1. The doctor **prescribed** a new medicine.

   _____

2. That volcano no longer **erupts**.

   _____

3. Anneliese is **conducting** a survey.

   _____

4. I've made **various** types of fruit smoothies.

   _____

Math

Find the total volume of the appliance using the formula $V = lwh$.

1.2 ft
1.7 ft
2.9 ft
3.5 ft

5. freezer: _____

6. refrigerator: _____

7. total volume: _____

Reading

Read the paragraph. Then answer the items.

     Maria and Marjorie Tallchief showed great promise in both music and dance, even when quite young. Their mother wanted the girls to have careers on the stage. She felt they would have a better chance in Hollywood. So the family moved to Los Angeles, California, when the girls were in elementary school.

8. Is the narrator's knowledge limited or unlimited? Explain how you know.

   _____

   _____

9. Rewrite the paragraph with Mrs. Tallchief as the narrator.

   _____

   _____

   _____

   _____

Language

Read the paragraph. Write the name of the type of figurative language above each underlined part.

1. As Stormalong neared the English Channel, he remarked, "It's the size of a

    plastic straw!" The ship groaned as it began to squeeze through the narrow passageway.

    "Round up all the soap you can find," Stormalong bellowed. "Soap the sides of the ship.

    I want to see suds as thick as whale blubber." After the crew used up every sliver of soap,

    the ship slid right through, leaving a clean channel in its wake.

Math

Plot the points on the coordinate grid and connect them. Then answer the item.

2. (−3, 5)   (−3, −4)

   (2, 3)   (2, −2)

3. What shape did you draw?

   _____

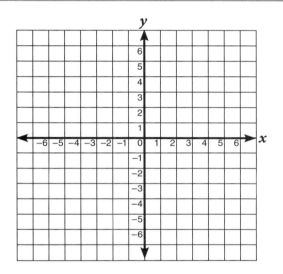

Reading

Read the paragraph. Then answer the item.

   Weeds can be sources of calcium, which is an important mineral for the healthy growth of bones and teeth. When an animal dies, its bones deposit calcium in the soil. The roots of weeds and other plants absorb the calcium. The plant you eat today might contain calcium that was in the skull of a saber-toothed tiger!

4. Noah inferred that calcium is stored in human and animal bones. Which statement provides evidence of this?

   Ⓐ Weeds can be sources of calcium.

   Ⓑ When an animal dies, its bones deposit calcium in the soil.

   Ⓒ The roots of weeds and other plants absorb the calcium.

   Ⓓ The plant you eat today might contain calcium.

Language

Read the sentence. Then answer the item.

Randy was as scared as a worm in a bird's nest.

1. Why is this simile effective? _____

_____

2. Write a sentence containing a simile.

_____

Math

Use the coordinate grid to answer the items.

3. Draw a square on the coordinate grid using the point given as one vertex.

4. Write the coordinates of each vertex.

_____ _____

_____ _____

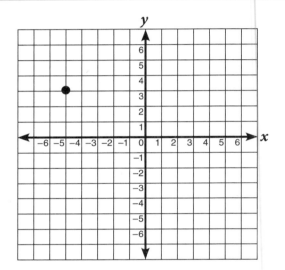

Reading

Read the paragraph. Then answer the item.

Helen Keller became famous for her remarkable achievements after a serious illness left her blind and deaf as an infant in 1882. At that time, blind and deaf kids could not go to public school. Textbooks weren't published in Braille. Tools such as white canes and sight or hearing dogs weren't available until the 1930s. Helen's work spread hope, raised funds, and supported laws to make independent living possible for people with physical challenges.

5. What laws did Helen probably promote? Underline supporting evidence in the text.

_____

_____

Language

Read the sentence. Then answer the item.

Following the scandal, Mr. Ito's political opponent sailed ahead at the ballot box.

1. Why is this metaphor effective? _____

_____

2. Write a sentence containing a metaphor.

_____

Math

Plot the points on the coordinate grid and connect them. Then answer the items.

3. (−2, 4)   (−2, 3)   (5, −4)

(2, 3)   (2, −4)   (5, 4)

4. What is the perimeter of the figure?

_____

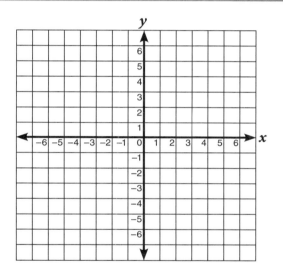

Reading

Read the paragraph. Then answer the item.

"Have you seen the flier in the cafeteria?" Dixie asked. "It says we can't eat fish!" she continued, exasperated. "Fish is a healthy food—I can't believe they're saying this!"

Lana hesitated. "Well, some people don't like the smell, and some are allergic."

"Oh, come on!" Dixie retorted. "I have a right to eat what I want. They can just eat outside."

"Or *you* could," Lana said. "Don't they have a right to eat without getting sick?"

5. With whom do you agree? _____ Use evidence to explain your opinion.

_____

_____

Language

Read the sentence. Then answer the item.

After I take this test, I want to <u>sleep for five days</u>!

1. Why is the underlined part hyperbole? _____

_____

2. When can hyperbole be used?

_____

Math

Use the coordinate grid to answer the item.

3. Draw a polygon with a perimeter
   of 38 units.

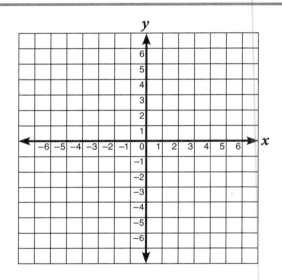

Reading

Read the paragraph. Then answer the item.

     Zach's grandfather was coming all the way from Wisconsin to watch the race. Grandpa
Morgan had been a track star and had even competed in the Olympics. As much as Zach
wanted his grandpa to watch him race and cheer for him, he was a little afraid. What if he
didn't like my technique? What if Jordan beat him again? As much as Zach had improved
his time, he didn't want to embarrass himself in front of his grandpa.

4. Why was Zach afraid of embarrassing himself? Underline supporting evidence in the paragraph.

_____

_____

Language

Read the sentence. Then answer the item.

After record highs, the temperature dove into the mid-forties.

1. Why is this personification effective? _____

_____

2. Write a sentence using personification.

_____

Math

Use the coordinate map to answer the items. Each line represents a street, and each square is a block.

3. Melina starts at her apartment (point *A*) and walks to the bank (point *B*), to city hall (point *C*), and to the deli (point *D*). Draw the shortest route she could take, staying on streets.

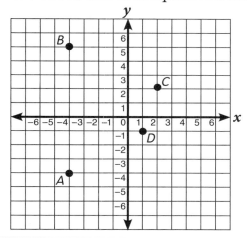

4. Write the number of blocks.

   A to *B* _____   *B* to *C* _____

   C to *D* _____   total distance _____

Reading

Read the paragraph. Then answer the items.

     A large 2013 study found that in schools in which boys and girls are in separate classes, 30% more boys in all-boy classes passed their state exams than boys in mixed classes. For all-girl classrooms, 16% more passed than in mixed classes. However, separate classes are less diverse, and class discussions may offer a narrower range of ideas. Students may be less prepared for a mixed work environment as an adult.

5. Should classes be mixed or separate? (Circle one.) Underline evidence that supports your view.

6. Why is it important to back up statements with evidence? _____

_____

Language

Read the sentence. Then add punctuation to set off the nonrestrictive element.

1. My music teacher Ms. Crawford is lending me a bassoon.

2. She introduced me to the other bassoonist Margie Wilke.

3. I recently found out that my father's only brother David played this instrument.

4. It would be wonderful if our family the Mullers continued the tradition.

Math

Use the figure to answer the item.

5.
8 in.

area of one face

_____

number of faces

_____

surface area of cube

_____

6.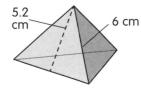
5.2 cm   6 cm

area of one face

_____

number of faces

_____

surface area of pyramid

_____

Reading

Read the ad. Then answer the item.

Super Sneaker athletic shoes outsell all other brands. Three out of four people surveyed chose Super Sneaker over other brands. Perfect for walking, jogging, aerobics, or tennis, Super Sneaker has the style you need. Be part of the team. Go Super Sneaker!

7. What is the ad designed to make the reader believe? How does it achieve its purpose?

_____

_____

_____

Language

Read the sentence. Then add punctuation to set off the nonrestrictive element.

1. George Washington the first U.S. president liked ice cream.

2. He treated Sweet Lips one of his hunting dogs like family.

3. Martha George's wife had two children from a previous marriage.

4. He was president before Washington, D.C. the nation's capital was founded.

Math

Use the figure to answer the item.

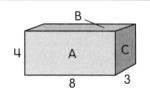

5. Draw all 6 faces of the rectangular prism. Label each face with its measurements.

face A _____ × _____ = _____ square units

face B _____ × _____ = _____ square units

face C _____ × _____ = _____ square units

total surface area _____ square units

Reading

Read the public service announcement. Then answer the item.

    Being prepared helps us avoid problems. For example, getting a dog will go smoothly if you're prepared with information and supplies the dog will need. Preparing for a test helps ensure a good grade. The same is true for unplanned events, such as a weather emergency. Prepare your home now—you'll be less likely to suffer damage or injury. Contact your local Office of Emergency Preparedness today so you won't have to call for help tomorrow.

6. What is the announcement trying to persuade the reader to do?

_____

_____

Language

Read the sentence. Then add punctuation to set off the nonrestrictive element.

1. The school bus which usually arrives at 7:55 was late today.

2. After school, I go to the library which is near my mom's job.

3. I'll stay after school when training starts for my favorite sport which is baseball.

4. The baseball coach who lives next door to me drives me home after practice.

Math

Use the figure to answer the item.

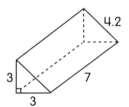

5. Draw all 5 faces of the triangular prism. Label each face with its measurements.

face A _____ × _____ = _____ square units

face B _____ × _____ = _____ square units

face C _____ × _____ = _____ square units

total surface area _____ square units

Reading

Read the speech. Then answer the item.

    Hello, fellow students! You all know me, Cynthia Nauja, but you may not know that I'm running for student council. Like you, I want to learn but have fun, too. I have some ideas for new clubs. Like you, I think some classes are hard. I'll work with the principal to start a tutoring center. And we need better cafeteria food! Wouldn't we all vote for that? Then vote for me, Cynthia Nauja, your sixth-grade student council representative!

6. What technique does Cynthia use to encourage students to vote for her? Give examples.

_____

_____

Language

Read the sentences. Then answer the item.

Ali's sister who is in high school is learning to drive.

Ali's sister, who is in high school, is learning to drive.

1. How do the sentences differ in meaning? _____

_____

_____

Math

Use the figure to answer the item.

2. Coletta is wrapping a gift in a rectangular box. She will need enough wrapping paper to cover the surface area of the box. What is the surface area of the box?

_____

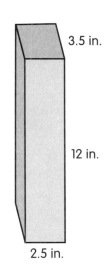

3.5 in.

12 in.

2.5 in.

Reading

Read the ad. Then answer the item.

Dentist Ana Lee recommends Glow toothpaste. "I recommend it for its fresh mint flavor and its decay-fighting ingredients. Glow keeps me smiling, and my kids love Glow, too! There's always a tube of Glow in every medicine cabinet at our home."

3. What technique does this ad use to sell Glow toothpaste? How valid is the ad's message?

_____

_____

_____

Language

Read the paragraph. Add a comma to set off any nonrestrictive elements.

1.   The Georgia Aquarium which I visited in April is shaped like a giant ship. The

largest exhibit Ocean Voyager features whale sharks. It also has a glass tunnel that you

can walk through and be surrounded by fish. I also saw a gigantic skeleton on display.

Its huge length about 18 steps long tells me it must be a whale of some kind.

Math

Use the figure and its net to answer the item.

2. Find the surface area of the figure.

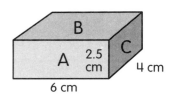
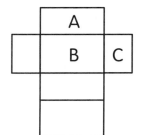

_____

Reading

Read the editorial. Then answer the item.

   Do you know someone who drove a car today? Tell that person to take the bus, train, or subway next time. First, it costs less, because the fares are cheaper than filling the gas tank. Also, with fewer cars releasing toxic carbon dioxide, public transportation reduces pollution. It makes life easier, too—no traffic or parking hassles.

3. How does the author show his or her bias? Give examples in your explanation.

_____

_____

_____

Language

Read the sentence. Complete it with a linking verb from the word box.

> felt   remains   smells   was

1. The air always _____ fresh after it rains.

2. Wanda _____ glad that she studied for the test.

3. Jiri _____ bad that he left without saying goodbye.

4. Kumail _____ loyal even after his favorite store raises its prices.

Math

Use the net to answer the item.

5. Circle the figure represented by the net.

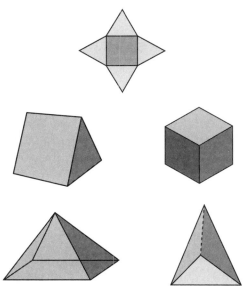

Reading

Read the essay. Then answer the items.

A GPS, or Global Positioning System, is better than a map. It is more accurate because the system can be updated quickly when new housing or business areas are developed. A GPS is also easier to use. It knows where you are and how much farther you have to go, and it can display your location in map view, in overhead view, or in street view. It is also useful in emergency situations, such as tracking a lost child or pet. Despite its higher cost, I'd choose a GPS.

6. Write two facts that support the argument for GPS.

_____

_____

7. Which fact does *not* support the argument for GPS?

_____

Language

Read the sentence. Circle the linking verb. Then write the modifier that correctly completes the sentence.

1. I am _____ that I have met you before. **(sure, surely)**

2. This restaurant is _____ for a graduation dinner. **(perfect, perfectly)**

3. Are you _____ in your new school? **(happily, happy)**

4. She has been _____ about her musical ability. **(honest, honestly)**

5. We were _____ until the director announced the audition results. **(nervously, nervous)**

Math

Use spatial reasoning to answer the item.

6. Look at the figure. Imagine you are tracing around the bottom of it all the way around. Draw what the tracing would look like.

Reading

Read the speech. Then answer the item.

As Dad and I got out of our new 1966 Chevy and walked toward the store's entrance, a woman approached us and handed Dad a flier. "Boycott California grapes!" she chanted. "The farmworkers are not paid enough to do their difficult job."

"Picking fruit sounds easy to me," I replied.

"They work long hours in the hot sun with no protection and no break. Usually there is no bathroom facility. And it's exhausting, back-breaking work," the woman retorted.

7. Was the woman's argument effective? Explain your answer.

_____

_____

_____

Language

Read the sentence. Circle the linking verb. Then choose the best modifier from the word box to complete the sentence.

correct	sour	calmly
sickly	wrongly	tired
sweetly	different	similarly

1. The children felt _____ after school.

2. This lemonade tastes too _____.

3. Tory's voice sounded _____ on the phone.

4. Does the grammar in this sentence look

   _____ to you?

Math

Use spatial reasoning to solve the item.

4. Look at the figure shown. Imagine you are looking at it straight on from the left side. Draw what you would see.

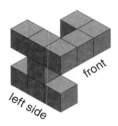

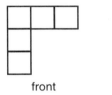

front   left side

Reading

Read the letter to the editor. Then answer the item.

  We've all heard the mantra "reduce, reuse, recycle" for years. Yet we still produce enormous amounts of garbage. Recycling reduces the amount of raw material needed for new products, but recycled material is weaker. We need to add a fourth "r" to the mantra: *refuse!* Refuse to buy every latest gadget that is made. Refuse to buy new things just because your friend did. Refuse to dump your wardrobe every season for the latest fad. If fewer goods are manufactured, our natural resources and our landfills will last longer.

6. Name a strength and a weakness in this argument.

   _____

   _____

   _____

   _____

Language

Read the sentence. If a word needs to be changed, cross it out and write the correct word above it.

1. Shani and her cousin from the East Coast became closely last summer.

2. Miguel's cat seemed nicely until Miguel left the room.

3. The apartment complex appears attractively from the outside.

4. The night grew coldly, with the temperature dropping 40 degrees.

Math

Use spatial reasoning to answer the item.

5. The distance around the whole circle is 24 cm. Estimate the distance from point A to point B.

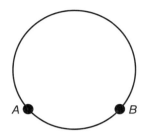

_____

Reading

Read the press release. Then answer the item.

N8Rlife Inc. announced today the release of a new food preservative called Azucan. "Unlike current preservatives, Azucan will not alter the flavor of the food it is preserving; the ingredients will still taste fresh and natural," according to product manager Loren Hamwi. "Double-blind studies show that Azucan boosts shelf life by 14%, without any health risks."

Azucan has been in development for eight years, including thorough testing by the U.S. FDA's lab for any potential dangers. Having been approved Friday, Azucan will be used in N8Rlife's fruit-based energy bars beginning next month.

6. Explain whether the claims about Azucan are supported.

_____

_____

_____

Language

Write three sentences using a linking verb from the word box and an adjective in each.

> seem   feel   stay   turn

1. _____

_____

2. _____

_____

3. _____

_____

Math

Use spatial reasoning to answer the item.

4. The circle graph shows the proportion of students at Northmont Middle School who take a music class. At Southmont, 3 times as many students take a music class. Draw and shade this amount on the second circle graph.

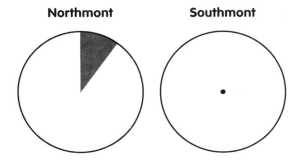

Northmont   Southmont

Reading

Read the letter to the editor. Then answer the item.

I don't think people should get tattoos, at least not kids under 18. I was thinking about getting one when I'm old enough. Then I learned that there are medical concerns with getting a tattoo. Also, it can hurt your future. Only delinquents get tattoos. Sometimes, people get them and then change their mind later on, but then they are stuck with the tattoo. People should really think about how they might feel in a few years, especially if they tattoo a name on their body.

5. How effective is the argument? Explain your reasons.

_____

_____

_____

_____

Language

Read the sentence. Use context to figure out the meaning of the underlined word.
Then match the sentence to the correct word meaning.

1. Ty devotes a lot to his garden, spending hours there daily. •   • to fight for a long time

2. Sana attended college, which propelled her career. •   • to commit or give

3. The two rival teams have been feuding for decades. •   • to reject or prohibit

4. Dad vetoed my idea, refusing to even listen to my reasons. •   • to push forward

Math

Find the mean of the data set.

5. test scores: 91, 88, 93, 79, 84   _____

6. ages of parents: 36, 40, 39, 38, 41, 39, 33   _____

7. books read: 11, 3, 4, 8, 6, 4   _____

Reading

Read the paragraph. Then answer the item.

Brief exposure to the sun allows our bodies to produce vitamin D. This essential vitamin can help prevent certain diseases and promotes bone growth. Just 10 to 20 minutes of sun each day can protect you. However, the sun can also cause wrinkles, skin cancer, and cataracts in the eyes.

8. Which of the following is a valid conclusion?
   Ⓐ The sun affects different people differently.
   Ⓑ The sun's benefits outweigh the risks.
   Ⓒ People should avoid being in the sun.
   Ⓓ Exposure to the sun should be limited.

Language

Read the sentence. Write the word from the sentence that helps you figure out the meaning of the underlined word.

1. Sara's cat is cooperative when she cuts his nails, but my cat is belligerent. _____

2. The gaudy curtains don't go with the plain furniture. _____

3. After the dentist extracted my tooth, he replaced it with an artificial tooth. _____

4. I've read the first book you mentioned but not the latter one. _____

Math

Find the median of the data set.

5. ages of contestants: 14, 15, 15, 14, 17, 16, 10   _____

6. blocks to school: 3, 10, 6, 1, 6, 7, 5, 3, 6, 3   _____

7. heights of trees: 23, 25, 16, 31, 89, 38   _____

Reading

Read the paragraph. Then answer the item.

      Laughter is good for our physical and psychological well-being. When we laugh, our brains release endorphins, which relax us and relieve stress. It can also boost immunity and lower blood pressure. Laughter works stomach, facial, leg, and back muscles. Laughing could replace your need to exercise.

8. Is the last sentence a valid conclusion? Explain your answer.

_____

_____

_____

Language

Read the sentence. Then answer the item.

A bird's unique <u>anatomy</u>, including its beak, highly flexible neck, and hollow bones, helps it eat, groom itself, and fly.

1. Write the meaning of the underlined word. _____

2. Explain how context in the given sentence helped you figure out the word's meaning.

_____

Math

Find the mode of the data set.

3. shoe sizes: 3, 5, 4, 4, 7, 5, 6, 4, 5, 2 _____

4. textbooks used in a year: 5, 7, 5, 4, 5, 6, 6, 4, 5 _____

5. rooms in a house: 6, 6, 7, 5, 8, 4, 6, 5, 5, 8, 6 _____

Reading

Read the paragraph. Then answer the item.

Cars need electricity to power headlights and radios, but those things don't make the car run. More importantly, gasoline engines need a constant supply of electric sparks, which ignite tiny controlled explosions that power the cars. When electromagnets spin around in engines, they make electricity. This electricity is used to power many things, including the plugs that create sparks.

6. Write a conclusion based on the information in the text.

_____

_____

Language

Read the sentence. Then answer the item.

Having grown up in a tiny town, Greyson dreamed of living in Los Angeles, Chicago, London, or another <u>metropolis</u> one day.

1. Write the meaning of the underlined word. _____

2. Explain how context in the given sentence helped you figure out the word's meaning.

_____

Math

Find the mean, median, and mode of the data set. Then answer the item.

Here are the 2010 populations of 8 western U.S. states (rounded):

Hawaii: 1.4 million   Alaska: 0.7 million   Washington: 6.7 million   Oregon: 3.8 million

California: 37.2 million   Arizona: 6.8 million   Nevada: 2.7 million   Idaho: 1.6 million

3. mean _____ median _____ mode _____

4. Which measure of center best represents the population of these western states? Explain.

_____

Reading

Read the journal entry. Then answer the item.

One of my father's clients came to San Francisco for a meeting. Father introduced me to the client's son, Danny, and asked me to show him around Chinatown. After walking past outdoor markets, we went to the Asian Art Museum in *dai fau*—the big city. There we saw all kinds of intricate woodcarvings, gold and jade jewelry, and Chinese watercolor paintings. "Wow, all Chinese people must be really talented artists!" Danny exclaimed.

5. Is Danny's generalization valid? Explain why or why not.

_____

_____

Language

Read the sentence. Use context to figure out what the underlined word means. Then write a new sentence using the underlined word.

1. The judges made a <u>unanimous</u> decision about who won the science fair.

   _____

2. Henry doesn't seem to react to poison oak, poison ivy, or any other <u>allergens</u>.

   _____

Math

Read the problem. Then answer the item.

Pierre recorded the weights in pounds of each animal examined by a veterinarian on one day. His data are shown in the table.

3. Find the mean, median, and mode for each type of animal.

   dogs: mean _____   median _____   mode _____

   cats: mean _____   median _____   mode _____

Dogs	Cats
18	11
18	8
107	10
55	8
34	9
98	17

Reading

Read the paragraph. Then answer the item.

Imagine being locked in a crowded, sweltering room for a 12-hour shift, six days a week. In New York factories in the early 1900s, factory owners gave employees only one 30-minute break. If employees took too long in the bathroom, they were sent home without pay. They could be fired just for talking to each other or singing to themselves. At this time in history, most factory owners treated employees like equipment.

4. Which statement from the text is a generalization? Is it valid? Explain.

   _____

   _____

Language

Read the sentence. Then cross out any unnecessary words or phrases.

1. Civilizations need access to natural resources like rivers, which are a natural resource.

2. People have different talents, and they want to contribute their talents to their society.

3. Some people build roads, and there are other people who build governments.

4. Ancient Chinese culture is interesting because of the fact that they invented so many things.

Math

Find the range of the data set.

5. prices of video games: $32, $35, $43, $33, $40, $31 _____

6. lengths of phone calls: 5, 2, 4, 36, 7, 4, 4, 20, 8, 22 _____

7. points scored: 12, 8, 6, 8, 14, 18, 12, 16, 10 _____

Reading

Read the paragraph. Then answer the item.

Deb's neighbor was madly shoveling dirt in his front yard. Mr. Caine never cleaned the leaves out of his rain gutters after fall. During winter, his gutters were always clogged with leaves, forcing rain to spill over. Today the rain had pounded out a trench several feet long. Deb thought about how her rain gutters emptied onto the driveway that sloped down toward the street. Little did she know it would wash away a problem she was having at school.

8. Which literary technique is used in the last sentence?
   Ⓐ imagery
   Ⓑ hyperbole
   Ⓒ foreshadowing
   Ⓓ figurative language

Language

Read the sentence. Rewrite it as a single sentence without duplicating any information.

1. Mesopotamia was an ancient culture. Mesopotamia was where Iraq is now.

   _____

2. The region is very fertile. The region has two large rivers. The rivers provide irrigation.

   _____

Math

Look at the data set. Then answer the items.

   high temperatures this week: 72°, 78°, 82°, 77°, 85°, 77°, 81°

3. Write the values in order from least to greatest. Circle the lowest, median, and highest values.

   _____

4. Find the distance from the bottom of the range to the median. _____

5. Find the distance from the median to the top of the range. _____

Reading

Read the paragraph. Then answer the item.

   Everyone in Laurence's family worked in the grocery store. Laurence and his brother stocked shelves, sorted bottles, and flattened boxes. Prices needed to be marked on groceries. When the family could leave the store, they enjoyed picnics and other outdoor activities. Laurence built a sandbox on the roof of their apartment building. It was there that he first created imaginary kingdoms that would later influence his life's work.

6. What part of the text shows foreshadowing? Explain how you know.

   _____

   _____

Language

Read the sentence. Then cross out any unnecessary words or phrases.

1. There are three kinds of rock, like for example, there is igneous, metamorphic, and sedimentary.

2. The types basically form in a bunch of different ways, such as heat, pressure, or cooling lava.

3. Rock can weather, which, what that is, is water or other material breaking the rock down.

4. Most different kinds of rock have totally unique combinations of particular minerals.

Math

Look at the data set. Then answer the items.

hours spent babysitting: 5, 3, 4, 7, 4, 6, 12, 8

5. Write the values in order from least to greatest. Circle the lowest, median, and highest values.

_____   Find the median. _____

6. Find the 1st quartile, midway between the bottom of the range and the median. _____

7. Find the 3rd quartile, midway between the median and the top of the range. _____

Reading

Read the paragraph. Then answer the item.

Tomorrow is Great-Grandma's ninety-first birthday. I made her a card and wrote a poem inside. Mom and I went shopping for the perfect gift last weekend, but nothing seemed quite right. Today when I visited Great-Grandma after school, she was in her kitchen, watching a tiny stray kitten eat scraps of leftover chicken. "I know I'm too old to care for a cat, but it sure has brightened my day," Great-Grandma admitted.

8. What future event might the last sentence foreshadow?

_____

_____

Language

Read the sentence. Rewrite it, eliminating wordiness and making it concise.

1. Every single living thing has its own individual pattern that is a pattern of DNA.

   _____

2. What DNA is, is like programming for each and every cell in your body.

   _____

Math

Look at the data set. Then answer the items.

   lengths of different whale species: 20, 110, 12, 15, 48, 59, 27, 45

3. Write the values in order from least to greatest. Circle the lowest, median, and highest values.

   _____   Find the median. _____

4. Find the 1st and 3rd quartiles: 1st quartile _____   3rd quartile _____

5. Find the interquartile range, the range between the 1st and 3rd quartiles. _____

Reading

Read the paragraph. Then answer the item.

   The kingdom knew that King Alexander's unreasonable demands would someday make him topple from the throne; they just didn't know how literally it would happen. King Alexander wanted the moon, which he believed was filled with gold. "Bring me the wisest person in the kingdom," the king demanded of his advisor. "I'll need help if I am to reach the moon."

6. Which sentence contains foreshadowing? What future event might that sentence foreshadow?

   _____

   _____

Language

Read the paragraph. Edit it, eliminating wordiness and making it concise.

1.   Everyone in the world cries, and there are quite a lot of reasons why. The most obvious

reason is that people cry if they are hurt. People also cry if they are becoming frustrated. Maybe

they're frustrated with having too much work to do, or they might be frustrated if they are having

an argument with, like, a friend. Experts who study crying believe that crying relieves stress.

Math

Read the problem. Then find the values.

In Chevauton, a haircut at eight hair salons costs $35, $43, $38, $52, $47, $49, $41, and $47.

2. range _____

3. median _____

4. 1st and 3rd quartiles: 1st quartile _____   3rd quartile _____

5. interquartile range _____

Reading

Read the paragraph. Then answer the item.

        It started as an assigned research paper about the value of clean water for science
class. Diego gathered a water sample from his own backyard and gave it to his cousin
Sofia for testing. Sofia was taking a chemistry course at the local community college,
and she gave the sample to her professor. Little did Diego know what a can of worms
the results would open.

6. Which sentence contains foreshadowing? Why do you think the author used this technique?

_____

_____

Language

Complete each row of the table to show different connotations of the same idea.

1.

Connotations

Positive	Neutral	Negative
modest	quiet	
	predictable	boring
innocent	inexperienced	
economical		stingy
	secure	egotistical

Math

Read the problem and the dot plot. Then answer the item.

A class survey asked how many bones each student had broken.

Number of Broken Bones

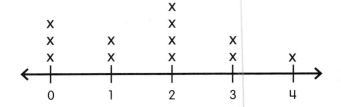

0   1   2   3   4

2. How many students have ever broken a bone?

_____

Reading

Read the paragraph. Then answer the item.

As the van rolled down the gravel road headed for the next work opportunity, Eduardo's dad turned up the radio and started singing. He always sang off-key, and it made everybody laugh. His mom passed food around. Next spring there'd be baseball somewhere. With a little more money, Eduardo could buy a ball and a bat. His brothers were getting bigger. Maybe they could all play on Sundays in a field or somewhere. Maybe he'd decide to play in the big leagues someday. He was sounding just like his dad.

3. What is the mood of the paragraph?

  Ⓐ frantic

  Ⓑ annoyed

  Ⓒ optimistic

  Ⓓ passionate

Language

Read the sentence. Complete it with a word from the word box that has the appropriate connotation.

observed   spied   watched

1. Bryan _____ on his older sister as she talked on the phone, and then he repeated the conversation to their father.

2. As the moon rose, Calista _____ its shape and described it in her notebook.

3. The audience _____ the brilliant actors bring the play to life.

Math

Read the problem and the circle graph. Then answer the item.

A class survey asked favorite book genres.

4. Write the genres in order from most to least popular.

_____

_____

Reading

Read the paragraph. Then answer the item.

As the Great Depression deepened, its effects were stamped on the faces of almost everyone; only the very young and the rich were spared. After my dad finished a government road repair project, we continued chasing the cotton harvest around Texas, as we had for the past three years. This time, however, we found that work opportunities had dried up with the land. A drought had struck with devastating results, and there were no crops to harvest.

5. What is the mood of the paragraph? What helped you figure it out?

_____

_____

_____

_____

Language

Answer the item.

1. What is the difference between these two words? When would you use *ambitious*?

pushy, ambitious

_____

_____

_____

_____

_____

_____

Math

Read the problem. Then answer the item.

Each week, Shineda spends 3 hours on language arts homework, 2 hours on math, 2 hours on Chinese, 2 hours on social studies, and 1 hour on science.

2. Make a circle graph to show how much time Shineda spends on each subject.

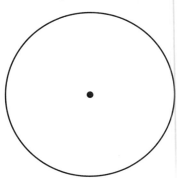

Reading

Read the paragraphs. Then answer the item.

   After ditching yet another cheerleading practice, I stayed secluded in my bed with a box of cookies. Why didn't I care about making practice or being with my friends? Who was this person leaving crumbs all over her pillow? How I wanted to point to some culprit—unreasonable family, difficult classes, homesickness, anything—but I couldn't.

   "Tamara, Callie's here to see you," Grandma announced through my door. When I failed to reply, she came in.

3. What is the mood of the paragraphs? Is the mood conveyed through word choice or Tamara's thoughts or actions? Explain with examples.

_____

_____

_____

_____

Language

Read the sentence. Choose the best word to complete it. Then explain your choice.

1. It was _____ of you to race across the train tracks after you heard the train whistle. **(daring, gutsy, reckless)**

   _____

   _____

2. The fans cheered the _____ winning play right at the end of the game. **(stealthy, devious, deceitful)**

   _____

   _____

Math

Read the problem and the histogram. Then answer the item.

A weather report showed daily snowfall.

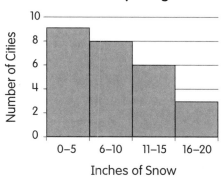

Snowfall in Wyoming Cities

3. How many cities had over 10 inches of snow?

   _____

Reading

Read the paragraph. Then answer the item.

   The next morning, Rachel awoke squinting at the sun streaming through a crack in the curtains. No longer was anything falling from the sky. No longer was the gale-force wind rattling the eaves of the roof and the fence gate. In fact, it was so silent that she had to speak to make sure she hadn't gone deaf overnight. Relieved, she opened the curtains and marveled at the sight—silky smooth snowdrifts piled high, and on the barren elm tree that is now entertaining pearls of ice, snow buntings huddled together on a white branch. Rachel and the birds had managed to survive a wild night.

4. What is the mood of the paragraph? Compare it to Rachel's emotions.

   _____

   _____

   _____

   _____

Language

Write a sentence with the given word. Make sure the word's connotation is clear.

1. **unusual**

   _____

   _____

   _____

2. **crazy**

   _____

   _____

   _____

Math

Read the problem. Then answer the item.

Students spent the following number of minutes exercising in one week:

| 23 | 55 | 60 | 45 | 38 | 45 | 95 |
| 110 | 90 | 120 | 48 | 60 | 75 | 82 |

3. Use the data to complete the histogram.

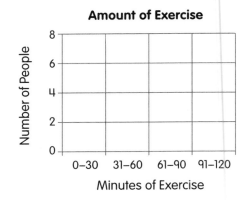

Amount of Exercise

Reading

Read the paragraphs. Then answer the item.

Wow, that was easy! The baby is in bed for the night, and I'm getting paid to do homework! I could get to like babysitting. Wait! *Squeak–thwap!* What was that? I think it's coming from the cellar. It's windy outside—maybe the air pressure is moving the cellar door. I'll go close it.

Hmm, it's closed alr... Hey! What's going on upstairs? That sounded like a utensil hitting the floor! Check on the baby first. Good, she's asleep. Should I venture into the kitchen now or call Dad for backup? I'll have my thumb ready on the phone when I enter the kitchen. My heart's pounding so loudly, I wouldn't even be able to hear him right now. Breathe in, breathe out; in the kitchen we go. HA! The Sotos didn't tell me they had a cat!

4. What is the mood of the paragraphs? Explain how the mood is conveyed.

   _____

   _____

   _____

Answer Key

✳ These answers will vary. Examples are given.

Page 11

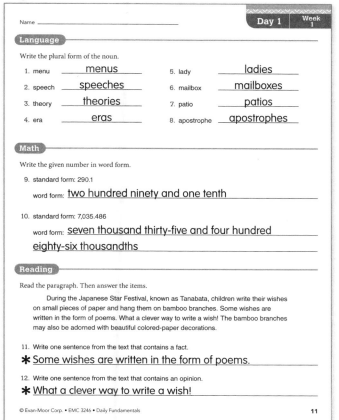

Name _____   Day 1 | Week 1

Language

Write the plural form of the noun.

1. menu — menus
2. speech — speeches
3. theory — theories
4. era — eras
5. lady — ladies
6. mailbox — mailboxes
7. patio — patios
8. apostrophe — apostrophes

Math

Write the given number in word form.

9. standard form: 290.1

   word form: two hundred ninety and one tenth

10. standard form: 7,035.486

    word form: seven thousand thirty-five and four hundred eighty-six thousandths

Reading

Read the paragraph. Then answer the items.

During the Japanese Star Festival, known as Tanabata, children write their wishes on small pieces of paper and hang them on bamboo branches. Some wishes are written in the form of poems. What a clever way to write a wish! The bamboo branches may also be adorned with beautiful colored-paper decorations.

11. Write one sentence from the text that contains a fact.

✳ Some wishes are written in the form of poems.

12. Write one sentence from the text that contains an opinion.

✳ What a clever way to write a wish!

© Evan-Moor Corp. • EMC 3246 • Daily Fundamentals   11

Page 12

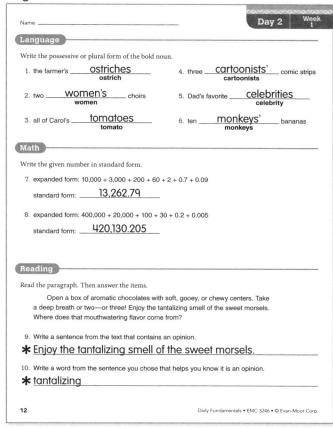

Name _____   Day 2 | Week 1

Language

Write the possessive or plural form of the bold noun.

1. the farmer's — ostriches / ostrich
2. two — women's / women — choirs
3. all of Carol's — tomatoes / tomato
4. three — cartoonists' / cartoonists — comic strips
5. Dad's favorite — celebrities / celebrity
6. ten — monkeys' / monkeys — bananas

Math

Write the given number in standard form.

7. expanded form: 10,000 + 3,000 + 200 + 60 + 2 + 0.7 + 0.09

   standard form: 13,262.79

8. expanded form: 400,000 + 20,000 + 100 + 30 + 0.2 + 0.005

   standard form: 420,130.205

Reading

Read the paragraph. Then answer the items.

Open a box of aromatic chocolates with soft, gooey, or chewy centers. Take a deep breath or two—or three! Enjoy the tantalizing smell of the sweet morsels. Where does that mouthwatering flavor come from?

9. Write a sentence from the text that contains an opinion.

✳ Enjoy the tantalizing smell of the sweet morsels.

10. Write a word from the sentence you chose that helps you know it is an opinion.

✳ tantalizing

12   Daily Fundamentals • EMC 3246 • © Evan-Moor Corp.

Page 13

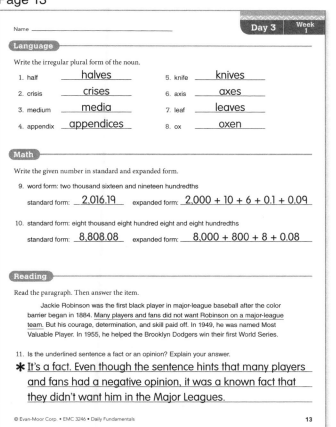

Name _____   Day 3 | Week 1

Language

Write the irregular plural form of the noun.

1. half — halves
2. crisis — crises
3. medium — media
4. appendix — appendices
5. knife — knives
6. axis — axes
7. leaf — leaves
8. ox — oxen

Math

Write the given number in standard and expanded form.

9. word form: two thousand sixteen and nineteen hundredths

   standard form: 2,016.19   expanded form: 2,000 + 10 + 6 + 0.1 + 0.09

10. standard form: eight thousand eight hundred eight and eight hundredths

    standard form: 8,808.08   expanded form: 8,000 + 800 + 8 + 0.08

Reading

Read the paragraph. Then answer the item.

Jackie Robinson was the first black player in major-league baseball after the color barrier began in 1884. Many players and fans did not want Robinson on a major-league team. But his courage, determination, and skill paid off. In 1949, he was named Most Valuable Player. In 1955, he helped the Brooklyn Dodgers win their first World Series.

11. Is the underlined sentence a fact or an opinion? Explain your answer.

✳ It's a fact. Even though the sentence hints that many players and fans had a negative opinion, it was a known fact that they didn't want him in the Major Leagues.

© Evan-Moor Corp. • EMC 3246 • Daily Fundamentals   13

Page 14

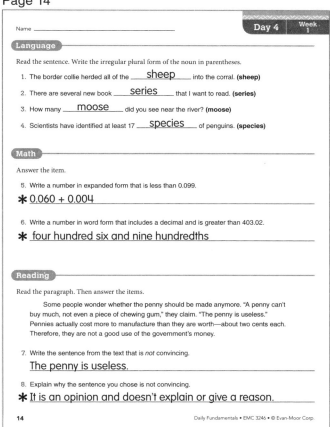

Name _____   Day 4 | Week 1

Language

Read the sentence. Write the irregular plural form of the noun in parentheses.

1. The border collie herded all of the sheep into the corral. (sheep)
2. There are several new book series that I want to read. (series)
3. How many moose did you see near the river? (moose)
4. Scientists have identified at least 17 species of penguins. (species)

Math

Answer the item.

5. Write a number in expanded form that is less than 0.099.

✳ 0.060 + 0.004

6. Write a number in word form that includes a decimal and is greater than 403.02.

✳ four hundred six and nine hundredths

Reading

Read the paragraph. Then answer the items.

Some people wonder whether the penny should be made anymore. "A penny can't buy much, not even a piece of chewing gum," they claim. "The penny is useless." Pennies actually cost more to manufacture than they are worth—about two cents each. Therefore, they are not a good use of the government's money.

7. Write the sentence from the text that is *not* convincing.

The penny is useless.

8. Explain why the sentence you chose is not convincing.

✳ It is an opinion and doesn't explain or give a reason.

14   Daily Fundamentals • EMC 3246 • © Evan-Moor Corp.

Page 15

Language

Write a sentence using a noun in the given form. Then circle the noun described.

1. proper noun: I am going to the (Northridge Mall) tonight.

* _____

2. irregular plural: They are having a sale on shoes for (children)

* _____

Math

Read the problem. Write the answer in standard form, expanded form, and word form.

3. Mike gave these clues to the cost of his new skateboard: There are five digits in all, and they add up to 16. The smallest digit is 1, which is in the hundreds place. The largest digit is 5, which is used twice. The 5's value in one place is 10 times greater than its value in the tenths place. The digit in the smallest place value is a 3. The value of the tens place is one-fifth the value of the number in the hundreds place.

standard form: $ 125.53   expanded form: $ 100 + 20 + 5 + 0.5 + 0.03

word form: $ one hundred twenty-five and fifty-three hundredths

Reading

Read the paragraph. Then answer the item.

Two colleagues were debating the grape boycott organized by César Chávez on behalf of farmworkers. "Morton, you know how business works," Jameson began. "It's the 1960s. You can't be successful in business if you worry about the comfort of your employees. And his methods! He's fasting to get attention. He'd get more respect from me if he used force. He's a weak leader."

4. Does Jameson's argument contain mostly facts or opinions? How effective is his argument?

* He used mostly opinions. It's not effective; it tells how Jameson feels but not if Chávez's efforts are working.

Page 16

Language

Read the sentence. Complete it with the correct pronoun to match the underlined antecedent.

1. After the dogs dug out under the fence, ___they___ chased the chickens.

2. Theresa, are ___you___ going to karate class tonight?

3. When Javier and I work together, ___we___ always get a good grade.

4. Mr. Schwartz built the cabin 50 years ago, and ___it___ is still in good shape.

Math

Write the expression using exponents. Then simplify.

5. $10 \times 10 \times 10 \times 10 \times 10$

10^5 100,000

6. $5 \times 5 \times 5$

5^3 125

7. $\frac{1}{3} \times \frac{1}{3} \times \frac{1}{3} \times \frac{1}{3} \times \frac{1}{3} \times \frac{1}{3}$

$\left(\frac{1}{3}\right)^6$ $\frac{1}{729}$

8. 2.1×2.1

2.1^2 4.41

Reading

Read the paragraph. Then answer the item.

Most computer hard drives use an electromagnet to write information onto a magnetic disk. MagLev trains use magnetism to float and propel trains forward on special tracks. Doctors use powerful magnets in magnetic reasonance imaging (MRI) machines to take detailed pictures of the insides of our bodies. You can see that, without harnessing the power of the magnet, much of today's technology wouldn't exist.

9. Underline the sentence that gives the main idea of the text. Then explain how you know.

* It is a general statement about magnets and technology. The other sentences are all examples of this technology.

Page 17

Language

Read the sentence. Complete it with the correct pronoun(s) to match the underlined antecedent(s).

1. After Paolo showed Kim and me the problem, he showed ___us___ how to fix it.

2. When Pam or I call you, bring up your project and give it to ___her___ or ___me___.

3. Even though they had good directions, our house was difficult for ___them___ to find.

4. Pointing to Juan, I said, "If it weren't for ___him___, my dog would still be missing."

Math

Write the term as an expression.

5. 16^4

$16 \times 16 \times 16 \times 16$

6. $\left(\frac{2}{7}\right)^3$

$\left(\frac{2}{7}\right) \times \left(\frac{2}{7}\right) \times \left(\frac{2}{7}\right)$

7. 12.5^2

12.5×12.5

Circle the expression that is equivalent to $\left(\frac{1}{8}\right)^5$. Then explain your choice.

8. $\frac{1}{8} \times 5$ $\frac{1}{8} \times \frac{1}{5}$ $\left(\frac{1}{8} \times \frac{1}{8} \times \frac{1}{8} \times \frac{1}{8} \times \frac{1}{8}\right)$

* It's the base $\left(\frac{1}{8}\right)$ multiplied by itself 5 times.

Reading

Read the paragraph. Then answer the items.

Koa Halpern was raised as a vegetarian, so he hadn't given much thought to fast food or the problems associated with it. That changed when his family hosted a foreign exchange student. Their guest's first goal was to eat at a fast-food restaurant. Halpern wondered what the appeal was. After a lot of research, his website was born.

9. Write what the text is mostly about in your own words.

* It's about what led Koa to start a website about fast food.

10. Write one supporting detail from the text in your own words.

* Koa Halpern didn't grow up eating fast food.

Page 18

Language

Read the sentences. Write a possessive pronoun to match the underlined antecedent.

1. That's not my notebook. ___Mine___ has a green cover.

2. Our seats are better than the Asadas' seats. ___Theirs___ are in row 23.

3. Your camera takes better pictures than my camera. May I borrow ___yours___?

4. Carla's apartment is at the end of the building. My apartment is right next to ___hers___.

Math

Simplify the expression.

5. 4.3×10^7

43,000,000

6. 9.9×10^{11}

990,000,000,000

7. 3.6×10^8

360,000,000

What is an advantage of writing very big numbers as an expression with a power of 10?

8. Really big numbers take up a lot of space, but they take up

* less space when written with a power of 10.

Reading

Read the paragraph. Then answer the items.

It seemed that 17-year-old Liu Wu's purpose in life was to play pranks on the gentle artisans who lived in the city. He spent his days stealing their goods or damaging their goods or playing tricks on them. His father was a well-respected merchant and a strict father. But most of the year he was away from the city, trading with other merchants.

9. How did Liu Wu treat the townspeople where he lived? Give an example.

* He played pranks on them. He broke things they made.

10. Why didn't Liu Wu's father discipline him better?

* He was often out of town working.

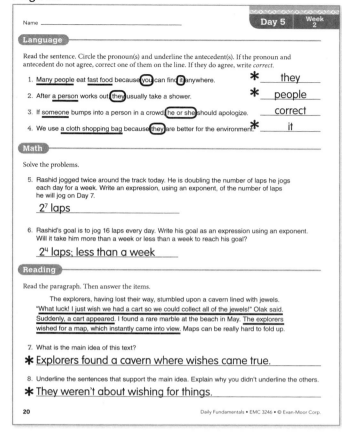

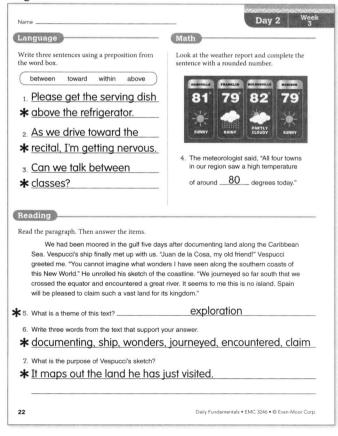

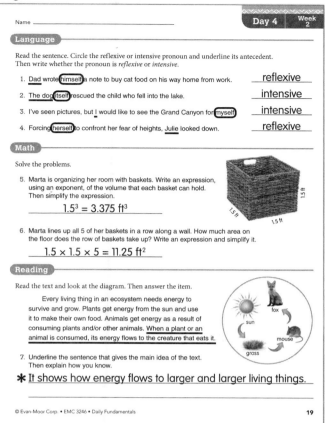

Page 19

Name _____

Day 4 | Week 2

Language

Read the sentence. Circle the reflexive or intensive pronoun and underline its antecedent. Then write whether the pronoun is *reflexive* or *intensive*.

1. Dad wrote (himself) a note to buy cat food on his way home from work. — reflexive
2. The dog (itself) rescued the child who fell into the lake. — intensive
3. I've seen pictures, but I would like to see the Grand Canyon for (myself). — intensive
4. Forcing (herself) to confront her fear of heights, Julie looked down. — reflexive

Math

Solve the problems.

5. Marta is organizing her room with baskets. Write an expression, using an exponent, of the volume that each basket can hold. Then simplify the expression.

$1.5^3 = 3.375$ ft^3

1.5 ft

6. Marta lines up all 5 of her baskets in a row along a wall. How much area on the floor does the row of baskets take up? Write an expression and simplify it.

$1.5 \times 1.5 \times 5 = 11.25$ ft^2

Reading

Read the text and look at the diagram. Then answer the item.

Every living thing in an ecosystem needs energy to survive and grow. Plants get energy from the sun and use it to make their own food. Animals get energy as a result of consuming plants and/or other animals. When a plant or an animal is consumed, its energy flows to the creature that eats it.

fox, sun, mouse, grass

7. Underline the sentence that gives the main idea of the text. Then explain how you know.

✳ It shows how energy flows to larger and larger living things.

© Evan-Moor Corp. • EMC 3246 • Daily Fundamentals — 19

Page 20

Name _____

Day 5 | Week 2

Language

Read the sentence. Circle the pronoun(s) and underline the antecedent(s). If the pronoun and antecedent do not agree, correct one of them on the line. If they do agree, write *correct*.

1. Many people eat fast food because (you) can find (it) anywhere. — ✳ they
2. After a person works out (they) usually take a shower. — ✳ people
3. If someone bumps into a person in a crowd (he or she) should apologize. — correct
4. We use a cloth shopping bag because (they) are better for the environment. — ✳ it

Math

Solve the problems.

5. Rashid jogged twice around the track today. He is doubling the number of laps he jogs each day for a week. Write an expression, using an exponent, of the number of laps he will jog on Day 7.

2^7 laps

6. Rashid's goal is to jog 16 laps every day. Write his goal as an expression using an exponent. Will it take him more than a week or less than a week to reach his goal?

2^4 laps; less than a week

Reading

Read the paragraph. Then answer the items.

The explorers, having lost their way, stumbled upon a cavern lined with jewels. "What luck! I just wish we had a cart so we could collect all of the jewels!" Olak said. Suddenly, a cart appeared. I found a rare marble at the beach in May. The explorers wished for a map, which instantly came into view. Maps can be really hard to fold up.

7. What is the main idea of this text?

✳ Explorers found a cavern where wishes came true.

8. Underline the sentences that support the main idea. Explain why you didn't underline the others.

✳ They weren't about wishing for things.

20 — Daily Fundamentals • EMC 3246 • © Evan-Moor Corp.

Page 21

Name _____

Day 1 | Week 3

Language

Read the sentence. Underline the prepositional phrase. Then circle the noun that it modifies.

1. The (geese) in the road are stopping traffic.
2. A (team) of doctors has invented a new treatment.
3. The purple (rose) among the white daisies really stands out.
4. A (bird) with blue wings sings softly.
5. The (dancers) behind the curtain are ready to start the show.
6. (Pizzas) cooked in a brick oven are crispier.

Math

Round to the nearest thousand.

7. 12,458 — 12,000
8. 764,842 — 765,000
9. 6,308,487 — 6,308,000
10. 51,949,083 — 51,949,000

Round to the nearest hundredth.

11. 15.375 — 15.38
12. 254.998 — 255.00
13. 39.0606 — 39.06
14. 4,857.3008 — 4,857.30

Reading

Read the paragraphs. Then answer the items.

Devin and his parents floated down the river toward the expedition site. "You might even have fun," Devin's mom said, smiling. "The Bindi-Way tribe has a completely different way of doing things than families in the U.S. You'll learn something new!"

Devin rested his chin on his hand and looked around gloomily. The sound of peculiar bird songs and rushing river water filled his ears as he peered into the strange deep, dark jungle. "I wish I could be at home playing a game on my tablet right now instead," he thought.

15. One possible theme of this text is ___.
  Ⓐ family
  ● change
  Ⓒ nature
  Ⓓ competition

16. Devin feels ___ about the expedition.
  Ⓐ cheerful
  Ⓑ enthusiastic
  ● depressed
  Ⓓ disgusted

© Evan-Moor Corp. • EMC 3246 • Daily Fundamentals — 21

Page 22

Name _____

Day 2 | Week 3

Language

Write three sentences using a preposition from the word box.

between | toward | within | above

1. Please get the serving dish ✳ above the refrigerator.
2. As we drive toward the ✳ recital, I'm getting nervous.
3. Can we talk between ✳ classes?

Math

Look at the weather report and complete the sentence with a rounded number.

NASHVILLE 81 SUNNY | FRANKLIN 79 RAINY | NOLENSVILLE 82 PARTLY CLOUDY | MADISON 79 SUNNY

4. The meteorologist said, "All four towns in our region saw a high temperature of around 80 degrees today."

Reading

Read the paragraph. Then answer the items.

We had been moored in the gulf five days after documenting land along the Caribbean Sea. Vespucci's ship finally met up with us. "Juan de la Cosa, my old friend!" Vespucci greeted me. "You cannot imagine what wonders I have seen along the southern coasts of this New World." He unrolled his sketch of the coastline. "We journeyed so far south that we crossed the equator and encountered a great river. It seems to me this is no island. Spain will be pleased to claim such a vast land for its kingdom."

5. What is a theme of this text? ✳ exploration

6. Write three words from the text that support your answer.

✳ documenting, ship, wonders, journeyed, encountered, claim

7. What is the purpose of Vespucci's sketch?

✳ It maps out the land he has just visited.

22 — Daily Fundamentals • EMC 3246 • © Evan-Moor Corp.

Page 23

Name _____

Day 3 | **Week 3**

Language

Read the sentence. Underline the prepositional phrase(s). Then circle the object of the preposition(s).

1. Give a permission slip to (each student)

2. You'll find the stairs just beyond (the kitchen)

3. Please buy some fruit for (our guests)

4. We bought Dad a new camera to take on (our vacation)

5. The store where we usually shop is right around (the corner)

6. Look at (the stars) falling across (the sky)

Math

Complete the sentence with a rounded number.

7. School Stuff sells color markers for about

$ __5__ per set.

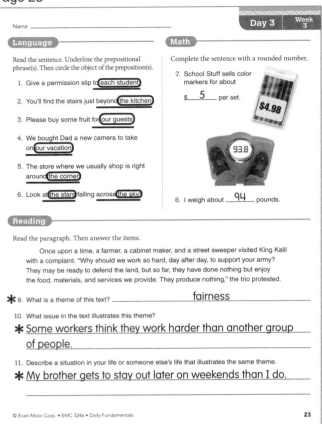

$4.98

93.8

8. I weigh about __94__ pounds.

Reading

Read the paragraph. Then answer the items.

Once upon a time, a farmer, a cabinet maker, and a street sweeper visited King Kalil with a complaint. "Why should we work so hard, day after day, to support your army? They may be ready to defend the land, but so far, they have done nothing but enjoy the food, materials, and services we provide. They produce nothing," the trio protested.

❋ 9. What is a theme of this text? __fairness__

10. What issue in the text illustrates this theme?

❋ Some workers think they work harder than another group of people.

11. Describe a situation in your life or someone else's life that illustrates the same theme.

❋ My brother gets to stay out later on weekends than I do.

© Evan-Moor Corp. • EMC 3246 • Daily Fundamentals | 23

Page 24

Name _____

Day 4 | **Week 3**

Language

Read the sentence. Underline the prepositional phrase(s). Then circle the object of the preposition(s).

1. Please send the package to (us) soon.

2. Tate's favorite teacher is right next to (me) in (the photo)

3. Our grandparents always hide little gifts for (my sister and me) to find.

4. The Goldfarbs found a park near (them) after they moved.

5. The student beside (you) is my math tutor.

6. Make your bed and clean beneath (it)

Math

Complete the paragraph with rounded numbers. Then answer the item.

7. Khalid was trying to decide where to vacation in March. In Coalville, the average March rainfall is 2.31 inches. In Stagway, it is 8.14 inches. Khalid said, "I'd rather go to Coalville because it rains only about __2__ inches that month. I'd need an umbrella to deal with the __8__ inches of rain we might get in Stagway!"

8. Why are rounded measurements more appropriate in this situation?

❋ He is comparing numbers that are not close together.

Reading

Read the paragraph. Then answer the items.

On a shelf inside the barn were bricks of aging cheese. Crow pranced around the cheeses, stopping to peck at each brick, until he finally found the perfect flavor. Crow boldly pulled off such a large piece of the cheese that he had trouble flying back to his nest. The farmer heard the crow flapping his wings madly and gave chase. The bird narrowly missed the farmer's grasp and almost dropped his treasure! When the rest of the flock returned from eating bugs and worms in the farmer's freshly plowed field, Crow would show off the cheese and devour it in front of them.

9. Explain how the theme of greed relates to the action in the text.

❋ Crow stole something really tasty and nearly lost it because he tried to take so much.

10. Would the theme be the same if Crow had found a large bug in the field? Explain your answer.

❋ No, he wouldn't have had to escape—he could eat it there.

24 | Daily Fundamentals • EMC 3246 • © Evan-Moor Corp.

Page 25

Name _____

Day 5 | **Week 3**

Language

Read the sentence. Underline the prepositional phrase(s). Read the sentence again without the prepositional phrase. Then explain the phrase's function.

1. Passengers on the Denver flight have arrived at Gate 15.

❋ It tells which passengers have arrived and where.

2. A colony of bees includes a queen, workers, scouts, and drones.

❋ It tells what kind of colony it is.

Math

Circle any of the situations in which rounding a number would make sense.

3. (a) deciding how much money to bring to a store

b) measuring ingredients in a recipe

c) timing a race

d) measuring lumber to construct a desk

(e) determining whether it's cold enough to wear a wool sweater

(f) figuring out the fastest route to school

g) weighing vegetables at the cash register

Reading

Read the paragraph. Then answer the items.

Traveling to Alta California with mules and cattle proved to be a challenge for our families. After the hot summer days had passed, it was windy and barren, and the desert provided little water and grass for our animals. After a month, we reached the banks of the Colorado River. The cold, bitter winter had made fording the river impossible. We had never seen such a wide river and such rushing water. Finally, a narrow flow was found to the north, where thick brush scratched our arms and legs and icy winds tossed dust at us.

4. Write one theme that you think is explored in this text. Explain how you identified the theme.

❋ Overcoming hardships is being explored. The text mentions/describes difficult, unpleasant conditions.

5. Write a sentence that could be added to the text that supports the theme.

❋ There was scarcely enough water to drink, let alone bathe in.

© Evan-Moor Corp. • EMC 3246 • Daily Fundamentals | 25

Page 26

Name _____

Day 1 | **Week 4**

Language

Read the sentence. Draw a line to separate the complete subject from the complete predicate.

1. The family of field mice | ran when they heard the foreign noise.

2. The loud buzzing sound from the forest | whined on and on.

3. Suddenly, the mice in their hideout | heard a tremendous crashing sound!

4. The largest spruce tree in the woods | landed with a huge thud that echoed.

Math

Write all the factors of the given number.

5. 64 __1, 64, 2, 32, 4, 16, 8__

6. 120 __1, 120, 2, 60, 3, 40, 4, 30, 5, 24, 6, 20, 8, 15, 10, 12__

7. 79 __1, 79__

8. 51 __1, 51, 3, 17__

9. 143 __1, 143, 11, 13__

Reading

Read the paragraphs. Then answer the items.

"I can't just *not* go," Christine said exasperated. Tamara was not even trying to understand. "My parents are going!"

Tamara's fingers pushed through the cool grass. "Actually," she said, "you could stay with us. My parents would take care of you if you didn't want to go. I know they would."

10. What is most likely Christine and Tamara's relationship?

❋ They're probably close friends.

11. What is Tamara probably unhappy about?

❋ Christine is moving far away.

26 | Daily Fundamentals • EMC 3246 • © Evan-Moor Corp.

Page 27

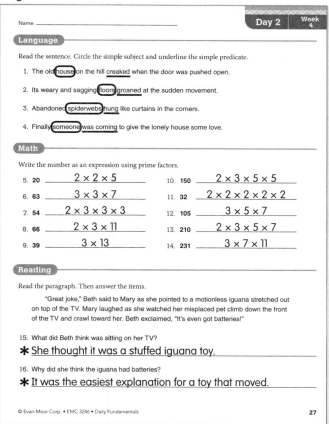

Name _____

Day 2 | Week 4

Language

Read the sentence. Circle the simple subject and underline the simple predicate.

1. The old (house) on the hill <u>creaked</u> when the door was pushed open.

2. Its weary and sagging (floors) <u>groaned</u> at the sudden movement.

3. Abandoned (spiderwebs) <u>hung</u> like curtains in the corners.

4. Finally (someone) <u>was coming</u> to give the lonely house some love.

Math

Write the number as an expression using prime factors.

5. 20 ___ $2 \times 2 \times 5$
6. 63 ___ $3 \times 3 \times 7$
7. 54 ___ $2 \times 3 \times 3 \times 3$
8. 66 ___ $2 \times 3 \times 11$
9. 39 ___ 3×13
10. 150 ___ $2 \times 3 \times 5 \times 5$
11. 32 ___ $2 \times 2 \times 2 \times 2 \times 2$
12. 105 ___ $3 \times 5 \times 7$
13. 210 ___ $2 \times 3 \times 5 \times 7$
14. 231 ___ $3 \times 7 \times 11$

Reading

Read the paragraph. Then answer the items.

"Great joke," Beth said to Mary as she pointed to a motionless iguana stretched out on top of the TV. Mary laughed as she watched her misplaced pet climb down the front of the TV and crawl toward the camera. Beth exclaimed, "It's even got batteries!"

15. What did Beth think was sitting on her TV?

✱ <u>She thought it was a stuffed iguana toy.</u>

16. Why did she think the iguana had batteries?

✱ <u>It was the easiest explanation for a toy that moved.</u>

© Evan-Moor Corp. • EMC 3246 • Daily Fundamentals   27

Page 28

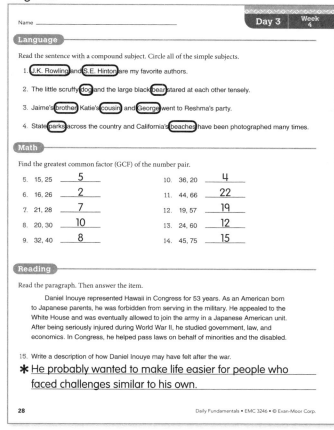

Name _____

Day 3 | Week 4

Language

Read the sentence with a compound subject. Circle all of the simple subjects.

1. (J.K. Rowling) and (S.E. Hinton) are my favorite authors.

2. The little scruffy (dog) and the large black (bear) stared at each other tensely.

3. Jaime's (brother) Katie's (cousin) and (George) went to Reshma's party.

4. State (parks) across the country and California's (beaches) have been photographed many times.

Math

Find the greatest common factor (GCF) of the number pair.

5. 15, 25 ___ 5
6. 16, 26 ___ 2
7. 21, 28 ___ 7
8. 20, 30 ___ 10
9. 32, 40 ___ 8
10. 36, 20 ___ 4
11. 44, 66 ___ 22
12. 19, 57 ___ 19
13. 24, 60 ___ 12
14. 45, 75 ___ 15

Reading

Read the paragraph. Then answer the item.

Daniel Inouye represented Hawaii in Congress for 53 years. As an American born to Japanese parents, he was forbidden from serving in the military. He appealed to the White House and was eventually allowed to join the army in a Japanese American unit. After being seriously injured during World War II, he studied government, law, and economics. In Congress, he helped pass laws on behalf of minorities and the disabled.

15. Write a description of how Daniel Inouye may have felt after the war.

✱ <u>He probably wanted to make life easier for people who</u>
<u>faced challenges similar to his own.</u>

28   Daily Fundamentals • EMC 3246 • © Evan-Moor Corp.

Page 29

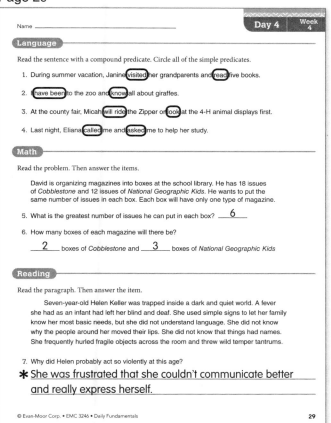

Name _____

Day 4 | Week 4

Language

Read the sentence with a compound predicate. Circle all of the simple predicates.

1. During summer vacation, Janine (visited) her grandparents and (read) five books.

2. I (have been) to the zoo and (know) all about giraffes.

3. At the county fair, Micah (will ride) the Zipper or (look) at the 4-H animal displays first.

4. Last night, Eliana (called) me and (asked) me to help her study.

Math

Read the problem. Then answer the items.

David is organizing magazines into boxes at the school library. He has 18 issues of *Cobblestone* and 12 issues of *National Geographic Kids*. He wants to put the same number of issues in each box. Each box will have only one type of magazine.

5. What is the greatest number of issues he can put in each box? ___ 6

6. How many boxes of each magazine will there be?

___ 2 ___ boxes of *Cobblestone* and ___ 3 ___ boxes of *National Geographic Kids*

Reading

Read the paragraph. Then answer the item.

Seven-year-old Helen Keller was trapped inside a dark and quiet world. A fever she had as an infant had left her blind and deaf. She used simple signs to let her family know her most basic needs, but she did not understand language. She did not know why the people around her moved their lips. She did not know that things had names. She frequently hurled fragile objects across the room and threw wild temper tantrums.

7. Why did Helen probably act so violently at this age?

✱ <u>She was frustrated that she couldn't communicate better</u>
<u>and really express herself.</u>

© Evan-Moor Corp. • EMC 3246 • Daily Fundamentals   29

Page 30

Name _____

Day 5 | Week 4

Language

Write one sentence with a compound subject and another sentence with a compound predicate. Circle the simple subject(s) and underline the simple predicate(s) in each sentence.

✱ 1. The (beach) and the (lake) <u>are</u> my two favorite vacation places.

✱ 2. (I) <u>make</u> sand castles and <u>go</u> swimming.

Math

Read the problem. Then answer the items.

Makela is filling grocery bags at a food pantry. Each bag's contents will be identical, and there will be no food left over. Makela has 27 boxes of oatmeal and 18 boxes of raisins.

3. What is the greatest number of bags can she fill? ___ 9

4. How many boxes of each food will go in each bag?

___ 3 ___ boxes of oatmeal and ___ 2 ___ boxes of raisins

Reading

Read the proclamation. Then answer the item.

In accordance with a proclamation from the Executive of the United States, all slaves are free. This involves an absolute equality of personal rights and rights of property between former masters and slaves, and the connection … between them becomes that between employer and hired labor. The freedmen are advised to remain quietly at their present homes and work for wages. They … will not be supported in idleness either there or elsewhere.

5. How do you think life changed for the freedmen who stayed with their employers?

✱ <u>They probably continued to work hard as long as they were</u>
<u>treated fairly.</u>

30   Daily Fundamentals • EMC 3246 • © Evan-Moor Corp.

Page 31

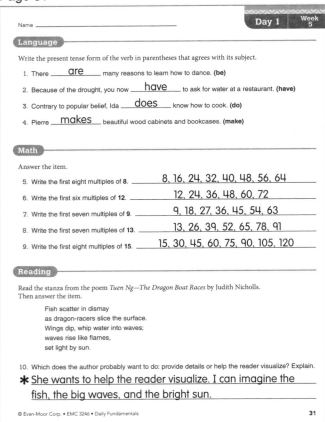

Name _____

Day 1 | **Week 5**

Language

Write the present tense form of the verb in parentheses that agrees with its subject.

1. There ___are___ many reasons to learn how to dance. **(be)**

2. Because of the drought, you now ___have___ to ask for water at a restaurant. **(have)**

3. Contrary to popular belief, Ida ___does___ know how to cook. **(do)**

4. Pierre ___makes___ beautiful wood cabinets and bookcases. **(make)**

Math

Answer the item.

5. Write the first eight multiples of **8**. ___8, 16, 24, 32, 40, 48, 56, 64___

6. Write the first six multiples of **12**. ___12, 24, 36, 48, 60, 72___

7. Write the first seven multiples of **9**. ___9, 18, 27, 36, 45, 54, 63___

8. Write the first seven multiples of **13**. ___13, 26, 39, 52, 65, 78, 91___

9. Write the first eight multiples of **15**. ___15, 30, 45, 60, 75, 90, 105, 120___

Reading

Read the stanza from the poem *Tuen Ng—The Dragon Boat Races* by Judith Nicholls. Then answer the item.

Fish scatter in dismay
as dragon-racers slice the surface.
Wings dip, whip water into waves;
waves rise like flames,
set light by sun.

10. Which does the author probably want to do: provide details or help the reader visualize? Explain.
* ___She wants to help the reader visualize. I can imagine the fish, the big waves, and the bright sun.___

© Evan-Moor Corp. • EMC 3246 • Daily Fundamentals   31

Page 32

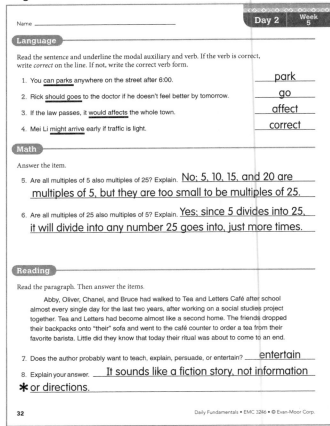

Name _____

Day 2 | **Week 5**

Language

Read the sentence and underline the modal auxiliary and verb. If the verb is correct, write *correct* on the line. If not, write the correct verb form.

1. You <u>can parks</u> anywhere on the street after 6:00. ___park___

2. Rick <u>should goes</u> to the doctor if he doesn't feel better by tomorrow. ___go___

3. If the law passes, it <u>would affects</u> the whole town. ___affect___

4. Mei Li <u>might arrive</u> early if traffic is light. ___correct___

Math

Answer the item.

5. Are all multiples of 5 also multiples of 25? Explain. ___No; 5, 10, 15, and 20 are multiples of 5, but they are too small to be multiples of 25.___

6. Are all multiples of 25 also multiples of 5? Explain. ___Yes; since 5 divides into 25, it will divide into any number 25 goes into, just more times.___

Reading

Read the paragraph. Then answer the items.

Abby, Oliver, Chanel, and Bruce had walked to Tea and Letters Café after school almost every single day for the last two years, after working on a social studies project together. Tea and Letters had become almost like a second home. The friends dropped their backpacks onto "their" sofa and went to the café counter to order a tea from their favorite barista. Little did they know that today their ritual was about to come to an end.

7. Does the author probably want to teach, explain, persuade, or entertain? ___entertain___

8. Explain your answer. ___It sounds like a fiction story, not information___
* ___or directions.___

32   Daily Fundamentals • EMC 3246 • © Evan-Moor Corp.

Page 33

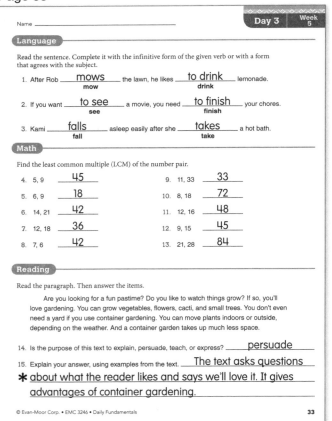

Name _____

Day 3 | **Week 5**

Language

Read the sentence. Complete it with the infinitive form of the given verb or with a form that agrees with the subject.

1. After Rob ___mows___ (**mow**) the lawn, he likes ___to drink___ (**drink**) lemonade.

2. If you want ___to see___ (**see**) a movie, you need ___to finish___ (**finish**) your chores.

3. Kami ___falls___ (**fall**) asleep easily after she ___takes___ (**take**) a hot bath.

Math

Find the least common multiple (LCM) of the number pair.

4. 5, 9 ___45___
5. 6, 9 ___18___
6. 14, 21 ___42___
7. 12, 18 ___36___
8. 7, 6 ___42___

9. 11, 33 ___33___
10. 8, 18 ___72___
11. 12, 16 ___48___
12. 9, 15 ___45___
13. 21, 28 ___84___

Reading

Read the paragraph. Then answer the items.

Are you looking for a fun pastime? Do you like to watch things grow? If so, you'll love gardening. You can grow vegetables, flowers, cacti, and small trees. You don't even need a yard if you use container gardening. You can move plants indoors or outside, depending on the weather. And a container garden takes up much less space.

14. Is the purpose of this text to explain, persuade, teach, or express? ___persuade___

15. Explain your answer, using examples from the text. ___The text asks questions___
* ___about what the reader likes and says we'll love it. It gives advantages of container gardening.___

© Evan-Moor Corp. • EMC 3246 • Daily Fundamentals   33

Page 34

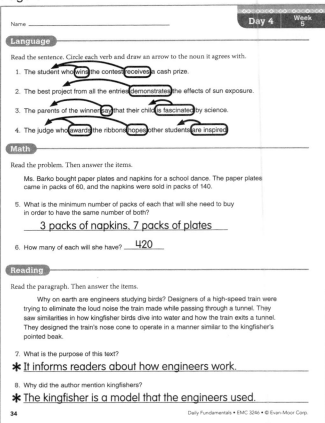

Name _____

Day 4 | **Week 5**

Language

Read the sentence. Circle each verb and draw an arrow to the noun it agrees with.

1. The student who wins the contest receives a cash prize.

2. The best project from all the entries demonstrates the effects of sun exposure.

3. The parents of the winner say that their child is fascinated by science.

4. The judge who awards the ribbons hopes other students are inspired.

Math

Read the problem. Then answer the items.

Ms. Barko bought paper plates and napkins for a school dance. The paper plates came in packs of 60, and the napkins were sold in packs of 140.

5. What is the minimum number of packs of each that will she need to buy in order to have the same number of both?
___3 packs of napkins, 7 packs of plates___

6. How many of each will she have? ___420___

Reading

Read the paragraph. Then answer the items.

Why on earth are engineers studying birds? Designers of a high-speed train were trying to eliminate the loud noise the train made while passing through a tunnel. They saw similarities in how kingfisher birds dive into water and how the train exits a tunnel. They designed the train's nose cone to operate in a manner similar to the kingfisher's pointed beak.

7. What is the purpose of this text?
* ___It informs readers about how engineers work.___

8. Why did the author mention kingfishers?
* ___The kingfisher is a model that the engineers used.___

34   Daily Fundamentals • EMC 3246 • © Evan-Moor Corp.

Page 35

Language

Read the paragraph. Complete it with verbs that make sense and agree with their subjects.

*1. One of the best places I __like__ to visit __is__ Juneau, Alaska. Everywhere you __look__, there __are__ rugged mountains, even on the coast! You can __see__ totem poles that __stand__ tall and __tell__ stories of local clans. One of the prettiest glaciers that are receding quickly __is__ Mendenhall Glacier.

Math

Solve the problem.

2. Jamal walks once around the track in 5 minutes. Keisha jogs once around the track in 3 minutes. If they start from the same place on the track at the same time, how long will it take them to arrive together at the start again?

__15 minutes__

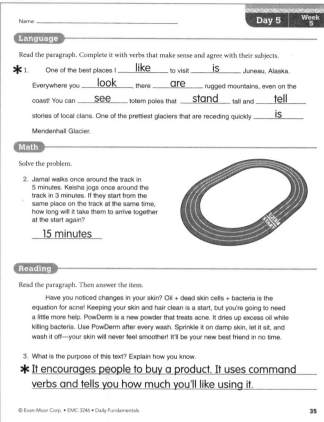

Reading

Read the paragraph. Then answer the item.

Have you noticed changes in your skin? Oil + dead skin cells + bacteria is the equation for acne! Keeping your skin and hair clean is a start, but you're going to need a little more help. PowDerm is a new powder that treats acne. It dries up excess oil while killing bacteria. Use PowDerm after every wash. Sprinkle it on damp skin, let it sit, and wash it off—your skin will never feel smoother! It'll be your new best friend in no time.

3. What is the purpose of this text? Explain how you know.

* __It encourages people to buy a product. It uses command__
__verbs and tells you how much you'll like using it.__

Page 36

Language

Read the sentence. Draw three lines (≡) under any letter that should be capitalized.

1. In mary's first issue of *national geographic*, she read an article on the great wall of china.

2. The magazine said that emperor qin shi huang ordered the wall built to keep out invaders.

3. In the mid-1600s, the manchus broke through the wall and ended the ming dynasty.

Math

Add.

4. 651.73 + 41.88
__693.61__

5. 3.125 + 11.894
__15.019__

6. 17.29 + 24.504
__41.794__

7. 32.1857 + 687.43
__719.6157__

Reading

Read the paragraph from a fiction story. Then look at the plot diagram and answer the items.

After I moved in with my grandparents in northern Maine, I realized how much I missed Florida, playing beach volleyball in the warm sand after school and waterskiing in the sultry Gulf of Mexico. I first realized how much my new surroundings were affecting me when I skipped two morning cheerleading practices. Callie asked if I had the flu, and my coach asked if something was bothering me—before giving me a warning. All I knew is that I was tired for no reason.

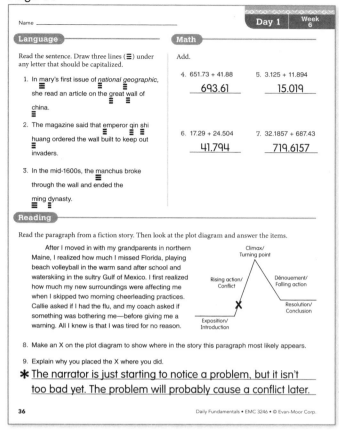

8. Make an X on the plot diagram to show where in the story this paragraph most likely appears.

9. Explain why you placed the X where you did.

* __The narrator is just starting to notice a problem, but it isn't__
__too bad yet. The problem will probably cause a conflict later.__

Page 37

Language

Write three sentences that include the name of a holiday. Capitalize the holidays.

1. We get two days off for
* Thanksgiving.

2. The lights during Diwali
* are beautiful.

3. During Rosh Hashanah,
* we play the shofar.

Math

Read the problem. Then answer the items.

Nigel is making butterscotch pudding. The recipe requires 0.473 liter of milk. He is also making oatmeal that calls for 0.237 liter of milk.

4. How much milk should Nigel have on hand before he starts cooking?
__0.710 liter__

5. Nigel has 0.059 liter milk more than he needs. How much does he have when he starts?
__0.769 liter__

Reading

Read the paragraph from a fiction story. Then answer the items.

When I returned to the dining room, my ordinary Saturday turned really strange. Mickey's mom was combing her hair with a fork. Mickey's dad jumped up from his chair and ran to a nearby wall. He pressed his body against the wall, making himself as flat as he could. Mickey himself was acting bizarre, squeezing all the food between his fingers—even his soup and salad! I felt confused and sweaty. Can I help, or should I escape? Suddenly, I remembered something my mom had said this morning, and I knew the problem was with *me*, not with Mickey's family.

6. Which part of the plot is this paragraph most likely from?
Ⓐ introduction
● conflict
Ⓒ falling action
Ⓓ resolution

7. Which of these will probably happen next?
● The problem will get worse.
Ⓑ The problem will be solved.
Ⓒ We'll learn more about the characters.
Ⓓ We'll learn more about the setting.

Page 38

Language

Read the sentence. Draw three lines (≡) under any letter that should be capitalized.

1. The store clerk said, "your cat will really like this brand of cat food."

2. "as I was saying," Mrs. Palacios continued, "your assignments are due tomorrow."

3. "where can I find tarpey road?" Terry asked the gas station attendant.

4. Just as the race started, he heard shouts of "go adelberto!" and "you can do it!"

Math

Subtract.

5. 95.34 − 94.36
__0.98__

6. 213.476 − 11.680
__201.796__

7. 57.29 − 35.355
__21.935__

8. 157.6 − 42.89
__114.71__

Reading

These notes were taken from a story to write a plot outline, but they are not in plot order. Read each note. On the line, write the part of the plot it belongs to, using the terms from the word box.

introduction   rising action   climax   falling action   resolution

9. __climax__ The mice come up with a way to always know where the cat is.

__rising action__ The mice meet to discuss what to do about the cat.

__resolution__ The mice see how their plan is working.

__introduction__ The household cat has hurt several mice.

__falling action__ The mice vote on the plan.

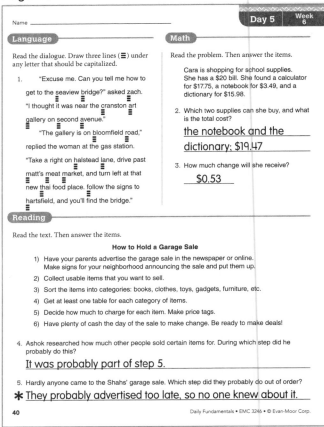

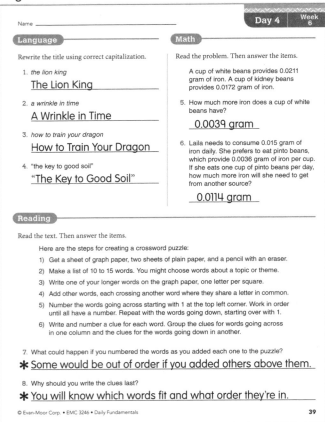

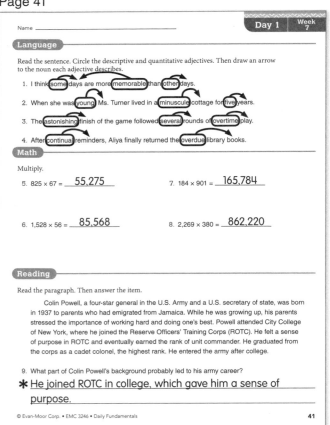

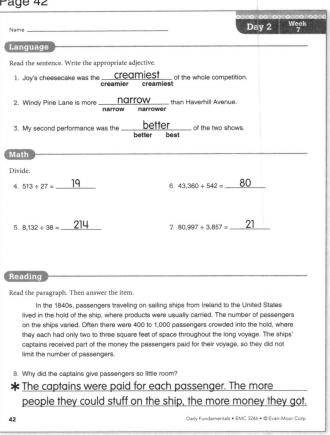

These answers will vary. Examples are given.

Page 39

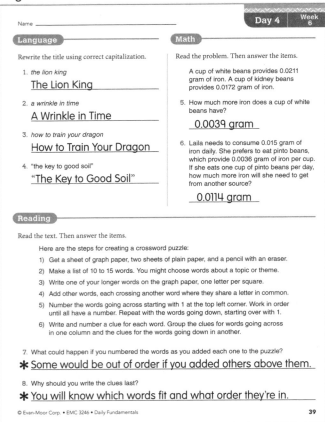

Name ____

Day 4 Week 6

Language

Rewrite the title using correct capitalization.

1. *the lion king*
   The Lion King

2. *a wrinkle in time*
   A Wrinkle in Time

3. *how to train your dragon*
   How to Train Your Dragon

4. *"the key to good soil"*
   "The Key to Good Soil"

Math

Read the problem. Then answer the items.

A cup of white beans provides 0.0211 gram of iron. A cup of kidney beans provides 0.0172 gram of iron.

5. How much more iron does a cup of white beans have?
   0.0039 gram

6. Laila needs to consume 0.015 gram of iron daily. She prefers to eat pinto beans, which provide 0.0036 gram of iron per cup. If she eats one cup of pinto beans per day, how much more iron will she need to get from another source?
   0.0114 gram

Reading

Read the text. Then answer the items.

Here are the steps for creating a crossword puzzle:

1) Get a sheet of graph paper, two sheets of plain paper, and a pencil with an eraser.
2) Make a list of 10 to 15 words. You might choose words about a topic or theme.
3) Write one of your longer words on the graph paper, one letter per square.
4) Add other words, each crossing another word where they share a letter in common.
5) Number the words going across starting with 1 at the top left corner. Work in order until all have a number. Repeat with the words going down, starting over with 1.
6) Write and number a clue for each word. Group the clues for words going across in one column and the clues for the words going down in another.

7. What could happen if you numbered the words as you added each one to the puzzle?
   ✱ Some would be out of order if you added others above them.

8. Why should you write the clues last?
   ✱ You will know which words fit and what order they're in.

© Evan-Moor Corp. • EMC 3246 • Daily Fundamentals   39

Page 40

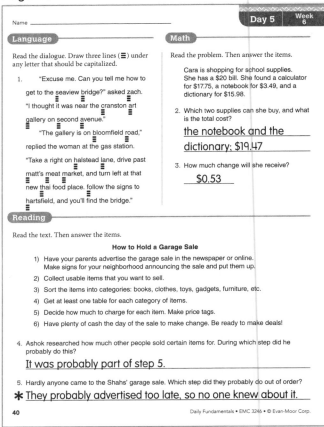

Name ____

Day 5 Week 6

Language

Read the dialogue. Draw three lines (≡) under any letter that should be capitalized.

1. "Excuse me. Can you tell me how to get to the seaview bridge?" asked zach. "I thought it was near the cranston art gallery on second avenue."
   "The gallery is on bloomfield road," replied the woman at the gas station.
   "Take a right on halstead lane, drive past matt's meat market, and turn left at that new thai food place. follow the signs to hartsfield, and you'll find the bridge."

Math

Read the problem. Then answer the items.

Cara is shopping for school supplies. She has a $20 bill. She found a calculator for $17.75, a notebook for $3.49, and a dictionary for $15.98.

2. Which two supplies can she buy, and what is the total cost?
   the notebook and the dictionary; $19.47

3. How much change will she receive?
   $0.53

Reading

Read the text. Then answer the items.

How to Hold a Garage Sale

1) Have your parents advertise the garage sale in the newspaper or online. Make signs for your neighborhood announcing the sale and put them up.
2) Collect usable items that you want to sell.
3) Sort the items into categories: books, clothes, toys, gadgets, furniture, etc.
4) Get at least one table for each category of items.
5) Decide how much to charge for each item. Make price tags.
6) Have plenty of cash the day of the sale to make change. Be ready to make deals!

4. Ashok researched how much other people sold certain items for. During which step did he probably do this?
   It was probably part of step 5.

5. Hardly anyone came to the Shahs' garage sale. Which step did they probably do out of order?
   ✱ They probably advertised too late, so no one knew about it.

40   Daily Fundamentals • EMC 3246 • © Evan-Moor Corp.

Page 41

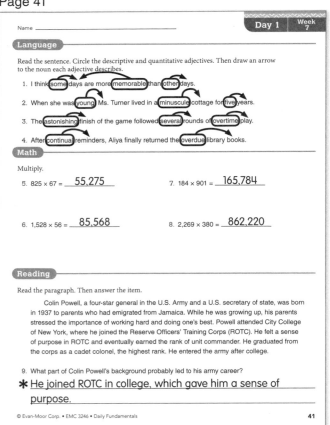

Name ____

Day 1 Week 7

Language

Read the sentence. Circle the descriptive and quantitative adjectives. Then draw an arrow to the noun each adjective describes.

1. I think some days are more memorable than other days.
2. When she was young, Ms. Turner lived in a minuscule cottage for five years.
3. The astonishing finish of the game followed several rounds of overtime play.
4. After continual reminders, Aliya finally returned the overdue library books.

Math

Multiply.

5. 825 × 67 = 55,275

7. 184 × 901 = 165,784

6. 1,528 × 56 = 85,568

8. 2,269 × 380 = 862,220

Reading

Read the paragraph. Then answer the item.

Colin Powell, a four-star general in the U.S. Army and a U.S. secretary of state, was born in 1937 to parents who had emigrated from Jamaica. While he was growing up, his parents stressed the importance of working hard and doing one's best. Powell attended City College of New York, where he joined the Reserve Officers' Training Corps (ROTC). He felt a sense of purpose in ROTC and eventually earned the rank of unit commander. He graduated from the corps as a cadet colonel, the highest rank. He entered the army after college.

9. What part of Colin Powell's background probably led to his army career?
   ✱ He joined ROTC in college, which gave him a sense of purpose.

© Evan-Moor Corp. • EMC 3246 • Daily Fundamentals   41

Page 42

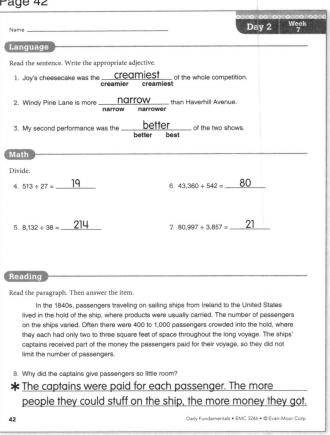

Name ____

Day 2 Week 7

Language

Read the sentence. Write the appropriate adjective.

1. Joy's cheesecake was the **creamiest** of the whole competition.
   creamier creamiest

2. Windy Pine Lane is more **narrow** than Haverhill Avenue.
   narrow narrower

3. My second performance was the **better** of the two shows.
   better best

Math

Divide.

4. 513 ÷ 27 = 19

6. 43,360 ÷ 542 = 80

5. 8,132 ÷ 38 = 214

7. 80,997 ÷ 3,857 = 21

Reading

Read the paragraph. Then answer the item.

In the 1840s, passengers traveling on sailing ships from Ireland to the United States lived in the hold of the ship, where products were usually carried. The number of passengers on the ships varied. Often there were 400 to 1,000 passengers crowded into the hold, where they each had only two to three square feet of space throughout the long voyage. The ships' captains received part of the money the passengers paid for their voyage, so they did not limit the number of passengers.

8. Why did the captains give passengers so little room?
   ✱ The captains were paid for each passenger. The more people they could stuff on the ship, the more money they got.

42   Daily Fundamentals • EMC 3246 • © Evan-Moor Corp.

168   Daily Fundamentals • EMC 3246 • © Evan-Moor Corp.

These answers will vary. Examples are given.

Page 43

Name _____

Language

Read the sentence. Write the proper adjective of the proper noun in parentheses.

1. The bouzouki is a __Greek__ musical stringed instrument. **(Greece)**
2. Did you know that bagels are a __Jewish__ food that originated in Poland? **(Jew)**
3. The __African__ savanna has a five-month-long rainy season. **(Africa)**
4. __Parisian__ architecture represents many historical building styles. **(Paris)**

Math

Multiply or divide.

5. 1,008 × 56 = __56,448__   7. 37,380 ÷ 35 = __1,068__

6. 5,790 ÷ 965 = __6__   8. 48,568 × 13 = __631,384__

Reading

Read the paragraph. Then answer the item.

Lisa's cousin Elena was coming from Mexico to live with her for the rest of the school year. Mom had insisted that Lisa give up her activities after school. "I can't drive back and forth all day," Mom had said. "I have to pick you both up right after school. It wouldn't be fair to have Elena wait an hour for you to finish play practice." Lisa had a big part in the school play. She hadn't yet told Mr. Blake, the drama teacher, that she couldn't come to rehearsals. She was hoping Mom would change her mind.

9. Why was Lisa going to have to drop out of the school play?

*__Her mother was going to have to pick up Lisa and Elena at the same time after school.__

Page 44

Name _____

Language

Read the sentence. Write *this, that, these,* or *those* on the line. Then circle the word it refers to.

1. I much prefer __these__ fresh (berries) to the berries you bought last week.
2. Please check on __that__ (customer) at the corner table.
3. My grandparents had one of __those__ old (phones) with a round dial.
4. I'm almost finished with __this__ (chapter) and then I'll eat lunch.

Math

Solve the problem.

5. Max will haul 1,235 cubic feet of gravel to a construction site. His truck can carry 95 cubic feet of gravel at a time. How many trips will he have to make to deliver all the gravel?

__13 trips__

6. A sled dog running in the Iditarod race needs 2,750 calories from beef per day. There are 16 dogs on a racing team. The race usually lasts 9 days. How many calories from beef will the team of dogs consume over 9 days of the race?

__396,000 calories__

Reading

Read the paragraphs. Then answer the item.

Mrs. Griffin explained that the class was a melting pot of its own. To demonstrate how they all meshed together to create one unique class, she asked her students to bring in things that represented their heritages. "If you have nothing that represents your heritage, draw a picture of something that does," she said. "If you don't know where your ancestors are from, bring in something from a culture that has influenced you."

At lunch, Tom, who was adopted, sullenly complained to classmate Carlos. "I don't want to choose a culture that has influenced me. I wish I knew where my ancestors were from."

7. What effect did the assignment have on Tom? __It made him curious about__
*__his own heritage.__

Page 45

Name _____

Language

Read the sentence. Complete it with the possessive adjective that matches the underlined antecedent.

1. My aunt and uncle sold __their__ house and moved next door to me.
2. They planted a garden, and __its__ flowers smell quite fragrant.
3. They said, "If you plant certain flowers, __your__ garden will smell good, too."
4. When the flowers bloom, __their__ scent will attract butterflies and bees.

Math

Solve the problems.

5. Simone's company sells custom T-shirts for $35 each. Last year, she sold 1,857 T-shirts. How much money did she receive?

__$64,995__

6. The income from the T-shirts is split evenly between Simone, the artist, the marketer, the order processor, and the materials supplier. How much does Simone get to keep?

__$12,999__

Reading

Read the paragraph. Then answer the item.

On a shoe-shopping trip, a salesman refused service because Martin Luther King, Jr.'s father, a civil rights leader, would not sit in the "black section" of the store. While the younger King was angry, he saw that anger would not defeat injustice. After King finished his schooling in the North, he became the pastor of a church in Montgomery, Alabama. When an African American named Rosa Parks was arrested for not giving up her bus seat to a white rider, King organized the community with a plan of nonviolent boycotts, marches, and sit-ins.

7. What effect did Martin Luther King, Jr.'s childhood experiences have on his adult life?

*__It inspired him to react calmly and to involve a lot of people in protests that got attention and put pressure on businesses.__

Page 46

Name _____

Language

Read the sentence. Circle the word that correctly completes the sentence.

1. Marco sang _____ in the talent show.   amazing   (amazingly)
2. Ms. Sharma bought a new car that is very _____.   (safe)   safely
3. I'll get to the hospital as _____ as I can.   quick   (quickly)
4. You did an _____ job on your science fair project!   (awesome)   awesomely

Math

Multiply.

5. 6.92 × 4 = __27.68__   7. 37.22 × 0.6 = __22.332__

6. 55.2 × 3.1 = __171.12__   8. 804.3 × 0.08 = __64.344__

Reading

Read the paragraphs. Then answer the item.

Sam set his books on the table and looked for Gramps. Gramps was in charge of the house while Sam's mom and dad were at work. The patio door was open. Gramps was sitting on a garden bench. He didn't look at Sam or say hello.

"He's probably tired of waiting for me," Sam thought. "I'm late, but Gramps shouldn't be mad. I was working on my science project. He's always telling me to study."

9. Is the setting for this story a school, a home, or a place of work? Explain your answer.

*__The setting is a home. Gramps is there waiting for Sam. The setting has a table, a patio, and a garden.__

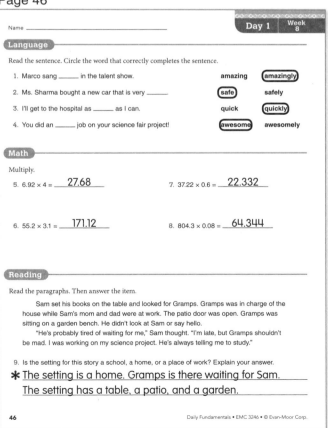

These answers will vary. Examples are given.

Page 47

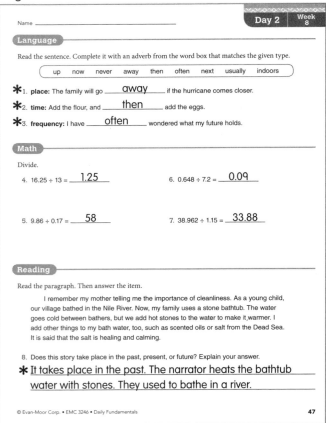

Day 2 · Week 8

Language

Read the sentence. Complete it with an adverb from the word box that matches the given type.

| up | now | never | away | then | often | next | usually | indoors |

✱1. **place:** The family will go ___away___ if the hurricane comes closer.

✱2. **time:** Add the flour, and ___then___ add the eggs.

✱3. **frequency:** I have ___often___ wondered what my future holds.

Math

Divide.

4. 16.25 ÷ 13 = __1.25__

6. 0.648 ÷ 7.2 = __0.09__

5. 9.86 ÷ 0.17 = __58__

7. 38.962 ÷ 1.15 = __33.88__

Reading

Read the paragraph. Then answer the item.

I remember my mother telling me the importance of cleanliness. As a young child, our village bathed in the Nile River. Now, my family uses a stone bathtub. The water goes cold between bathers, but we add hot stones to the water to make it warmer. I add other things to my bath water, too, such as scented oils or salt from the Dead Sea. It is said that the salt is healing and calming.

8. Does this story take place in the past, present, or future? Explain your answer.

✱ It takes place in the past. The narrator heats the bathtub water with stones. They used to bathe in a river.

© Evan-Moor Corp. • EMC 3246 • Daily Fundamentals — 47

Page 48

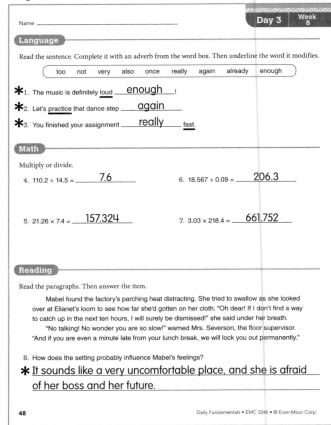

Day 3 · Week 8

Language

Read the sentence. Complete it with an adverb from the word box. Then underline the word it modifies.

| too | not | very | also | once | really | again | already | enough |

✱1. The music is definitely loud ___enough___ .

✱2. Let's practice that dance step ___again___

✱3. You finished your assignment ___really___ fast.

Math

Multiply or divide.

4. 110.2 ÷ 14.5 = __7.6__

6. 18.567 ÷ 0.09 = __206.3__

5. 21.26 × 7.4 = __157.324__

7. 3.03 × 218.4 = __661.752__

Reading

Read the paragraphs. Then answer the item.

Mabel found the factory's parching heat distracting. She tried to swallow as she looked over at Elianet's loom to see how far she'd gotten on her cloth. "Oh dear! If I don't find a way to catch up in the next ten hours, I will surely be dismissed!" she said under her breath.

"No talking! No wonder you are so slow!" warned Mrs. Severson, the floor supervisor. "And if you are even a minute late from your lunch break, we will lock you out permanently."

8. How does the setting probably influence Mabel's feelings?

✱ It sounds like a very uncomfortable place, and she is afraid of her boss and her future.

48 — Daily Fundamentals • EMC 3246 • © Evan-Moor Corp.

Page 49

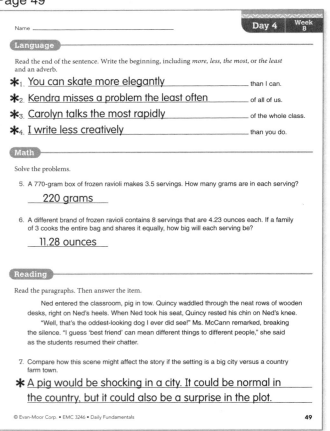

Day 4 · Week 8

Language

Read the end of the sentence. Write the beginning, including *more, less, the most,* or *the least* and an adverb.

✱1. You can skate more elegantly than I can.

✱2. Kendra misses a problem the least often of all of us.

✱3. Carolyn talks the most rapidly of the whole class.

✱4. I write less creatively than you do.

Math

Solve the problems.

5. A 770-gram box of frozen ravioli makes 3.5 servings. How many grams are in each serving?

__220 grams__

6. A different brand of frozen ravioli contains 8 servings that are 4.23 ounces each. If a family of 3 cooks the entire bag and shares it equally, how big will each serving be?

__11.28 ounces__

Reading

Read the paragraphs. Then answer the item.

Ned entered the classroom, pig in tow. Quincy waddled through the neat rows of wooden desks, right on Ned's heels. When Ned took his seat, Quincy rested his chin on Ned's knee.

"Well, that's the oddest-looking dog I ever did see!" Ms. McCann remarked, breaking the silence. "I guess 'best friend' can mean different things to different people," she said as the students resumed their chatter.

7. Compare how this scene might affect the story if the setting is a big city versus a country farm town.

✱ A pig would be shocking in a city. It could be normal in the country, but it could also be a surprise in the plot.

© Evan-Moor Corp. • EMC 3246 • Daily Fundamentals — 49

Page 50

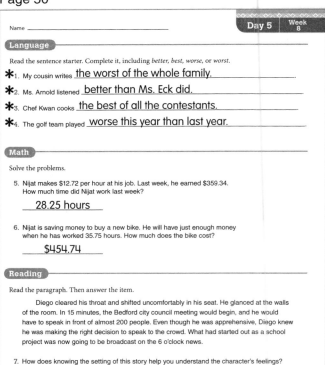

Day 5 · Week 8

Language

Read the sentence starter. Complete it, including *better, best, worse,* or *worst.*

✱1. My cousin writes the worst of the whole family.

✱2. Ms. Arnold listened better than Ms. Eck did.

✱3. Chef Kwan cooks the best of all the contestants.

✱4. The golf team played worse this year than last year.

Math

Solve the problems.

5. Nijat makes $12.72 per hour at his job. Last week, he earned $359.34. How much time did Nijat work last week?

__28.25 hours__

6. Nijat is saving money to buy a new bike. He will have just enough money when he has worked 35.75 hours. How much does the bike cost?

__$454.74__

Reading

Read the paragraph. Then answer the item.

Diego cleared his throat and shifted uncomfortably in his seat. He glanced at the walls of the room. In 15 minutes, the Bedford city council meeting would begin, and he would have to speak in front of almost 200 people. Even though he was apprehensive, Diego knew he was making the right decision to speak to the crowd. What had started out as a school project was now going to be broadcast on the 6 o'clock news.

7. How does knowing the setting of this story help you understand the character's feelings?

✱ If he was speaking to his class, friends, or family, he might not be as nervous. The city council and TV cameras are scary!

50 — Daily Fundamentals • EMC 3246 • © Evan-Moor Corp.

170

Daily Fundamentals • EMC 3246 • © Evan-Moor Corp.

Page 51

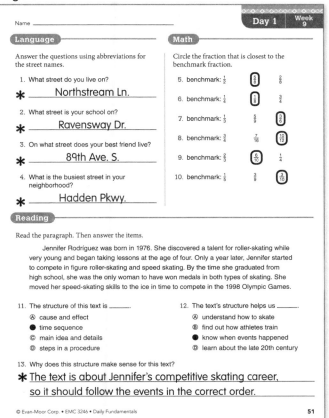

Name _____

Day 1 | Week 9

Language

Answer the questions using abbreviations for the street names.

1. What street do you live on?

  * Northstream Ln.

2. What street is your school on?

  * Ravensway Dr.

3. On what street does your best friend live?

  * 89th Ave. S.

4. What is the busiest street in your neighborhood?

  * Hadden Pkwy.

Math

Circle the fraction that is closest to the benchmark fraction.

5. benchmark: $\frac{1}{2}$ (8/15)   2/21

6. benchmark: $\frac{1}{4}$ (2/9)   3/4

7. benchmark: $\frac{1}{3}$ 5/9   (3/10)

8. benchmark: $\frac{3}{4}$ 7/16   (10/12)

9. benchmark: $\frac{2}{3}$ (6/10)   1/4

10. benchmark: $\frac{1}{5}$ 3/9   (3/10)

Reading

Read the paragraph. Then answer the items.

Jennifer Rodríguez was born in 1976. She discovered a talent for roller-skating while very young and began taking lessons at the age of four. Only a year later, Jennifer started to compete in figure roller-skating and speed skating. By the time she graduated from high school, she was the only woman to have won medals in both types of skating. She moved her speed-skating skills to the ice in time to compete in the 1998 Olympic Games.

11. The structure of this text is _____.
  Ⓐ cause and effect
  ● time sequence
  Ⓒ main idea and details
  Ⓓ steps in a procedure

12. The text's structure helps us _____.
  Ⓐ understand how to skate
  Ⓑ find out how athletes train
  ● know when events happened
  Ⓓ learn about the late 20th century

13. Why does this structure make sense for this text?

  * The text is about Jennifer's competitive skating career, so it should follow the events in the correct order.

Page 52

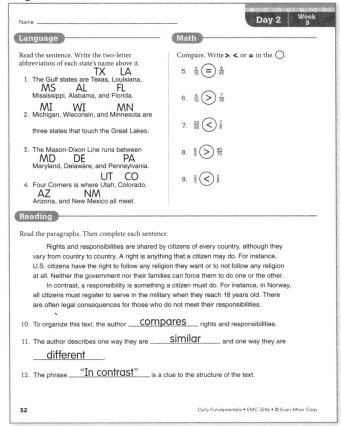

Name _____

Day 2 | Week 9

Language

Read the sentence. Write the two-letter abbreviation of each state's name above it.

1. The Gulf states are Texas, Louisiana, TX LA   Mississippi, Alabama, and Florida.   MS AL FL

2. Michigan, Wisconsin, and Minnesota are   MI WI MN   three states that touch the Great Lakes.

3. The Mason-Dixon Line runs between   MD DE PA   Maryland, Delaware, and Pennsylvania.

4. Four Corners is where Utah, Colorado,   UT CO   Arizona, and New Mexico all meet.   AZ NM

Math

Compare. Write >, <, or = in the ◯.

5. $\frac{3}{15}$ (=) $\frac{9}{45}$

6. $\frac{4}{10}$ (>) $\frac{7}{35}$

7. $\frac{23}{50}$ (<) $\frac{7}{8}$

8. $\frac{6}{8}$ (>) $\frac{40}{70}$

9. $\frac{2}{3}$ (<) $\frac{6}{8}$

Reading

Read the paragraphs. Then complete each sentence.

Rights and responsibilities are shared by citizens of every country, although they vary from country to country. A right is anything that a citizen may do. For instance, U.S. citizens have the right to follow any religion they want or to not follow any religion at all. Neither the government nor their families can force them to do one or the other.
In contrast, a responsibility is something a citizen must do. For instance, in Norway, all citizens must register to serve in the military when they reach 18 years old. There are often legal consequences for those who do not meet their responsibilities.

10. To organize this text, the author __compares__ rights and responsibilities.

11. The author describes one way they are __similar__ and one way they are __different__.

12. The phrase __"In contrast"__ is a clue to the structure of the text.

Page 53

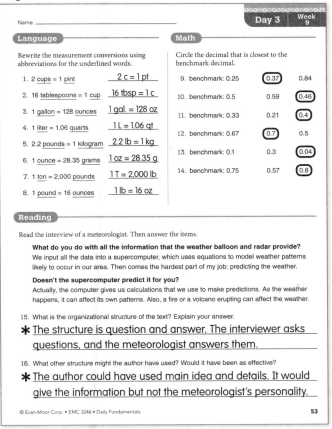

Name _____

Day 3 | Week 9

Language

Rewrite the measurement conversions using abbreviations for the underlined words.

1. 2 cups = 1 pint   2 c = 1 pt

2. 16 tablespoons = 1 cup   16 tbsp = 1 c

3. 1 gallon = 128 ounces   1 gal. = 128 oz

4. 1 liter = 1.06 quarts   1 L = 1.06 qt

5. 2.2 pounds = 1 kilogram   2.2 lb = 1 kg

6. 1 ounce = 28.35 grams   1 oz = 28.35 g

7. 1 ton = 2,000 pounds   1 T = 2,000 lb

8. 1 pound = 16 ounces   1 lb = 16 oz

Math

Circle the decimal that is closest to the benchmark decimal.

9. benchmark: 0.25   (0.37)   0.84

10. benchmark: 0.5   0.59   (0.46)

11. benchmark: 0.33   0.21   (0.4)

12. benchmark: 0.67   (0.7)   0.5

13. benchmark: 0.1   0.3   (0.04)

14. benchmark: 0.75   0.57   (0.8)

Reading

Read the interview of a meteorologist. Then answer the items.

What do you do with all the information that the weather balloon and radar provide?
We input all the data into a supercomputer, which uses equations to model weather patterns likely to occur in our area. Then comes the hardest part of my job: predicting the weather.

Doesn't the supercomputer predict it for you?
Actually, the computer gives us calculations that we use to make predictions. As the weather happens, it can affect its own patterns. Also, a fire or a volcano erupting can affect the weather.

15. What is the organizational structure of the text? Explain your answer.

  * The structure is question and answer. The interviewer asks questions, and the meteorologist answers them.

16. What other structure might the author have used? Would it have been as effective?

  * The author could have used main idea and details. It would give the information but not the meteorologist's personality.

Page 54

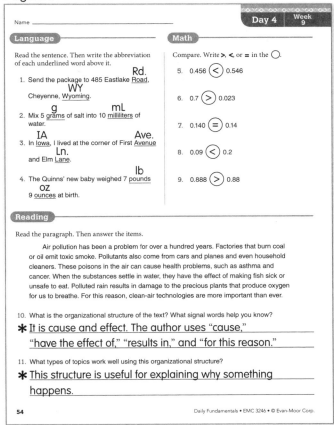

Name _____

Day 4 | Week 9

Language

Read the sentence. Then write the abbreviation of each underlined word above it.

1. Send the package to 485 Eastlake Road,   Rd.   Cheyenne, Wyoming.   WY

2. Mix 5 grams of salt into 10 milliliters of   g   mL   water.

3. In Iowa, I lived at the corner of First Avenue   IA   Ave.   and Elm Lane.   Ln.

4. The Quinns' new baby weighed 7 pounds   lb   9 ounces at birth.   oz

Math

Compare. Write >, <, or = in the ◯.

5. 0.456 (<) 0.546

6. 0.7 (>) 0.023

7. 0.140 (=) 0.14

8. 0.09 (<) 0.2

9. 0.888 (>) 0.88

Reading

Read the paragraph. Then answer the items.

Air pollution has been a problem for over a hundred years. Factories that burn coal or oil emit toxic smoke. Pollutants also come from cars and planes and even household cleaners. These poisons in the air can cause health problems, such as asthma and cancer. When the substances settle in water, they have the effect of making fish sick or unsafe to eat. Polluted rain results in damage to the precious plants that produce oxygen for us to breathe. For this reason, clean-air technologies are more important than ever.

10. What is the organizational structure of the text? What signal words help you know?

  * It is cause and effect. The author uses "cause," "have the effect of," "results in," and "for this reason."

11. What types of topics work well using this organizational structure?

  * This structure is useful for explaining why something happens.

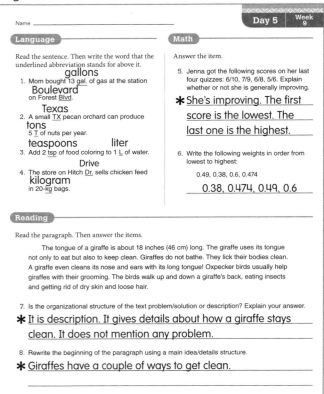
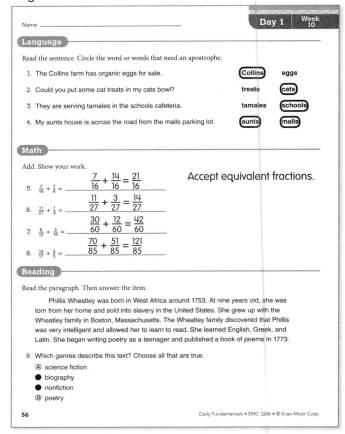
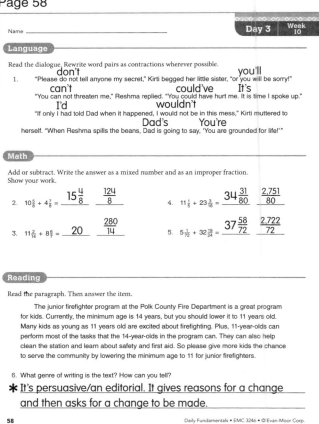

These answers will vary. Examples are given.

Page 55

Name _____

Day 5 | Week 9

Language

Read the sentence. Then write the word that the underlined abbreviation stands for above it.

gallons
1. Mom bought 13 gal. of gas at the station
   Boulevard
   on Forest Blvd.
   Texas
2. A small TX pecan orchard can produce
   tons
   5 T of nuts per year.
   teaspoons   liter
3. Add 2 tsp of food coloring to 1 L of water.
   Drive
4. The store on Hitch Dr. sells chicken feed
   kilogram
   in 20-kg bags.

Math

Answer the item.

5. Jenna got the following scores on her last four quizzes: 6/10, 7/9, 6/8, 5/6. Explain whether or not she is generally improving.

* She's improving. The first score is the lowest. The last one is the highest.

6. Write the following weights in order from lowest to highest:
   0.49, 0.38, 0.6, 0.474
   0.38, 0.474, 0.49, 0.6

Reading

Read the paragraph. Then answer the items.

The tongue of a giraffe is about 18 inches (46 cm) long. The giraffe uses its tongue not only to eat but also to keep clean. Giraffes do not bathe. They lick their bodies clean. A giraffe even cleans its nose and ears with its long tongue! Oxpecker birds usually help giraffes with their grooming. The birds walk up and down a giraffe's back, eating insects and getting rid of dry skin and loose hair.

7. Is the organizational structure of the text problem/solution or description? Explain your answer.

* It is description. It gives details about how a giraffe stays clean. It does not mention any problem.

8. Rewrite the beginning of the paragraph using a main idea/details structure.

* Giraffes have a couple of ways to get clean.

© Evan-Moor Corp. • EMC 3246 • Daily Fundamentals   55

Page 56

Name _____

Day 1 | Week 10

Language

Read the sentence. Circle the word or words that need an apostrophe.

1. The Collins farm has organic eggs for sale.   (Collins)   eggs
2. Could you put some cat treats in my cats bowl?   treats   (cats)
3. They are serving tamales in the schools cafeteria. tamales (schools)
4. My aunts house is across the road from the malls parking lot. (aunts) (malls)

Math

Add. Show your work.

5. $\frac{7}{16} + \frac{7}{8}$ = $\frac{7}{16} + \frac{14}{16} = \frac{21}{16}$

6. $\frac{11}{27} + \frac{1}{9}$ = $\frac{11}{27} + \frac{3}{27} = \frac{14}{27}$

7. $\frac{6}{12} + \frac{3}{15}$ = $\frac{30}{60} + \frac{12}{60} = \frac{42}{60}$

8. $\frac{14}{17} + \frac{3}{5}$ = $\frac{70}{85} + \frac{51}{85} = \frac{121}{85}$

Accept equivalent fractions.

Reading

Read the paragraph. Then answer the item.

Phillis Wheatley was born in West Africa around 1753. At nine years old, she was torn from her home and sold into slavery in the United States. She grew up with the Wheatley family in Boston, Massachusetts. The Wheatley family discovered that Phillis was very intelligent and allowed her to learn to read. She learned English, Greek, and Latin. She began writing poetry as a teenager and published a book of poems in 1773.

9. Which genres describe this text? Choose all that are true.
Ⓐ science fiction
● biography
● nonfiction
Ⓓ poetry

56   Daily Fundamentals • EMC 3246 • © Evan-Moor Corp.

Page 57

Name _____

Day 2 | Week 10

Language

Read the sentence. Rewrite it, correcting any errors in apostrophe use.

1. Look at the color's of the rainforest's deciduous trees' leave's!
   Look at the colors of the rainforest's deciduous trees' leaves!

2. Chinas and Germanys famous walls were created for different purposes.
   China's and Germany's famous walls were created for different purposes.

Math

Subtract. Show your work.

3. $\frac{9}{18} - \frac{6}{6}$ = $\frac{9}{18} - \frac{6}{18} = \frac{3}{18}$

4. $\frac{34}{52} - \frac{6}{13}$ = $\frac{34}{52} - \frac{24}{52} = \frac{10}{52}$

5. $\frac{4}{14} - \frac{1}{4}$ = $\frac{8}{28} - \frac{7}{28} = \frac{1}{28}$

6. $\frac{11}{13} - \frac{5}{7}$ = $\frac{77}{91} - \frac{65}{91} = \frac{12}{91}$

Accept equivalent fractions.

Reading

Read the paragraph. Then answer the item.

Once upon a time, there were three smart pigs. No, these aren't the ones you may have heard about whose houses were blown down, but their younger cousins. These pigs had learned from the misfortunes of their relatives and had constructed houses that were sturdy, secure, and comfortable. And while an earthquake or flood might cause damage, a wolf certainly would not.

7. Is this probably the beginning of a myth, a fable, or a legend? Explain your answer.

* It's a fable. It begins with "Once upon a time." It doesn't sound like it will explain nature or describe a hero.

© Evan-Moor Corp. • EMC 3246 • Daily Fundamentals   57

Page 58

Name _____

Day 3 | Week 10

Language

Read the dialogue. Rewrite word pairs as contractions wherever possible.

                    don't   you'll
1. "Please do not tell anyone my secret," Kirti begged her little sister, "or you will be sorry!"
   can't   could've   It's
   "You can not threaten me," Reshma replied. "You could have hurt me. It is time I spoke up."
   I'd   wouldn't
   "If only I had told Dad when it happened, I would not be in this mess," Kirti muttered to
              Dad's   You're
   herself. "When Reshma spills the beans, Dad is going to say, 'You are grounded for life!'"

Math

Add or subtract. Write the answer as a mixed number and as an improper fraction. Show your work.

2. $10\frac{5}{8} + 4\frac{7}{8}$ = $15\frac{4}{8}$ $\frac{124}{8}$

3. $11\frac{2}{14} + 8\frac{6}{7}$ = 20 $\frac{280}{14}$

4. $11\frac{1}{5} + 23\frac{3}{16}$ = $34\frac{31}{80}$ $\frac{2,751}{80}$

5. $5\frac{1}{12} + 32\frac{19}{24}$ = $37\frac{58}{72}$ $\frac{2,722}{72}$

Reading

Read the paragraph. Then answer the item.

The junior firefighter program at the Polk County Fire Department is a great program for kids. Currently, the minimum age is 14 years, but you should lower it to 11 years old. Many kids as young as 11 years old are excited about firefighting. Plus, 11-year-olds can perform most of the tasks that the 14-year-olds in the program can. They can also help clean the station and learn about safety and first aid. So please give more kids the chance to serve the community by lowering the minimum age to 11 for junior firefighters.

6. What genre of writing is the text? How can you tell?

* It's persuasive/an editorial. It gives reasons for a change and then asks for a change to be made.

58   Daily Fundamentals • EMC 3246 • © Evan-Moor Corp.

172   Daily Fundamentals • EMC 3246 • © Evan-Moor Corp.

Page 59

Name _____

Day 4 Week 10

Language

Read the sentence. Circle the word that completes the sentence.

1. If _____ going to the store, please buy me some gum. your **(you're)**
2. Next month, _____ try out for the play together. lets **(let's)**
3. The opossum seems to have hurt _____ paw. **(its)** it's
4. Oh no, my brand-new _____ been stolen! bikes **(bike's)**

Math

Read the problem. Then answer the items.

Roger is in a clam-collecting contest. He has collected two buckets of clams weighing $31\frac{5}{8}$ pounds and $33\frac{3}{16}$ pounds. The first person to collect 80 pounds wins.

5. How many pounds of clams has he collected so far? $64\frac{13}{16}$ pounds
6. How many pounds of clams does he still need to find? $15\frac{3}{16}$ pounds

Reading

Read the text. Then answer the item.

Jerome: I have a personal favor to ask. I heard that you speak Italian.
Lee: Well, I've heard enough at home to fake it pretty well.
Jerome: Yeah? Well, I'm going to Italy this summer. Do you think you could teach me?
Lee: I could probably teach you some phrases. Do you think you could show me the secret of your long-distance football pass?

7. Is the text from a play or an interview? Explain your answer.

※ It's from a play. It's a conversation, not asking for information.

Page 60

Name _____

Day 5 Week 10

Language

Read the paragraph. Add apostrophes where needed.

1. Kevin's got the next two months planned out. Now that he's finished his school projects, he and his brother are driving to their cousin's cabin. They're going to borrow Valerie's train passes and head east through the Rockies. "I'm hoping its not too hot," he thought while turning on the car's radio. "We're expecting a freak snowstorm in the Rockies foothills," the announcer began.

Math

Read the problem. Then answer the items.

Mrs. Norris is using a 30-foot roll of green paper to cover her bulletin boards. So far, she has cut lengths measuring $10\frac{7}{12}$ feet, $10\frac{7}{12}$ feet, and $6\frac{1}{3}$ feet. She will need $4\frac{5}{6}$ feet for the last bulletin board.

2. How much paper has she used so far? $27\frac{1}{2}$ feet
3. Will there be enough left on the roll for the last bulletin board? Explain your answer.

※ No. She has only $2\frac{1}{2}$ feet left over, which is less than $4\frac{5}{6}$.

Reading

Read the paragraph. Then answer the item.

Alfred Bullfrog Stormalong was the tallest and strongest sailor that ever lived. No ordinary sailing ship was big enough for him. Every time he stepped from the port to the starboard side of a ship, it rocked around like it was hit by a hurricane. Stormalong had to sleep on the deck because of his size. Several times he almost tipped over a ship when he rolled about in his sleep. The sailors complained about the splashing, but Stormalong always turned the ship right-side up before they fell into the water.

4. Underline one sentence from the text that shows it is a tall tale. Explain your choice.

※ Rocking a big ship by stepping from one side to the other is
※ a big exaggeration. Tall tales have lots of exaggeration.

Page 61

Name _____

Day 1 Week 11

Language

Write a helping verb to complete the progressive tense in the sentence.

1. I **was/had been** having a bad dream when my alarm clock went off.
2. Melissa **is** working on her social studies project right now.
3. The twins **will be** celebrating their twelfth birthday this weekend.
4. The squirrels **were/had been** gathering nuts when they noticed the snarling dog.

Math

Accept equivalent answers.

Multiply. Then answer the item.

5. $\frac{5}{9} \times 15 = \frac{75}{9}$ OR $8\frac{1}{3}$
6. $\frac{9}{11} \times \frac{5}{6} = \frac{45}{66}$
7. $\frac{10}{23} \times \frac{3}{8} = \frac{30}{184}$
8. $\frac{15}{4} \times \frac{17}{32} = \frac{255}{128}$ OR $1\frac{127}{128}$

9. Write a math problem that can be solved using $\frac{3}{4} \times \frac{1}{2}$. Neela cut a $\frac{3}{4}$-meter

※ plank in half. How long are the pieces?

Reading

Read the paragraph. Then answer the item.

Homesickness hit David's *abuela* like a tidal wave. He could see how much his grandmother missed Mexico as they walked slowly along the quiet beach. She talked about the green hills that spread out like a wrinkled blanket. She talked about the friends she had left behind. David rattled the seashells in his pockets and listened.

10. Circle the two similes in the text. What is being compared in each?

※ a. The narrator compares homesickness and a tidal wave.
※ b. The narrator compares green hills and a wrinkled blanket.

Page 62

Name _____

Day 2 Week 11

Language

Write the correct form of the verb in parentheses to complete the sentence.

1. I am **running** late this morning. **(run)**
2. Who will be **doing** the extra-credit assignment this week? **(do)**
3. The pollen has been **irritating** my eyes, so I went to the doctor. **(irritate)**
4. Diego is **reciting** a famous poem in the talent show. **(recite)**

Math

Accept equivalent answers.

Divide. Then answer the item.

5. $\frac{2}{13} \div 5 = \frac{2}{65}$
6. $\frac{8}{31} \div \frac{3}{12} = \frac{96}{93}$
7. $\frac{24}{55} \div \frac{6}{7} = \frac{168}{330}$
8. $\frac{20}{9} \div \frac{11}{12} = \frac{240}{99}$ OR $2\frac{42}{99}$

9. Write a math problem that can be solved using $\frac{7}{10} \div \frac{1}{4}$. You are cooking $\frac{7}{10}$ pound of fish. How many $\frac{1}{4}$-pound servings will it make?

Reading

Read the paragraph. Then answer the items.

You've probably heard about Pecos Bill, the Texas wrangler who was as tall as a two-story house and as strong as an ox. When it was time to round up the cattle and drive 'em to Abilene, Bill would just point his nose toward the sky and let out a coyote howl that echoed all across Texas.

10. Underline all the uses of hyperbole in the text.
11. Choose one hyperbole from the text. Explain its meaning.

※ The narrator says Bill was "as tall as a two-story house." It means he was unusually tall, but not actually that tall.

Page 63

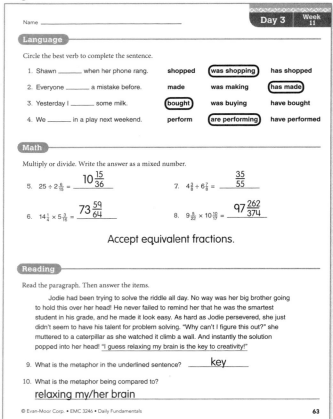

Name _____

Day 3 | **Week 11**

Language

Circle the best verb to complete the sentence.

1. Shawn _____ when her phone rang.　shopped　(was shopping)　has shopped

2. Everyone _____ a mistake before.　made　was making　(has made)

3. Yesterday I _____ some milk.　(bought)　was buying　have bought

4. We _____ in a play next weekend.　perform　(are performing)　have performed

Math

Multiply or divide. Write the answer as a mixed number.

5. $25 \div 2\frac{6}{15} = 10\frac{15}{36}$

7. $4\frac{3}{8} \div 6\frac{7}{8} = \frac{35}{55}$

6. $14\frac{1}{4} \times 5\frac{3}{16} = 73\frac{59}{64}$

8. $9\frac{5}{22} \times 10\frac{10}{17} = 97\frac{262}{374}$

Accept equivalent fractions.

Reading

Read the paragraph. Then answer the items.

Jodie had been trying to solve the riddle all day. No way was her big brother going to hold this over her head! He never failed to remind her that he was the smartest student in his grade, and he made it look easy. As hard as Jodie persevered, she just didn't seem to have his talent for problem solving. "Why can't I figure this out?" she muttered to a caterpillar as she watched it climb a wall. And instantly the solution popped into her head! "I guess relaxing my brain is the key to creativity!"

9. What is the metaphor in the underlined sentence?　key

10. What is the metaphor being compared to?　relaxing my/her brain

© Evan-Moor Corp. • EMC 3246 • Daily Fundamentals　63

Page 64

Name _____

Day 4 | **Week 11**

Language

Write a sentence using the given verb and tense.

1. **wonder** (past progressive): _____

✳ I was wondering when you'd arrive.

2. **save** (present progressive): _____

✳ They are saving money for a new video game.

Math

Read the problem. Then answer the items.

Nancy jogs every day. She covers a mile every $\frac{1}{6}$ hour. Yesterday she jogged for $1\frac{1}{4}$ hours.

3. How many miles did she jog yesterday?　$7\frac{1}{2}$ miles

4. Nancy wants to jog on a park path that is $12\frac{3}{4}$ miles long. How many hours will it take?

$2\frac{3}{24}$ hours

Reading

Read the paragraph. Then answer the item.

Her fascination with bicycle racing began with that book Aunt Linda had given her. It transformed her love of riding into a personal challenge and a new set of goals. Now, though, Marisol realized that the book had given her a little bit of tunnel vision, as well. When she mounted a bike now, fun was not part of the ride; it was all about building strength, technique, speed, and control. Today she was just a little weary.

5. Explain what the idiom *tunnel vision* means.

✳ It means a focus that is too narrow. She was missing the fun part of bike riding.

64　Daily Fundamentals • EMC 3246 • © Evan-Moor Corp.

Page 65

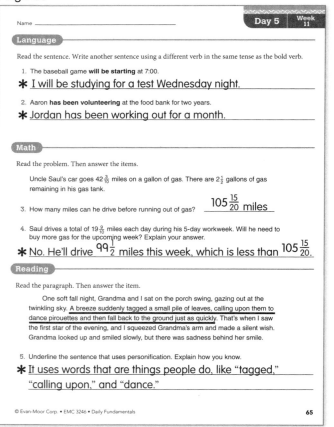

Name _____

Day 5 | **Week 11**

Language

Read the sentence. Write another sentence using a different verb in the same tense as the bold verb.

1. The baseball game **will be starting** at 7:00.

✳ I will be studying for a test Wednesday night.

2. Aaron **has been volunteering** at the food bank for two years.

✳ Jordan has been working out for a month.

Math

Read the problem. Then answer the items.

Uncle Saul's car goes $42\frac{3}{10}$ miles on a gallon of gas. There are $2\frac{1}{2}$ gallons of gas remaining in his gas tank.

3. How many miles can he drive before running out of gas?　$105\frac{15}{20}$ miles

4. Saul drives a total of $19\frac{9}{10}$ miles each day during his 5-day workweek. Will he need to buy more gas for the upcoming week? Explain your answer.

✳ No. He'll drive $99\frac{1}{2}$ miles this week, which is less than $105\frac{15}{20}$.

Reading

Read the paragraph. Then answer the item.

One soft fall night, Grandma and I sat on the porch swing, gazing out at the twinkling sky. A breeze suddenly tagged a small pile of leaves, calling upon them to dance pirouettes and then fall back to the ground just as quickly. That's when I saw the first star of the evening, and I squeezed Grandma's arm and made a silent wish. Grandma looked up and smiled slowly, but there was sadness behind her smile.

5. Underline the sentence that uses personification. Explain how you know.

✳ It uses words that are things people do, like "tagged," "calling upon," and "dance."

© Evan-Moor Corp. • EMC 3246 • Daily Fundamentals　65

Page 66

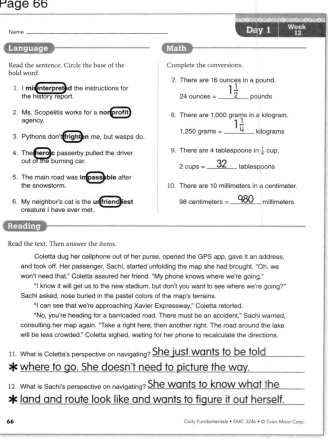

Name _____

Day 1 | **Week 12**

Language

Read the sentence. Circle the base of the bold word.

1. I **mis(interpret)ed** the instructions for the history report.

2. Ms. Scopelitis works for a **non(profit)** agency.

3. Pythons don't **(frighten)** me, but wasps do.

4. The **(hero)ic** passerby pulled the driver out of the burning car.

5. The main road was **im(pass)able** after the snowstorm.

6. My neighbor's cat is the **un(friend)liest** creature I have ever met.

Math

Complete the conversions.

7. There are 16 ounces in a pound.

24 ounces = $1\frac{1}{2}$ pounds

8. There are 1,000 grams in a kilogram.

1,250 grams = $1\frac{1}{4}$ kilograms

9. There are 4 tablespoons in $\frac{1}{4}$ cup.

2 cups = 32 tablespoons

10. There are 10 millimeters in a centimeter.

98 centimeters = 980 millimeters

Reading

Read the text. Then answer the items.

Coletta dug her cellphone out of her purse, opened the GPS app, gave it an address, and took off. Her passenger, Sachi, started unfolding the map she had brought. "Oh, we won't need that," Coletta assured her friend. "My phone knows where we're going."

"I know it will get us to the new stadium, but don't you want to see where we're going?" Sachi asked, nose buried in the pastel colors of the map's terrains.

"I can see that we're approaching Xavier Expressway," Coletta retorted.

"No, you're heading for a barricaded road. There must be an accident," Sachi warned, consulting her map again. "Take a right here, then another right. The road around the lake will be less crowded." Coletta sighed, waiting for her phone to recalculate the directions.

11. What is Coletta's perspective on navigating? She just wants to be told

✳ where to go. She doesn't need to picture the way.

12. What is Sachi's perspective on navigating? She wants to know what the

✳ land and route look like and wants to figure it out herself.

66　Daily Fundamentals • EMC 3246 • © Evan-Moor Corp.

Page 67

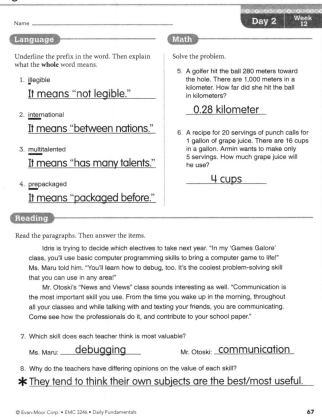

Name _____

Day 2 Week 12

Language

Underline the prefix in the word. Then explain what the **whole** word means.

1. <u>il</u>legible

It means "not legible."

2. <u>inter</u>national

It means "between nations."

3. <u>multi</u>talented

It means "has many talents."

4. <u>pre</u>packaged

It means "packaged before."

Math

Solve the problem.

5. A golfer hit the ball 280 meters toward the hole. There are 1,000 meters in a kilometer. How far did she hit the ball in kilometers?

0.28 kilometer

6. A recipe for 20 servings of punch calls for 1 gallon of grape juice. There are 16 cups in a gallon. Armin wants to make only 5 servings. How much grape juice will he use?

4 cups

Reading

Read the paragraphs. Then answer the items.

Idris is trying to decide which electives to take next year. "In my 'Games Galore' class, you'll use basic computer programming skills to bring a computer game to life!" Ms. Maru told him. "You'll learn how to debug, too. It's the coolest problem-solving skill that you can use in any area!"

Mr. Otoski's "News and Views" class sounds interesting as well. "Communication is the most important skill you use. From the time you wake up in the morning, throughout all your classes and while talking with and texting your friends, you are communicating. Come see how the professionals do it, and contribute to your school paper."

7. Which skill does each teacher think is most valuable?

Ms. Maru: debugging   Mr. Otoski: communication

8. Why do the teachers have differing opinions on the value of each skill?

* They tend to think their own subjects are the best/most useful.

Page 68

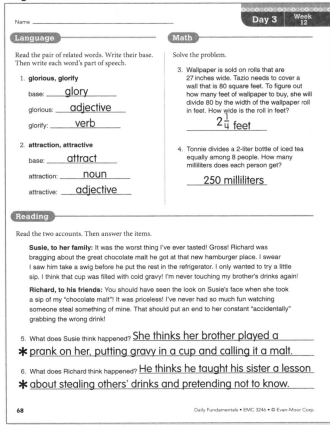

Name _____

Day 3 Week 12

Language

Read the pair of related words. Write their base. Then write each word's part of speech.

1. **glorious, glorify**

base: glory

glorious: adjective

glorify: verb

2. **attraction, attractive**

base: attract

attraction: noun

attractive: adjective

Math

Solve the problem.

3. Wallpaper is sold on rolls that are 27 inches wide. Tazio needs to cover a wall that is 80 square feet. To figure out how many feet of wallpaper to buy, she will divide 80 by the width of the wallpaper roll in feet. How wide is the roll in feet?

$2\frac{1}{4}$ feet

4. Tonnie divides a 2-liter bottle of iced tea equally among 8 people. How many milliliters does each person get?

250 milliliters

Reading

Read the two accounts. Then answer the items.

Susie, to her family: It was the worst thing I've ever tasted! Gross! Richard was bragging about the great chocolate malt he got at that new hamburger place. I swear I saw him take a swig before he put the rest in the refrigerator. I only wanted to try a little sip. I think that cup was filled with cold gravy! I'm never touching my brother's drinks again!

Richard, to his friends: You should have seen the look on Susie's face when she took a sip of my "chocolate malt"! It was priceless! I've never had so much fun watching someone steal something of mine. That should put an end to her constant "accidentally" grabbing the wrong drink!

5. What does Susie think happened? She thinks her brother played a
* prank on her, putting gravy in a cup and calling it a malt.

6. What does Richard think happened? He thinks he taught his sister a lesson
* about stealing others' drinks and pretending not to know.

Page 69

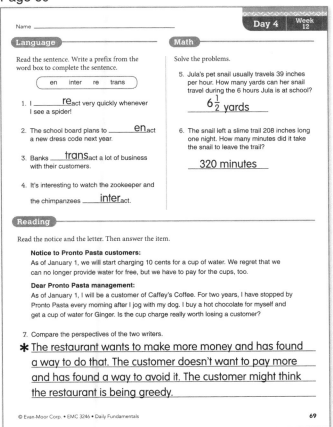

Name _____

Day 4 Week 12

Language

Read the sentence. Write a prefix from the word box to complete the sentence.

| en   inter   re   trans |

1. I **re**act very quickly whenever I see a spider!

2. The school board plans to **en**act a new dress code next year.

3. Banks **trans**act a lot of business with their customers.

4. It's interesting to watch the zookeeper and the chimpanzees **inter**act.

Math

Solve the problems.

5. Jula's pet snail usually travels 39 inches per hour. How many yards can her snail travel during the 6 hours Jula is at school?

$6\frac{1}{2}$ yards

6. The snail left a slime trail 208 inches long one night. How many minutes did it take the snail to leave the trail?

320 minutes

Reading

Read the notice and the letter. Then answer the item.

Notice to Pronto Pasta customers:
As of January 1, we will start charging 10 cents for a cup of water. We regret that we can no longer provide water for free, but we have to pay for the cups, too.

Dear Pronto Pasta management:
As of January 1, I will be a customer of Caffey's Coffee. For two years, I have stopped by Pronto Pasta every morning after I jog with my dog. I buy a hot chocolate for myself and get a cup of water for Ginger. Is the cup charge really worth losing a customer?

7. Compare the perspectives of the two writers.

* The restaurant wants to make more money and has found a way to do that. The customer doesn't want to pay more and has found a way to avoid it. The customer might think the restaurant is being greedy.

Page 70

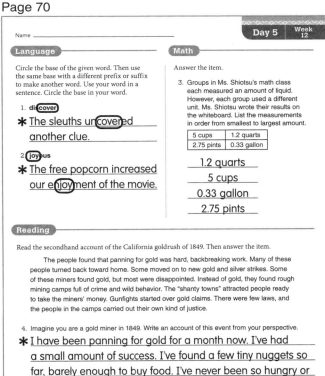

Name _____

Day 5 Week 12

Language

Circle the base of the given word. Then use the same base with a different prefix or suffix to make another word. Use your word in a sentence. Circle the base in your word.

1. dis(cover)
* The sleuths un(covered) another clue.

2. (joy)ous
* The free popcorn increased our en(joy)ment of the movie.

Math

Answer the item.

3. Groups in Ms. Shiotsu's math class each measured an amount of liquid. However, each group used a different unit. Ms. Shiotsu wrote their results on the whiteboard. List the measurements in order from smallest to largest amount.

| 5 cups | 1.2 quarts |
| 2.75 pints | 0.33 gallon |

1.2 quarts

5 cups

0.33 gallon

2.75 pints

Reading

Read the secondhand account of the California goldrush of 1849. Then answer the item.

The people found that panning for gold was hard, backbreaking work. Many of these people turned back toward home. Some moved on to new gold and silver strikes. Some of these miners found gold, but most were disappointed. Instead of gold, they found rough mining camps full of crime and wild behavior. The "shanty towns" attracted people ready to take the miners' money. Gunfights started over gold claims. There were few laws, and the people in the camps carried out their own kind of justice.

4. Imagine you are a gold miner in 1849. Write an account of this event from your perspective.

* I have been panning for gold for a month now. I've had a small amount of success. I've found a few tiny nuggets so far, barely enough to buy food. I've never been so hungry or sore. I might try another town, but I saw what happened to a miner from Placerville. He looked pretty beat up.

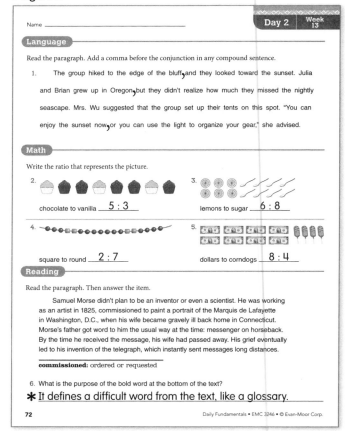
Page 71

Name _____

Day 1 | Week 13

Language

Read the sentence. Determine whether it is a compound sentence.
Write *yes* if it is a compound sentence. Write *no* if it is not.

1. The driver honked his horn, and the stray dog jumped out of the way. — **yes**

2. Wanda brushed her long, dark hair and put it in a ponytail. — **no**

3. The girl I met while I was in Boston, Massachusetts, just texted me. — **no**

4. First you add the flour, and then you measure the milk. — **yes**

Math

Read the phrase. Match it to its corresponding ratio.

5. 2 staples for every 10 pages
6. 3 teaspoons of cocoa for every 8 ounces of milk
7. 10 dollars spent on ads for every new customer
8. 1 egg for every 3 pancakes

- 1 : 3
- 1 : 10
- 2 : 10
- 3 : 1
- 3 : 8
- 10 : 1

Reading

Read the chart on being safe. Then answer the item.

Emergency Situation	Action Plan	Supplies
Downed Power Line	Call the power company and emergency (911); do not approach the power line.	power company's phone number; cellphone or corded landline phone
Tornado	Seek shelter in a basement, a room without windows, or a bathtub.	radio with batteries, water, flashlights
Earthquake	Go outside into an open area or take shelter under a desk or table, or against an inside wall.	radio with batteries, water, flashlights, food and supplies for three days

9. If a power line is down, what should you do, and what will you use to do it? **Call 911 and**
* **the power company from a cellphone or corded landline phone.**

Page 72

Name _____

Day 2 | Week 13

Language

Read the paragraph. Add a comma before the conjunction in any compound sentence.

1.   The group hiked to the edge of the bluff, and they looked toward the sunset. Julia and Brian grew up in Oregon, but they didn't realize how much they missed the nightly seascape. Mrs. Wu suggested that the group set up their tents on this spot. "You can enjoy the sunset now, or you can use the light to organize your gear," she advised.

Math

Write the ratio that represents the picture.

2. chocolate to vanilla **5 : 3**

3. lemons to sugar **6 : 8**

4. square to round **2 : 7**

5. dollars to corndogs **8 : 4**

Reading

Read the paragraph. Then answer the item.

    Samuel Morse didn't plan to be an inventor or even a scientist. He was working as an artist in 1825, commissioned to paint a portrait of the Marquis de Lafayette in Washington, D.C., when his wife became gravely ill back home in Connecticut. Morse's father got word to him the usual way at the time: messenger on horseback. By the time he received the message, his wife had passed away. His grief eventually led to his invention of the telegraph, which instantly sent messages long distances.

commissioned: ordered or requested

6. What is the purpose of the bold word at the bottom of the text?
* **It defines a difficult word from the text, like a glossary.**

Page 73

Name _____

Day 3 | Week 13

Language

Read the sentences. Rewrite them as a single compound sentence, adding a coordinating conjunction.

1. Guillermo tried to be careful. He lost his key anyway.

   Guillermo tried to be careful, but he lost his key anyway.

2. Tanika had never been to Argentina. The terrain seemed very familiar.

   Tanika had never been to Argentina, yet the terrain seemed very familiar.

Math

A map key shows a scale of 2 inches = 30 miles. Use the graph to answer the items.

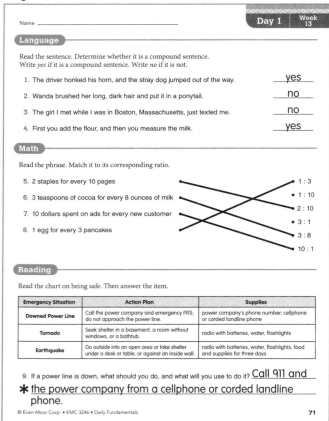

3. Two cities are 3 inches apart on the map. How far apart are they in real life?

   45 miles

4. Cindy knows that Dawes is 90 miles from her hometown. How many inches from her hometown is Dawes on the map?

   6 inches

Reading

Read the page from an index in a book on weaving. Then answer the item.

shuttle, 13, 15, 22, 33, 54–56	warp, 5–9, 12, 22, 33, 54, 55–61
spinning jenny, 13	weft, 5–8, 12, 22, 55–60
tapestry needle, 15–18	yarn
twill weave fabrics	cotton, 28
denim, 32	linen (flax), 28
gabardine, 34	silk, 17, 27
wool twill, 33	wool, 18, 29

5. On what pages would you find information about wool?

   Wool is on pages 33, 18, and 29.

Page 74

Name _____

Day 4 | Week 13

Language

Read the sentence. Rewrite it as a compound sentence, making two independent clauses.

1. The festival is held every May and attracts lots of visitors.

   The festival is held every May, and it attracts lots of visitors.

2. We guarantee your carpets will be clean or give you your money back.

   We guarantee your carpets will be clean, or we give you your money back.

Math

Read the problem. Then answer the items.

A 50-pound sack of chicken scratch feeds Kim's 30 chickens for a week.

3. What is the ratio of pounds of scratch to chickens? **50 : 30**

4. How many pounds of scratch will 15 chickens eat in a week? **25 pounds**

5. Kim's 15 hens lay 84 eggs in a week. What is the ratio of pounds of scratch to eggs laid?

   25 : 84

Reading

Look at the photo and its caption. Then answer the item.

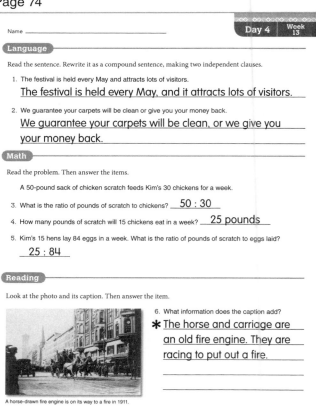

A horse-drawn fire engine is on its way to a fire in 1911.

6. What information does the caption add?
* **The horse and carriage are an old fire engine. They are racing to put out a fire.**

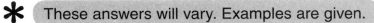
Page 75

Name _____

Day 5 | Week 13

Language

Write two compound sentences about your favorite hobby.

* 1. I love to bake, and everyone likes my chocolate chip cookies.

* 2. Chocolate is my favorite ingredient, but I also like to use cinnamon.

Math

Solve the problem.

3. A recipe that makes 4 servings uses 10 ounces of chicken. Kenichi needs to make 6 servings. How much chicken will he need?

15 ounces

4. Sarah wants to build a doghouse, but first she builds a smaller model to practice. The biggest piece of wood she will need for the full-size doghouse is 39 inches wide and 24 inches tall. If she uses a piece for the model that is 8 inches tall, how wide should it be?

13 inches

Reading

Read the text and the sidebar. Then answer the item.

Many people use the Internet for research. Since anyone can post information, it's important to make sure you use worthy sources. Find out the sponsor, the author's sources, and the posting date.

Look at the URL ending for the sponsor:
• edu = a college
• org = an organization
• com = a business
• gov = government

5. Who is the likely sponsor of a website at www.MiceAreUs.com?

* It's probably a company that sells mice, toy mice, or pest-control services.

© Evan-Moor Corp. • EMC 3246 • Daily Fundamentals   75

Page 76

Name _____

Day 1 | Week 14

Language

Read the dependent clause. Write an independent clause to complete the complex sentence.

* 1. When the phone rang, Miranda looked to see who was calling

* 2. After Pierre fed the dog, he made dinner for himself

* 3. You should see the new Star Trek movie if you like science fiction.

* 4. Let's meet before breakfast unless that's too early.

Math

Read the statement and write the unit rate as a ratio.

5. Dad's car gets 33 miles per gallon. $\frac{33}{1}$

6. Rachel reads 124 words per minute. $\frac{124}{1}$

7. The speed limit is 75 kilometers per hour. $\frac{75}{1}$

8. Salmon costs 22 dollars per pound. $\frac{22}{1}$

Reading

Read the paragraph. Then answer the item.

In the shower that evening, Deb thought about her science project. She had to create a concept for a new kind of energy. She tried to conjure up images of magnets, windmills, and falling marbles as she enjoyed the warm water beating on her tired leg muscles. It reminded her of the electric massage chair at the mall. Deb was sore from riding her muddy bike home in the rain through soggy piles of leaves. As she rinsed the soap off and watched the suds swirl through the drain, an idea finally hit her!

9. What kind of idea do you think Deb had? Why do you think so?

* I think she wants to do something with rain or water power. She thinks of rain, water massaging, rinsing, and swirling.

76   Daily Fundamentals • EMC 3246 • © Evan-Moor Corp.

Page 77

Name _____

Day 2 | Week 14

Language

Read the independent clause. Write a dependent clause to complete the complex sentence.

* 1. Because you study so hard, you get good grades.

* 2. Even though I've been here a year, I still miss my old school.

* 3. While it is snowing, I'm going to sit by the fireplace

* 4. When Phoebe goes hiking, she takes awesome photos

Math

A parking lot in Hamilton City charges $2.50 per hour. Figure out how much drivers with these parking stubs would owe.

5. Time In: 11:30 a.m.   Time Out: 12:30 p.m.
Rate: $2.50 per hour   1 hour of parking
Total Due: $2.50

6. Time In: 1:15 p.m.   Time Out: 6:15 p.m.
Rate: $2.50 per hour   5 hours of parking
Total Due: $12.50

7. Time In: 8:42 a.m.   Time Out: 11:42 a.m.
Rate: $2.50 per hour   3 hours of parking
Total Due: $7.50

8. Time In: 7:05 a.m.   Time Out: 6:05 p.m.
Rate: $2.50 per hour   11 hours of parking
Total Due: $27.50

Reading

Read this introduction to an article. Then answer the item.

When you walk through your yard or a park, do you want to see weeds? They are often the tallest plants, hiding prettier flowers or competing with vegetables for water and nutrients. Many weeds have sharp stickers that hurt skin if grasped or stepped on. Weeds are the uninvited guests of the plant world. They sprout up in yards, gardens, forests, pastures, and even in the cracks of streets and sidewalks. They can put down roots in places where other plants can't grow at all. You may not like to see weeds, but they are important in many ways.

9. What kind of information would you probably read in the rest of this article?

* I would probably read that weeds are not all bad.

© Evan-Moor Corp. • EMC 3246 • Daily Fundamentals   77

Page 78

Name _____

Day 3 | Week 14

Language

Read the sentences. Rewrite them as a single complex sentence, adding a transition word.

1. Mayra scores another goal. The Kangaroos win the game!

* If Mayra scores another goal, the Kangaroos win the game!

2. The traffic has been much worse. The new mall opened last month.

* The traffic has been much worse since the new mall opened last month.

Math

A cheerleading squad holds a car wash to raise money. Use the graph to answer the items.

The graph shows how many cars they wash in a given time.

3. What is the cheerleaders' car-washing rate?

5 cars per hour

4. At this rate, how long would it take the cheerleading squad to wash 45 cars?

9 hours

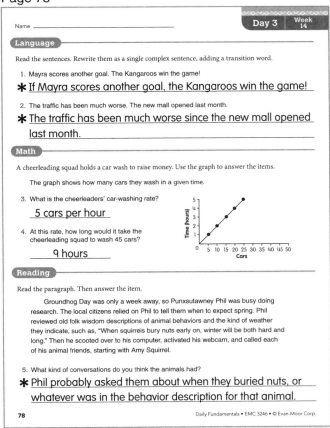

Reading

Read the paragraph. Then answer the item.

Groundhog Day was only a week away, so Punxsutawney Phil was busy doing research. The local citizens relied on Phil to tell them when to expect spring. Phil reviewed old folk wisdom descriptions of animal behaviors and the kind of weather they indicate, such as, "When squirrels bury nuts early on, winter will be both hard and long." Then he scooted over to his computer, activated his webcam, and called each of his animal friends, starting with Amy Squirrel.

5. What kind of conversations do you think the animals had?

* Phil probably asked them about when they buried nuts, or whatever was in the behavior description for that animal.

78   Daily Fundamentals • EMC 3246 • © Evan-Moor Corp.

Page 79

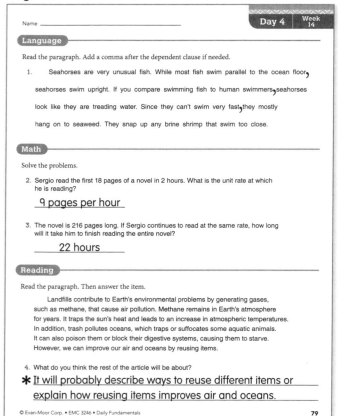

Name _____

Day 4 | Week 14

Language

Read the paragraph. Add a comma after the dependent clause if needed.

1. Seahorses are very unusual fish. While most fish swim parallel to the ocean floor**,** seahorses swim upright. If you compare swimming fish to human swimmers**,** seahorses look like they are treading water. Since they can't swim very fast**,** they mostly hang on to seaweed. They snap up any brine shrimp that swim too close.

Math

Solve the problems.

2. Sergio read the first 18 pages of a novel in 2 hours. What is the unit rate at which he is reading?

__9 pages per hour__

3. The novel is 216 pages long. If Sergio continues to read at the same rate, how long will it take him to finish reading the entire novel?

__22 hours__

Reading

Read the paragraph. Then answer the item.

Landfills contribute to Earth's environmental problems by generating gases, such as methane, that cause air pollution. Methane remains in Earth's atmosphere for years. It traps the sun's heat and leads to an increase in atmospheric temperatures. In addition, trash pollutes oceans, which traps or suffocates some aquatic animals. It can also poison them or block their digestive systems, causing them to starve. However, we can improve our air and oceans by reusing items.

4. What do you think the rest of the article will be about?

✳ It will probably describe ways to reuse different items or explain how reusing items improves air and oceans.

Page 80

Name _____

Day 5 | Week 14

Language

Write two complex sentences about a sport.

✳ 1. Whenever figure skating is on TV, I watch it with great interest.

✳ 2. I can't go skating anymore because they closed our local ice rink.

Math

Solve the problems.

3. Between 2001 and 2016, the Columbia glacier in Prince William Sound has retreated, or shrunk, a total of 165 km. What is its rate of retreat?

__11 km per year__

4. In 2016, the glacier was 51 km long. If the glacier continues to retreat at the same rate, about how long will it take before it disappears from the Sound?

✳ Accept any answer between 4 and 5 years.

Reading

Read the text titles. Then answer the items.

a. **Genes for Survival (nonfiction)**   b. **A Winter to Forget (fiction)**

5. What do you think each text will be about?

✳ a. It will explain how certain genes help animals/people survive.

✳ b. It's a story about something bad happening in winter.

6. Write a question that can be answered by making predictions based on the title of a text.

✳ Does it have the information I need?/Will it be interesting?

Page 81

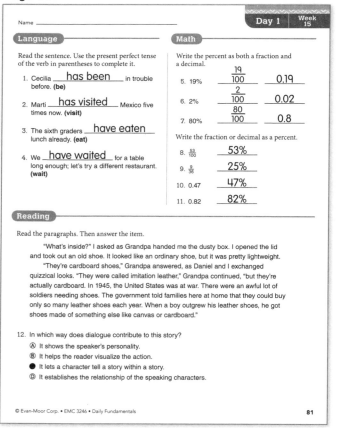

Name _____

Day 1 | Week 15

Language

Read the sentence. Use the present perfect tense of the verb in parentheses to complete it.

1. Cecilia __has been__ in trouble before. **(be)**

2. Marti __has visited__ Mexico five times now. **(visit)**

3. The sixth graders __have eaten__ lunch already. **(eat)**

4. We __have waited__ for a table long enough; let's try a different restaurant. **(wait)**

Math

Write the percent as both a fraction and a decimal.

5. 19% $\frac{19}{100}$ 0.19

6. 2% $\frac{2}{100}$ 0.02

7. 80% $\frac{80}{100}$ 0.8

Write the fraction or decimal as a percent.

8. $\frac{53}{100}$ __53%__

9. $\frac{9}{36}$ __25%__

10. 0.47   __47%__

11. 0.82   __82%__

Reading

Read the paragraphs. Then answer the item.

"What's inside?" I asked as Grandpa handed me the dusty box. I opened the lid and took out an old shoe. It looked like an ordinary shoe, but it was pretty lightweight.

"They're cardboard shoes," Grandpa answered, as Daniel and I exchanged quizzical looks. "They were called imitation leather," Grandpa continued, "but they're actually cardboard. In 1945, the United States was at war. There were an awful lot of soldiers needing shoes. The government told families here at home that they could buy only so many leather shoes each year. When a boy outgrew his leather shoes, he got shoes made of something else like canvas or cardboard."

12. In which way does dialogue contribute to this story?
- Ⓐ It shows the speaker's personality.
- Ⓑ It helps the reader visualize the action.
- ● It lets a character tell a story within a story.
- Ⓓ It establishes the relationship of the speaking characters.

Page 82

Name _____

Day 2 | Week 15

Language

Read the sentence. Use the past perfect tense of the verb in parentheses to complete it.

1. We __had worked__ on our project for three days when Al joined the group. **(work)**

2. Terry __had heard__ of that book before Saleh mentioned it. **(hear)**

3. There __had been__ four accidents by the time the city finally installed a stoplight. **(be)**

4. I __had crossed__ the street when I heard someone call out my name. **(cross)**

Math

Find the part of the whole.

5. 5% of 200 is __10__

6. 25% of 496 is __124__

7. 75% of 12 is __9__

8. 56% of 5,550 is __3,108__

Solve the problem.

9. Johan buys a backpack for $41. He has to pay 8% sales tax. How much is the tax?

__$3.28__

Reading

Read the paragraphs. Then answer the item.

Suddenly, Jordan made his move, crossing the finish line just ahead of Zach. Wiping his face with a damp towel, Zach headed for the bleachers.

"Whoa," said a voice behind Zach. "Great race, buddy. Thanks for tiring out the other runners with that fast start. It made winning a lot easier for me."

Zach turned to see Jordan grinning at him. "Save a little speed for the last half," Jordan continued. "Then, next time, maybe you'll finish ahead of me—if I'm not so far out in front that you can't catch me, that is."

"Yeah, thanks," Zach said to Jordan once he had his breath and his temper under control. "I'll keep that in mind."

10. What can you tell about Jordan from the dialogue?

✳ Jordan acts like he is better than Zach. He seems stuck-up. He has a very superior/arrogant attitude. He acts like a coach, but he's just a runner. He's condescending.

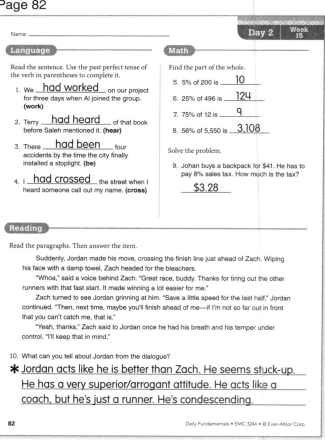

Page 83

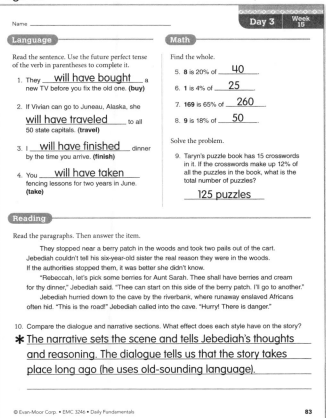

Day 3 • Week 15

Language

Read the sentence. Use the future perfect tense of the verb in parentheses to complete it.

1. They __will have bought__ a new TV before you fix the old one. **(buy)**

2. If Vivian can go to Juneau, Alaska, she __will have traveled__ to all 50 state capitals. **(travel)**

3. I __will have finished__ dinner by the time you arrive. **(finish)**

4. You __will have taken__ fencing lessons for two years in June. **(take)**

Math

Find the whole.

5. **8** is 20% of __40__
6. **1** is 4% of __25__
7. **169** is 65% of __260__
8. **9** is 18% of __50__

Solve the problem.

9. Taryn's puzzle book has 15 crosswords in it. If the crosswords make up 12% of all the puzzles in the book, what is the total number of puzzles?
__125 puzzles__

Reading

Read the paragraphs. Then answer the item.

They stopped near a berry patch in the woods and took two pails out of the cart. Jebediah couldn't tell his six-year-old sister the real reason they were in the woods. If the authorities stopped them, it was better she didn't know.

"Rebeccah, let's pick some berries for Aunt Sarah. Thee shall have berries and cream for thy dinner," Jebediah said. "Thee can start on this side of the berry patch. I'll go to another."

Jebediah hurried down to the cave by the riverbank, where runaway enslaved Africans often hid. "This is the road!" Jebediah called into the cave. "Hurry! There is danger."

10. Compare the dialogue and narrative sections. What effect does each style have on the story?

✱ The narrative sets the scene and tells Jebediah's thoughts and reasoning. The dialogue tells us that the story takes place long ago (he uses old-sounding language).

© Evan-Moor Corp. • EMC 3246 • Daily Fundamentals   83

Page 84

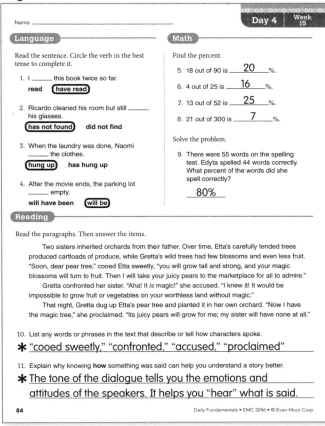

Day 4 • Week 15

Language

Read the sentence. Circle the verb in the best tense to complete it.

1. I _____ this book twice so far.
   read (**have read**)

2. Ricardo cleaned his room but still _____ his glasses.
   (**has not found**) did not find

3. When the laundry was done, Naomi _____ the clothes.
   (**hung up**) has hung up

4. After the movie ends, the parking lot _____ empty.
   will have been (**will be**)

Math

Find the percent.

5. 18 out of 90 is __20__%.
6. 4 out of 25 is __16__%.
7. 13 out of 52 is __25__%.
8. 21 out of 300 is __7__%.

Solve the problem.

9. There were 55 words on the spelling test. Edyta spelled 44 words correctly. What percent of the words did she spell correctly?
__80%__

Reading

Read the paragraphs. Then answer the items.

Two sisters inherited orchards from their father. Over time, Etta's carefully tended trees produced cartloads of produce, while Gretta's wild trees had few blossoms and even less fruit. "Soon, dear pear tree," cooed Etta sweetly, "you will grow tall and strong, and your magic blossoms will turn to fruit. Then I will take your juicy pears to the marketplace for all to admire."

Gretta confronted her sister. "Aha! It is magic!" she accused. "I knew it! It would be impossible to grow fruit or vegetables on your worthless land without magic."

That night, Gretta dug up Etta's pear tree and planted it in her own orchard. "Now I have the magic tree," she proclaimed. "Its juicy pears will grow for me; my sister will have none at all."

10. List any words or phrases in the text that describe or tell how characters spoke.

✱ "cooed sweetly," "confronted," "accused," "proclaimed"

11. Explain why knowing **how** something was said can help you understand a story better.

✱ The tone of the dialogue tells you the emotions and attitudes of the speakers. It helps you "hear" what is said.

84   Daily Fundamentals • EMC 3246 • © Evan-Moor Corp.

Page 85

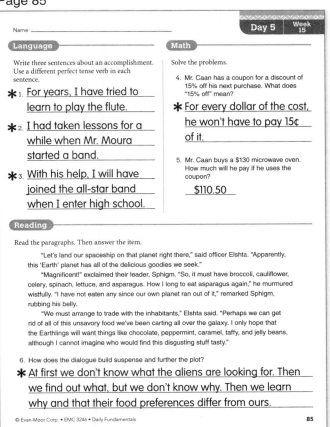

Day 5 • Week 15

Language

Write three sentences about an accomplishment. Use a different perfect tense verb in each sentence.

✱1. For years, I have tried to learn to play the flute.

✱2. I had taken lessons for a while when Mr. Moura started a band.

✱3. With his help, I will have joined the all-star band when I enter high school.

Math

Solve the problems.

4. Mr. Caan has a coupon for a discount of 15% off his next purchase. What does "15% off" mean?

✱ For every dollar of the cost, he won't have to pay 15¢ of it.

5. Mr. Caan buys a $130 microwave oven. How much will he pay if he uses the coupon?
__$110.50__

Reading

Read the paragraphs. Then answer the item.

"Let's land our spaceship on that planet right there," said officer Elshta. "Apparently, this 'Earth' planet has all of the delicious goodies we seek."

"Magnificent!" exclaimed their leader, Sphigm. "So, it must have broccoli, cauliflower, celery, spinach, lettuce, and asparagus. How long to eat asparagus again," he murmured wistfully. "I have not eaten any since our own planet ran out of it," remarked Sphigm, rubbing his belly.

"We must arrange to trade with the inhabitants," Elshta said. "Perhaps we can get rid of all of this unsavory food we've been carting all over the galaxy. I only hope that the Earthlings will want things like chocolate, peppermint, caramel, taffy, and jelly beans, although I cannot imagine who would find this disgusting stuff tasty."

6. How does the dialogue build suspense and further the plot?

✱ At first we don't know what the aliens are looking for. Then we find out what, but we don't know why. Then we learn why and that their food preferences differ from ours.

© Evan-Moor Corp. • EMC 3246 • Daily Fundamentals   85

Page 86

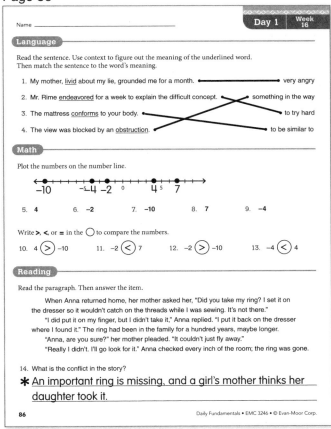

Day 1 • Week 16

Language

Read the sentence. Use context to figure out the meaning of the underlined word. Then match the sentence to the word's meaning.

1. My mother, livid about my lie, grounded me for a month. — very angry
2. Mr. Rime endeavored for a week to explain the difficult concept. — something in the way
3. The mattress conforms to your body. — to try hard
4. The view was blocked by an obstruction. — to be similar to

Math

Plot the numbers on the number line.

-10   -5 -4 -2 0   4 5 7

5. **4**   6. **-2**   7. **-10**   8. **7**   9. **-4**

Write >, <, or = in the ○ to compare the numbers.

10. 4 (>) -10   11. -2 (<) 7   12. -2 (>) -10   13. -4 (<) 4

Reading

Read the paragraph. Then answer the item.

When Anna returned home, her mother asked her, "Did you take my ring? I set it on the dresser so it wouldn't catch on the threads while I was sewing. It's not there."

"I did put it on my finger, but I didn't take it," Anna replied. "I put it back on the dresser where I found it." The ring had been in the family for a hundred years, maybe longer.

"Anna, are you sure?" her mother pleaded. "It couldn't just fly away."

"Really I didn't. I'll go look for it." Anna checked every inch of the room; the ring was gone.

14. What is the conflict in the story?

✱ An important ring is missing, and a girl's mother thinks her daughter took it.

86   Daily Fundamentals • EMC 3246 • © Evan-Moor Corp.

© Evan-Moor Corp. • EMC 3246 • Daily Fundamentals   **179**

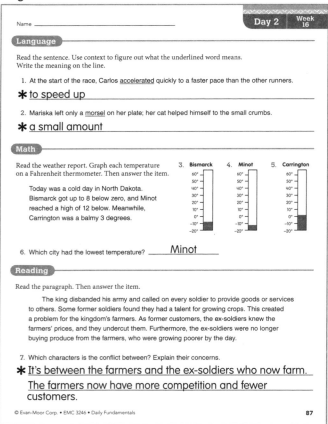
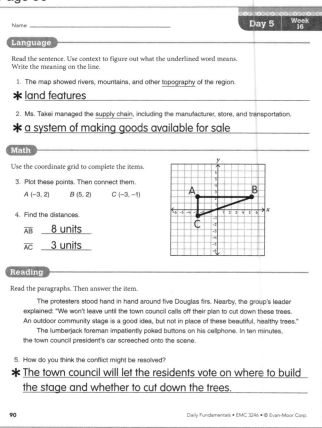

✻ These answers will vary. Examples are given.

Page 87

Name _____

Day 2 | Week 16

Language

Read the sentence. Use context to figure out what the underlined word means.
Write the meaning on the line.

1. At the start of the race, Carlos accelerated quickly to a faster pace than the other runners.

✻ to speed up

2. Mariska left only a morsel on her plate; her cat helped himself to the small crumbs.

✻ a small amount

Math

Read the weather report. Graph each temperature on a Fahrenheit thermometer. Then answer the item.

Today was a cold day in North Dakota. Bismarck got up to 8 below zero, and Minot reached a high of 12 below. Meanwhile, Carrington was a balmy 3 degrees.

3. Bismarck 4. Minot 5. Carrington

6. Which city had the lowest temperature? _____ Minot

Reading

Read the paragraph. Then answer the item.

The king disbanded his army and called on every soldier to provide goods or services to others. Some former soldiers found they had a talent for growing crops. This created a problem for the kingdom's farmers. As former customers, the ex-soldiers knew the farmers' prices, and they undercut them. Furthermore, the ex-soldiers were no longer buying produce from the farmers, who were growing poorer by the day.

7. Which characters is the conflict between? Explain their concerns.

✻ It's between the farmers and the ex-soldiers who now farm. The farmers now have more competition and fewer customers.

© Evan-Moor Corp. • EMC 3246 • Daily Fundamentals   87

Page 88

Name _____

Day 3 | Week 16

Language

Read the sentence. Use context to figure out what the underlined word means.
Write the meaning on the line.

1. The imposter ran off when the real magician arrived.

✻ fake; someone who is pretending to be someone different

2. The little fish was caught in the net, but it liberated itself and swam freely away from the boat.

✻ to make free

Math

Read the statement and write the positive or negative number described.

3. In the U.S., drones may not fly higher than 400 feet.   400

4. The city of Jericho sits at least 233 meters below sea level.   −233

5. The Cave of the Crystals in Mexico is located 951 feet underground.   −951

6. The zip line starts at 450 meters up in the forest's trees.   450

Reading

Read the paragraphs. Then answer the item.

"I could live here," thought Charmaine, "for the rest of my life." On the last day of vacation, Charmaine rowed her canoe out to the tiny mound in Lake Paz. It was like a private treehouse.
As she stroked toward the shore, she fantasized behind closed eyelids about buying a little cabin and working as a writer someday. The water seemed thicker with her eyes shut. When she opened them, she saw water seeping through a crack just as she felt her shoes getting wet.

7. Is the main conflict in the story internal or external? Explain your answer.

✻ It's external. Even though there is only one character, the conflict is coming from a leaky boat, not inside her head.

88   Daily Fundamentals • EMC 3246 • © Evan-Moor Corp.

Page 89

Name _____

Day 4 | Week 16

Language

Read the sentence. Use context to figure out what the underlined word means.
Write the meaning on the line.

1. Ungulates, such as deer, zebras, and moose, have hooves and eat grass.

✻ a type of animal

2. Dilip met the criteria for joining the group by paying dues and attending three meetings.

✻ requirements; standards

Math

Read the situation and write a positive or negative number to represent it.

3. earning $15 for weeding   15

4. donating $5 to charity   −5

5. lending a friend $1.50   −1.50

6. selling a guitar for $60   60

7. spending $25 at the movies   −25

Reading

Read the paragraphs. Then answer the item.

John heard the crack of the bat. He spotted the ball and took a few steps toward it as it dropped five feet away. Rob yelled, "You didn't even reach for it. Where is your head?"
Until recently, John's world was baseball. Lately, he'd been more concerned with his grades. Was he growing up? Caring about your future sounds mature, but not at the expense of losing your joy. Well, he'd have to figure it out later, because another ball was on its way toward the infield.

8. Is the main conflict in the story internal or external? Explain your answer.

✻ It's internal. John isn't playing well because he's starting to think about his future.

© Evan-Moor Corp. • EMC 3246 • Daily Fundamentals   89

Page 90

Name _____

Day 5 | Week 16

Language

Read the sentence. Use context to figure out what the underlined word means.
Write the meaning on the line.

1. The map showed rivers, mountains, and other topography of the region.

✻ land features

2. Ms. Takei managed the supply chain, including the manufacturer, store, and transportation.

✻ a system of making goods available for sale

Math

Use the coordinate grid to complete the items.

3. Plot these points. Then connect them.
   A (−3, 2)   B (5, 2)   C (−3, −1)

4. Find the distances.
   AB̄   8 units
   AC̄   3 units

Reading

Read the paragraphs. Then answer the item.

The protesters stood hand in hand around five Douglas firs. Nearby, the group's leader explained: "We won't leave until the town council calls off their plan to cut down these trees. An outdoor community stage is a good idea, but not in place of these beautiful, healthy trees." The lumberjack foreman impatiently poked buttons on his cellphone. In ten minutes, the town council president's car screeched onto the scene.

5. How do you think the conflict might be resolved?

✻ The town council will let the residents vote on where to build the stage and whether to cut down the trees.

90   Daily Fundamentals • EMC 3246 • © Evan-Moor Corp.

Daily Fundamentals • EMC 3246 • © Evan-Moor Corp.

These answers will vary. Examples are given.

Page 91

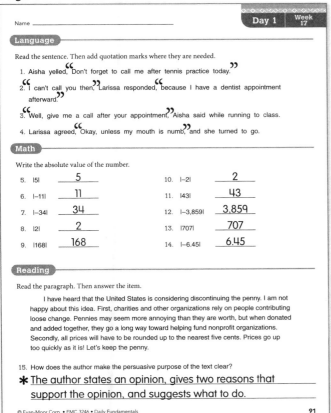

Day 1 | Week 17

Language

Read the sentence. Then add quotation marks where they are needed.

1. Aisha yelled, "Don't forget to call me after tennis practice today."

2. "I can't call you then," Larissa responded, "because I have a dentist appointment afterward."

3. "Well, give me a call after your appointment," Aisha said while running to class.

4. Larissa agreed, "Okay, unless my mouth is numb," and she turned to go.

Math

Write the absolute value of the number.

5. |5| 5
6. |−11| 11
7. |−34| 34
8. |2| 2
9. |168| 168
10. |−2| 2
11. |43| 43
12. |−3,859| 3,859
13. |707| 707
14. |−6.45| 6.45

Reading

Read the paragraph. Then answer the item.

I have heard that the United States is considering discontinuing the penny. I am not happy about this idea. First, charities and other organizations rely on people contributing loose change. Pennies may seem more annoying than they are worth, but when donated and added together, they go a long way toward helping fund nonprofit organizations. Secondly, all prices will have to be rounded up to the nearest five cents. Prices go up too quickly as it is! Let's keep the penny.

15. How does the author make the persuasive purpose of the text clear?

* The author states an opinion, gives two reasons that support the opinion, and suggests what to do.

© Evan-Moor Corp. • EMC 3246 • Daily Fundamentals — 91

Page 92

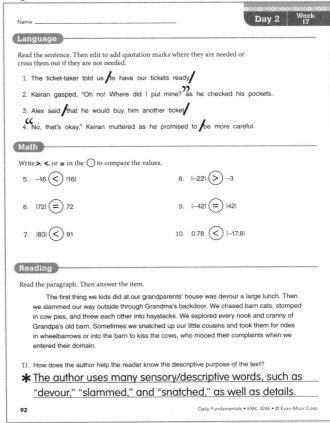

Day 2 | Week 17

Language

Read the sentence. Then edit to add quotation marks where they are needed or cross them out if they are not needed.

1. The ticket-taker told us /to have our tickets ready/

2. Keiran gasped, "Oh no! Where did I put mine?" as he checked his pockets.

3. Alex said /that he would buy him another ticket/

4. "No, that's okay," Keiran muttered as he promised to /be more careful.

Math

Write >, <, or = in the ○ to compare the values.

5. −16 < |16|
6. |72| = 72
7. |83| < 91
8. |−22| > −3
9. |−42| = |42|
10. 0.78 < |−17.8|

Reading

Read the paragraph. Then answer the item.

The first thing we kids did at our grandparents' house was devour a large lunch. Then we slammed our way outside through Grandma's backdoor. We chased barn cats, stomped in cow pies, and threw each other into haystacks. We explored every nook and cranny of Grandpa's old barn. Sometimes we snatched up our little cousins and took them for rides in wheelbarrows or into the barn to kiss the cows, who mooed their complaints when we entered their domain.

11. How does the author help the reader know the descriptive purpose of the text?

* The author uses many sensory/descriptive words, such as "devour," "slammed," and "snatched," as well as details.

92 — Daily Fundamentals • EMC 3246 • © Evan-Moor Corp.

Page 93

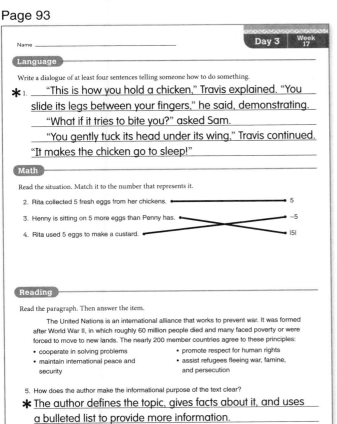

Day 3 | Week 17

Language

Write a dialogue of at least four sentences telling someone how to do something.

* 1. "This is how you hold a chicken," Travis explained. "You slide its legs between your fingers," he said, demonstrating. "What if it tries to bite you?" asked Sam. "You gently tuck its head under its wing," Travis continued. "It makes the chicken go to sleep!"

Math

Read the situation. Match it to the number that represents it.

2. Rita collected 5 fresh eggs from her chickens. — 5
3. Henny is sitting on 5 more eggs than Penny has. — −5
4. Rita used 5 eggs to make a custard. — |5|

Reading

Read the paragraph. Then answer the item.

The United Nations is an international alliance that works to prevent war. It was formed after World War II, in which roughly 60 million people died and many faced poverty or were forced to move to new lands. The nearly 200 member countries agree to these principles:

• cooperate in solving problems
• maintain international peace and security
• promote respect for human rights
• assist refugees fleeing war, famine, and persecution

5. How does the author make the informational purpose of the text clear?

* The author defines the topic, gives facts about it, and uses a bulleted list to provide more information.

© Evan-Moor Corp. • EMC 3246 • Daily Fundamentals — 93

Page 94

Day 4 | Week 17

Language

Read the sentence. Then add quotation marks around the title.

1. The poem "The Road Not Taken" is about making decisions for your future.

2. We read the article "The Two Carolinas," and it really made me think.

3. Australians voted in 1984 to make "Advance Australia Fair" their national anthem.

4. Turn to the story "Star in the Storm" in your reading book.

Math

Solve the problem.

5. A hot-air balloon is flying at an altitude of 1,240 feet. A bristlemouth fish is swimming at a depth of −3,362 feet. Which is closer to sea level?

the hot-air balloon

6. The daytime temperature on the moon reaches 107°C. The nighttime temperature reaches −183°C. Is it closer to freezing (0°C) during the day or night?

during the day

Reading

Read the paragraph. Then answer the item.

This bookcase is easy to assemble. First, fill the holes on one shelf with glue. Then fill a pair of holes on a side board with glue. Next, place two pegs in the glued holes on the side board and attach the shelf. Repeat with the remaining shelves. Tap each shelf with a hammer and wipe off the excess glue. After the glue sets, repeat the gluing, tapping, and wiping with the other side board and let set. Finally, attach the back of the bookcase with the screws provided.

7. How can the reader tell that the text's purpose is instructional?

* The verbs are mostly commands. There are sequence words. The topic is assembling a bookcase.

94 — Daily Fundamentals • EMC 3246 • © Evan-Moor Corp.

© Evan-Moor Corp. • EMC 3246 • Daily Fundamentals

181

Page 95

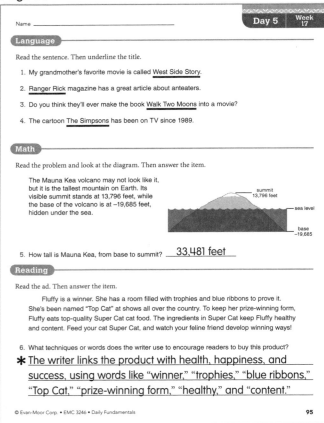

Name _____

Day 5 Week 17

Language

Read the sentence. Then underline the title.

1. My grandmother's favorite movie is called West Side Story.

2. Ranger Rick magazine has a great article about anteaters.

3. Do you think they'll ever make the book Walk Two Moons into a movie?

4. The cartoon The Simpsons has been on TV since 1989.

Math

Read the problem and look at the diagram. Then answer the item.

The Mauna Kea volcano may not look like it, but it is the tallest mountain on Earth. Its visible summit stands at 13,796 feet, while the base of the volcano is at −19,685 feet, hidden under the sea.

summit 13,796 feet
sea level
base −19,685

5. How tall is Mauna Kea, from base to summit? __33,481 feet__

Reading

Read the ad. Then answer the item.

Fluffy is a winner. She has a room filled with trophies and blue ribbons to prove it. She's been named "Top Cat" at shows all over the country. To keep her prize-winning form, Fluffy eats top-quality Super Cat cat food. The ingredients in Super Cat keep Fluffy healthy and content. Feed your cat Super Cat, and watch your feline friend develop winning ways!

6. What techniques or words does the writer use to encourage readers to buy this product?

✱ The writer links the product with health, happiness, and success, using words like "winner," "trophies," "blue ribbons," "Top Cat," "prize-winning form," "healthy," and "content."

© Evan-Moor Corp. • EMC 3246 • Daily Fundamentals ⋯ 95

Page 96

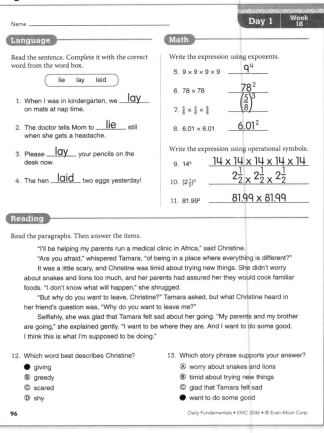

Name _____

Day 1 Week 18

Language

Read the sentence. Complete it with the correct word from the word box.

| lie | lay | laid |

1. When I was in kindergarten, we __lay__ on mats at nap time.

2. The doctor tells Mom to __lie__ still when she gets a headache.

3. Please __lay__ your pencils on the desk now.

4. The hen __laid__ two eggs yesterday!

Math

Write the expression using exponents.

5. $9 \times 9 \times 9 \times 9$ ___9^4___

6. 78×78 ___78^2___

7. $\frac{5}{8} \times \frac{5}{8} \times \frac{5}{8}$ ___$\left(\frac{5}{8}\right)^3$___

8. 6.01×6.01 ___6.01^2___

Write the expression using operational symbols.

9. 14^5 ___$14 \times 14 \times 14 \times 14 \times 14$___

10. $\left(2\frac{1}{2}\right)^3$ ___$2\frac{1}{2} \times 2\frac{1}{2} \times 2\frac{1}{2}$___

11. 81.99^2 ___81.99×81.99___

Reading

Read the paragraphs. Then answer the items.

"I'll be helping my parents run a medical clinic in Africa," said Christine.

"Are you afraid," whispered Tamara, "of being in a place where everything is different?"

It was a little scary, and Christine was timid about trying new things. She didn't worry about snakes and lions too much, and her parents had assured her they would cook familiar foods. "I don't know what will happen," she shrugged.

"But why do you want to leave, Christine?" Tamara asked, but what Christine heard in her friend's question was, "Why do you want to leave me?"

Selfishly, she was glad that Tamara felt sad about her going. "My parents and my brother are going," she explained gently. "I want to be where they are. And I want to do some good. I think this is what I'm supposed to be doing."

12. Which word best describes Christine?
- ● giving
- Ⓑ greedy
- Ⓒ scared
- Ⓓ shy

13. Which story phrase supports your answer?
- Ⓐ worry about snakes and lions
- Ⓑ timid about trying new things
- Ⓒ glad that Tamara felt sad
- ● want to do some good

96 ⋯ Daily Fundamentals • EMC 3246 • © Evan-Moor Corp.

Page 97

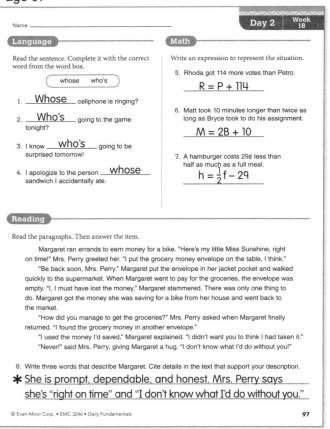

Name _____

Day 2 Week 18

Language

Read the sentence. Complete it with the correct word from the word box.

| whose | who's |

1. __Whose__ cellphone is ringing?

2. __Who's__ going to the game tonight?

3. I know __who's__ going to be surprised tomorrow!

4. I apologize to the person __whose__ sandwich I accidentally ate.

Math

Write an expression to represent the situation.

5. Rhoda got 114 more votes than Petro.

$R = P + 114$

6. Matt took 10 minutes longer than twice as long as Bryce took to do his assignment.

$M = 2B + 10$

7. A hamburger costs 29¢ less than half as much as a full meal.

$h = \frac{1}{2}f - 29$

Reading

Read the paragraphs. Then answer the item.

Margaret ran errands to earn money for a bike. "Here's my little Miss Sunshine, right on time!" Mrs. Perry greeted her. "I put the grocery money envelope on the table, I think."

"Be back soon, Mrs. Perry." Margaret put the envelope in her jacket pocket and walked quickly to the supermarket. When Margaret went to pay for the groceries, the envelope was empty. "I, I must have lost the money," Margaret stammered. There was only one thing to do. Margaret got the money she was saving for a bike from her house and went back to the market.

"How did you manage to get the groceries?" Mrs. Perry asked when Margaret finally returned. "I found the grocery money in another envelope."

"I used the money I'd saved," Margaret explained. "I didn't want you to think I had taken it."

"Never!" said Mrs. Perry, giving Margaret a hug. "I don't know what I'd do without you!"

8. Write three words that describe Margaret. Cite details in the text that support your description.

✱ She is prompt, dependable, and honest. Mrs. Perry says she's "right on time" and "I don't know what I'd do without you."

© Evan-Moor Corp. • EMC 3246 • Daily Fundamentals ⋯ 97

Page 98

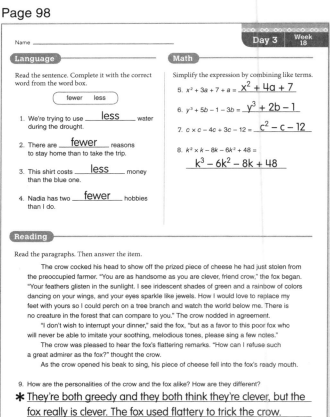

Name _____

Day 3 Week 18

Language

Read the sentence. Complete it with the correct word from the word box.

| fewer | less |

1. We're trying to use __less__ water during the drought.

2. There are __fewer__ reasons to stay home than to take the trip.

3. This shirt costs __less__ money than the blue one.

4. Nadia has two __fewer__ hobbies than I do.

Math

Simplify the expression by combining like terms.

5. $x^2 + 3a + 7 + a =$ ___$x^2 + 4a + 7$___

6. $y^3 + 5b - 1 - 3b =$ ___$y^3 + 2b - 1$___

7. $c \times c - 4c + 3c - 12 =$ ___$c^2 - c - 12$___

8. $k^2 \times k - 8k - 6k^2 + 48 =$

___$k^3 - 6k^2 - 8k + 48$___

Reading

Read the paragraphs. Then answer the item.

The crow cocked his head to show off the prized piece of cheese he had just stolen from the preoccupied farmer. "You are as handsome as you are clever, friend crow," the fox began. "Your feathers glisten in the sunlight. I see iridescent shades of green and a rainbow of colors dancing on your wings, and your eyes sparkle like jewels. How I would love to replace my feet with yours so I could perch on a tree branch and watch the world below me. There is no creature in the forest that can compare to you." The crow nodded in agreement.

"I don't wish to interrupt your dinner," said the fox, "but as a favor to this poor fox who will never be able to imitate your soothing, melodious tones, please sing a few notes."

The crow was pleased to hear the fox's flattering remarks. "How can I refuse such a great admirer as the fox?" thought the crow.

As the crow opened his beak to sing, his piece of cheese fell into the fox's ready mouth.

9. How are the personalities of the crow and the fox alike? How are they different?

✱ They're both greedy and they both think they're clever, but the fox really is clever. The fox used flattery to trick the crow.

98 ⋯ Daily Fundamentals • EMC 3246 • © Evan-Moor Corp.

These answers will vary. Examples are given.

Page 99

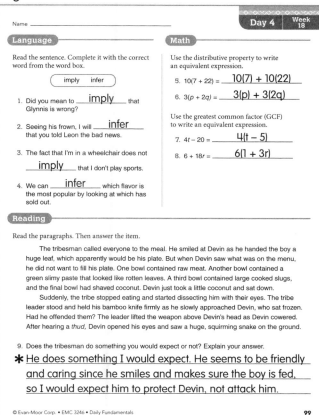

Day 4 | Week 18

Language

Read the sentence. Complete it with the correct word from the word box.

word box: imply   infer

1. Did you mean to **imply** that Glynnis is wrong?
2. Seeing his frown, I will **infer** that you told Leon the bad news.
3. The fact that I'm in a wheelchair does not **imply** that I don't play sports.
4. We can **infer** which flavor is the most popular by looking at which has sold out.

Math

Use the distributive property to write an equivalent expression.

5. $10(7 + 22) =$ **10(7) + 10(22)**
6. $3(p + 2q) =$ **3(p) + 3(2q)**

Use the greatest common factor (GCF) to write an equivalent expression.

7. $4t - 20 =$ **4(t − 5)**
8. $6 + 18r =$ **6(1 + 3r)**

Reading

Read the paragraphs. Then answer the item.

The tribesman called everyone to the meal. He smiled at Devin as he handed the boy a huge leaf, which apparently would be his plate. But when Devin saw what was on the menu, he did not want to fill his plate. One bowl contained raw meat. Another bowl contained a green slimy paste that looked like rotten leaves. A third bowl contained large cooked slugs, and the final bowl had shaved coconut. Devin just took a little coconut and sat down.

Suddenly, the tribe stopped eating and started dissecting him with their eyes. The tribe leader stood and held his bamboo knife firmly as he slowly approached Devin, who sat frozen. Had he offended them? The leader lifted the weapon above Devin's head as Devin cowered. After hearing a *thud,* Devin opened his eyes and saw a huge, squirming snake on the ground.

9. Does the tribesman do something you would expect or not? Explain your answer.

* He does something I would expect. He seems to be friendly and caring since he smiles and makes sure the boy is fed, so I would expect him to protect Devin, not attack him.

© Evan-Moor Corp. • EMC 3246 • Daily Fundamentals   99

Page 100

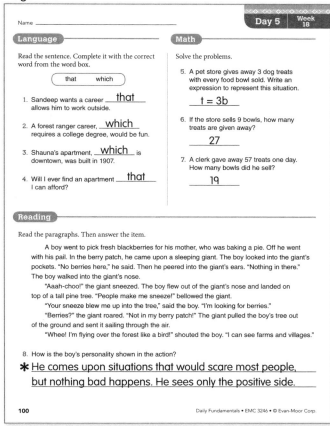

Day 5 | Week 18

Language

Read the sentence. Complete it with the correct word from the word box.

word box: that   which

1. Sandeep wants a career **that** allows him to work outside.
2. A forest ranger career, **which** requires a college degree, would be fun.
3. Shauna's apartment, **which** is downtown, was built in 1907.
4. Will I ever find an apartment **that** I can afford?

Math

Solve the problems.

5. A pet store gives away 3 dog treats with every food bowl sold. Write an expression to represent this situation.
   t = 3b
6. If the store sells 9 bowls, how many treats are given away?
   27
7. A clerk gave away 57 treats one day. How many bowls did he sell?
   19

Reading

Read the paragraphs. Then answer the item.

A boy went to pick fresh blackberries for his mother, who was baking a pie. Off he went with his pail. In the berry patch, he came upon a sleeping giant. The boy looked into the giant's pockets. "No berries here," he said. Then he peered into the giant's ears. "Nothing in there." The boy walked into the giant's nose.

"Aaah-choo!" the giant sneezed. The boy flew out of the giant's nose and landed on top of a tall pine tree. "People make me sneeze!" bellowed the giant.

"Your sneeze blew me up into the tree," said the boy. "I'm looking for berries."

"Berries?" the giant roared. "Not in my berry patch!" The giant pulled the boy's tree out of the ground and sent it sailing through the air.

"Whee! I'm flying over the forest like a bird!" shouted the boy. "I can see farms and villages."

8. How is the boy's personality shown in the action?

* He comes upon situations that would scare most people, but nothing bad happens. He sees only the positive side.

100   Daily Fundamentals • EMC 3246 • © Evan-Moor Corp.

Page 101

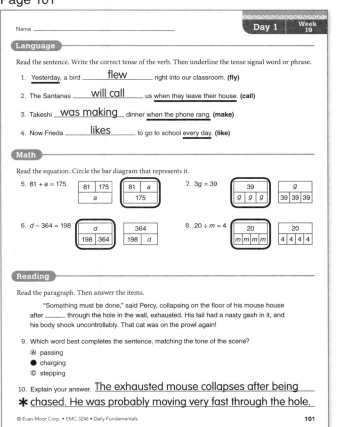

Day 1 | Week 19

Language

Read the sentence. Write the correct tense of the verb. Then underline the tense signal word or phrase.

1. Yesterday, a bird **flew** right into our classroom. **(fly)**
2. The Santanas **will call** us when they leave their house. **(call)**
3. Takeshi **was making** dinner when the phone rang. **(make)**
4. Now Frieda **likes** to go to school every day. **(like)**

Math

Read the equation. Circle the bar diagram that represents it.

5. $81 + a = 175$
6. $d - 364 = 198$
7. $3g = 39$
8. $20 \div m = 4$

Reading

Read the paragraph. Then answer the items.

"Something must be done," said Percy, collapsing on the floor of his mouse house after _____ through the hole in the wall, exhausted. His tail had a nasty gash in it, and his body shook uncontrollably. That cat was on the prowl again!

9. Which word best completes the sentence, matching the tone of the scene?
   Ⓐ passing
   ● charging
   Ⓒ stepping

10. Explain your answer. The exhausted mouse collapses after being
* chased. He was probably moving very fast through the hole.

© Evan-Moor Corp. • EMC 3246 • Daily Fundamentals   101

Page 102

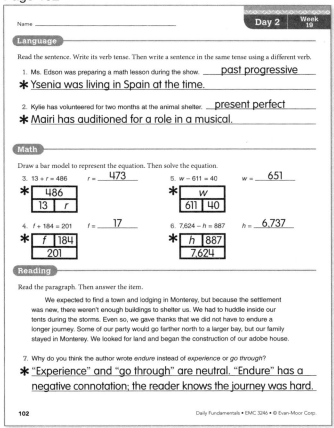

Day 2 | Week 19

Language

Read the sentence. Write its verb tense. Then write a sentence in the same tense using a different verb.

1. Ms. Edson was preparing a math lesson during the show. **past progressive**
* Ysenia was living in Spain at the time.
2. Kylie has volunteered for two months at the animal shelter. **present perfect**
* Mairi has auditioned for a role in a musical.

Math

Draw a bar model to represent the equation. Then solve the equation.

3. $13 + r = 486$ $r =$ **473**
4. $f + 184 = 201$ $f =$ **17**
5. $w - 611 = 40$ $w =$ **651**
6. $7,624 - h = 887$ $h =$ **6,737**

Reading

Read the paragraph. Then answer the item.

We expected to find a town and lodging in Monterey, but because the settlement was new, there weren't enough buildings to shelter us. We had to huddle inside our tents during the storms. Even so, we gave thanks that we did not have to endure a longer journey. Some of our party would go farther north to a larger bay, but our family stayed in Monterey. We looked for land and began the construction of our adobe house.

7. Why do you think the author wrote *endure* instead of *experience* or *go through*?

* "Experience" and "go through" are neutral. "Endure" has a negative connotation; the reader knows the journey was hard.

102   Daily Fundamentals • EMC 3246 • © Evan-Moor Corp.

© Evan-Moor Corp. • EMC 3246 • Daily Fundamentals   **183**

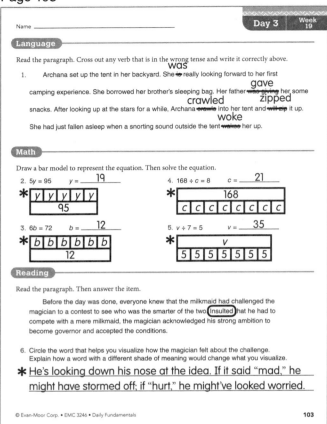

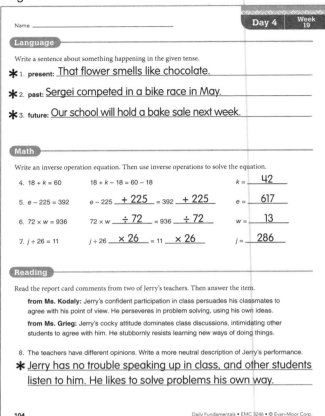

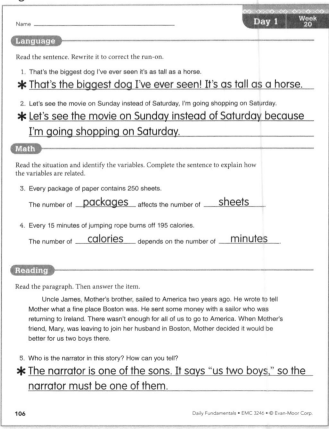

Page 103

Name _____

Day 3 | Week 19

Language

Read the paragraph. Cross out any verb that is in the wrong tense and write it correctly above.

1. Archana set up the tent in her backyard. She ~~is~~ **was** really looking forward to her first camping experience. She borrowed her brother's sleeping bag. Her father ~~was giving~~ **gave** her some snacks. After looking up at the stars for a while, Archana ~~crawls~~ **crawled** into her tent and ~~will zip~~ **zipped** it up. She had just fallen asleep when a snorting sound outside the tent ~~wakes~~ **woke** her up.

Math

Draw a bar model to represent the equation. Then solve the equation.

2. $5y = 95$ $y =$ **19**

✳ | y | y | y | y | y |
  | 95 | | | | |

3. $6b = 72$ $b =$ **12**

✳ | b | b | b | b | b | b |
  | 12 | | | | | |

4. $168 \div c = 8$ $c =$ **21**

✳ | 168 | | | | | | | |
  | c | c | c | c | c | c | c | c |

5. $v \div 7 = 5$ $v =$ **35**

✳ | v | | | | | | |
  | 5 | 5 | 5 | 5 | 5 | 5 | 5 |

Reading

Read the paragraph. Then answer the item.

Before the day was done, everyone knew that the milkmaid had challenged the magician to a contest to see who was the smarter of the two. (Insulted) that he had to compete with a mere milkmaid, the magician acknowledged his strong ambition to become governor and accepted the conditions.

6. Circle the word that helps you visualize how the magician felt about the challenge. Explain how a word with a different shade of meaning would change what you visualize.

✳ He's looking down his nose at the idea. If it said "mad," he might have stormed off; if "hurt," he might've looked worried.

Page 104

Name _____

Day 4 | Week 19

Language

Write a sentence about something happening in the given tense.

✳ 1. present: That flower smells like chocolate.

✳ 2. past: Sergei competed in a bike race in May.

✳ 3. future: Our school will hold a bake sale next week.

Math

Write an inverse operation equation. Then use inverse operations to solve the equation.

4. $18 + k = 60$ $18 + k - 18 = 60 - 18$ $k =$ **42**

5. $e - 225 = 392$ $e - 225$ **+ 225** $= 392$ **+ 225** $e =$ **617**

6. $72 \times w = 936$ $72 \times w$ **÷ 72** $= 936$ **÷ 72** $w =$ **13**

7. $j \div 26 = 11$ $j \div 26$ **× 26** $= 11$ **× 26** $j =$ **286**

Reading

Read the report card comments from two of Jerry's teachers. Then answer the item.

from Ms. Kodaly: Jerry's confident participation in class persuades his classmates to agree with his point of view. He perseveres in problem solving, using his own ideas.

from Ms. Grieg: Jerry's cocky attitude dominates class discussions, intimidating other students to agree with him. He stubbornly resists learning new ways of doing things.

8. The teachers have different opinions. Write a more neutral description of Jerry's performance.

✳ Jerry has no trouble speaking up in class, and other students listen to him. He likes to solve problems his own way.

Page 105

Name _____

Day 5 | Week 19

Language

Write a paragraph to convey a sequence of events.

✳ 1. ____ I went to a neighborhood potluck party last weekend. I had made a fruit salad, but the fruit turned brown before I left for the party. So I walked to the store and bought some grapes and cheese. The next day, Mom told me what to do with the fruit. From now on, I will dip cut fruit in lemon juice.

Math

Read the problem. Use any strategy to solve it. Show your work.

2. A craft fair sold $1,485 of Erynne's necklaces. Before the fair, Erynne had spent 198 hours making the necklaces.

How much money did Erynne earn per hour? **$7.50**

$198 \times m = 1,485$

$198 \div 198 \times m = 1,485 \div 198$ Work may vary.

$m = 7.5$

Reading

Read the paragraph. Then answer the item.

"Amy," the woman scolded, "I thought you had more sense than to go swimming this time of year. What would your mother say if she could see you playing in the water on a cold day like this? How careless of you! Some children just think of themselves."

3. How did *scolded* prepare you for the rest of the dialogue? Rewrite the first sentence, changing *scolded* to a word with another shade of meaning and making that which follows match.

✳ After "scolded," I expected to hear what Amy did wrong. "Amy," the woman warned, "you should get out of that cold water now before you catch a chill."

Page 106

Name _____

Day 1 | Week 20

Language

Read the sentence. Rewrite it to correct the run-on.

1. That's the biggest dog I've ever seen it's as tall as a horse.

✳ That's the biggest dog I've ever seen! It's as tall as a horse.

2. Let's see the movie on Sunday instead of Saturday, I'm going shopping on Saturday.

✳ Let's see the movie on Sunday instead of Saturday because I'm going shopping on Saturday.

Math

Read the situation and identify the variables. Complete the sentence to explain how the variables are related.

3. Every package of paper contains 250 sheets.

The number of **packages** affects the number of **sheets**.

4. Every 15 minutes of jumping rope burns off 195 calories.

The number of **calories** depends on the number of **minutes**.

Reading

Read the paragraph. Then answer the item.

Uncle James, Mother's brother, sailed to America two years ago. He wrote to tell Mother what a fine place Boston was. He sent some money with a sailor who was returning to Ireland. There wasn't enough for all of us to go to America. When Mother's friend, Mary, was leaving to join her husband in Boston, Mother decided it would be better for us two boys there.

5. Who is the narrator in this story? How can you tell?

✳ The narrator is one of the sons. It says "us two boys," so the narrator must be one of them.

Page 107

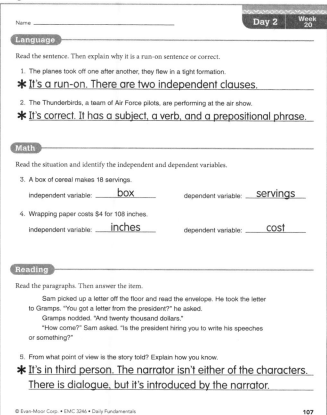

Name _____

Day 2 | **Week 20**

Language

Read the sentence. Then explain why it is a run-on sentence or correct.

1. The planes took off one after another, they flew in a tight formation.

✻ It's a run-on. There are two independent clauses.

2. The Thunderbirds, a team of Air Force pilots, are performing at the air show.

✻ It's correct. It has a subject, a verb, and a prepositional phrase.

Math

Read the situation and identify the independent and dependent variables.

3. A box of cereal makes 18 servings.

independent variable: ___box___   dependent variable: ___servings___

4. Wrapping paper costs $4 for 108 inches.

independent variable: ___inches___   dependent variable: ___cost___

Reading

Read the paragraphs. Then answer the item.

Sam picked up a letter off the floor and read the envelope. He took the letter to Gramps. "You got a letter from the president?" he asked.

Gramps nodded. "And twenty thousand dollars."

"How come?" Sam asked. "Is the president hiring you to write his speeches or something?"

5. From what point of view is the story told? Explain how you know.

✻ It's in third person. The narrator isn't either of the characters. There is dialogue, but it's introduced by the narrator.

© Evan-Moor Corp. • EMC 3246 • Daily Fundamentals   107

Page 108

Name _____

Day 3 | **Week 20**

Language

Read the sentence. Rewrite it to correct the fragment.

1. The jacket on the left side of the closet in the hallway.

✻ The jacket is on the left side of the closet in the hallway.

2. The science experiment that we did last Friday.

✻ We did a science experiment last Friday.

Math

Read the situation. Write a variable in each table heading. Then complete the table with data that represent the situation.

3. Carnival tickets cost $4 each.

Tickets	Dollars
1	4
2	8
3	12

4. Rides last 8 minutes each.

Rides	Min.
2	16
4	32
6	48

5. Win a prize for every 3 bottles knocked down.

Prizes	Bottles
1	3
3	9
6	18

Reading

Read the paragraph. Then answer the item.

It was about 105 degrees at Camp Clear Creek the day Hoa's parents dropped him off. Then he saw the cabin where he'd be staying for two weeks. There was no air conditioning, nor was there electricity. "The brochure said it was 'rustic,'" Hoa muttered, "but 'primitive' is more like it." Just then, his roommate appeared.

6. Is the narrator's knowledge limited or unlimited? Explain how you know.

✻ It's limited. We know what happened and what Hoa did, but we don't know what he thought until he said something.

108   Daily Fundamentals • EMC 3246 • © Evan-Moor Corp.

Page 109

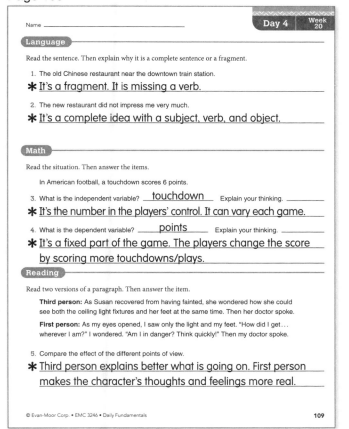

Name _____

Day 4 | **Week 20**

Language

Read the sentence. Then explain why it is a complete sentence or a fragment.

1. The old Chinese restaurant near the downtown train station.

✻ It's a fragment. It is missing a verb.

2. The new restaurant did not impress me very much.

✻ It's a complete idea with a subject, verb, and object.

Math

Read the situation. Then answer the items.

In American football, a touchdown scores 6 points.

3. What is the independent variable? ___touchdown___ Explain your thinking. _____

✻ It's the number in the players' control. It can vary each game.

4. What is the dependent variable? ___points___ Explain your thinking. _____

✻ It's a fixed part of the game. The players change the score by scoring more touchdowns/plays.

Reading

Read two versions of a paragraph. Then answer the item.

Third person: As Susan recovered from having fainted, she wondered how she could see both the ceiling light fixtures and her feet at the same time. Then her doctor spoke.

First person: As my eyes opened, I saw only the light and my feet. "How did I get... wherever I am?" I wondered. "Am I in danger? Think quickly!" Then my doctor spoke.

5. Compare the effect of the different points of view.

✻ Third person explains better what is going on. First person makes the character's thoughts and feelings more real.

© Evan-Moor Corp. • EMC 3246 • Daily Fundamentals   109

Page 110

Name _____

Day 5 | **Week 20**

Language

Read the paragraph. Then rewrite it, correcting the fragments and run-ons.

1. When Tamara went to the doctor. A twisted ankle and a bruised hip. Her doctor thought she'd run into another soccer player. Actually, she tripped on the curb then she fell on the sidewalk.

✻ Tamara went to the doctor with a twisted ankle and a bruised hip. Her doctor thought she'd run into another soccer player. Actually, she tripped on the curb and then fell on the sidewalk.

Math

Read the situation. Complete the table and answer the item.

2. Janelle's pancake recipe requires 2 eggs for every batch of 11 pancakes. Write the independent variable in the first column and the dependent variable in the second column of the table. Then complete the table for 2, 4, and 6 eggs.

Eggs	Pancakes
2	11
4	22
6	33

How many pancakes will 6 eggs make?

___33___

Reading

Read the paragraph. Then answer the item.

Billiken jumped up on Kaitlin's chair. His front paws kneaded her stomach while his back legs balanced delicately on the armrest. He blocked her view of both the TV and the computer on the table next to her. "Why don't you sit here next to me?" Kaitlin suggested as she patted the empty cat-sized spot next to her leg. He just purred and kept kneading.

3. Rewrite the paragraph with Billiken, the cat, as the narrator.

✻ I jumped up on Kaitlin's chair and kneaded her stomach. I managed to block her view of both the TV and the computer. Now she has to pay attention to me!

110   Daily Fundamentals • EMC 3246 • © Evan-Moor Corp.

Page 111

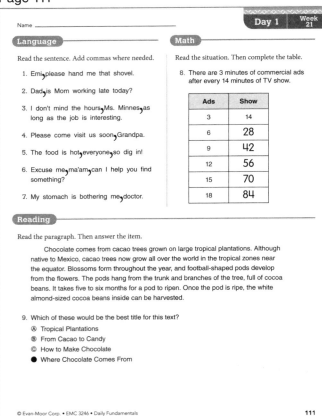

Name _____

Day 1 | **Week 21**

Language

Read the sentence. Add commas where needed.

1. Emi, please hand me that shovel.

2. Dad, is Mom working late today?

3. I don't mind the hours, Ms. Minnes, as long as the job is interesting.

4. Please come visit us soon, Grandpa.

5. The food is hot, everyone, so dig in!

6. Excuse me, ma'am, can I help you find something?

7. My stomach is bothering me, doctor.

Math

Read the situation. Then complete the table.

8. There are 3 minutes of commercial ads after every 14 minutes of TV show.

Ads	Show
3	14
6	28
9	42
12	56
15	70
18	84

Reading

Read the paragraph. Then answer the item.

Chocolate comes from cacao trees grown on large tropical plantations. Although native to Mexico, cacao trees now grow all over the world in the tropical zones near the equator. Blossoms form throughout the year, and football-shaped pods develop from the flowers. The pods hang from the trunk and branches of the tree, full of cocoa beans. It takes five to six months for a pod to ripen. Once the pod is ripe, the white almond-sized cocoa beans inside can be harvested.

9. Which of these would be the best title for this text?
   Ⓐ Tropical Plantations
   Ⓑ From Cacao to Candy
   Ⓒ How to Make Chocolate
   ● Where Chocolate Comes From

Page 112

Name _____

Day 2 | **Week 21**

Language

Read the sentence. Add a comma where needed.

1. No, I don't think that answer is right.

2. Yes, your plan sounds good to me.

3. This is that song you like, no?

4. You recommended this magazine, didn't you?

5. He doesn't give bad advice, does he?

6. Yes, please tell us more about Laos.

7. The twins will be in different classes, won't they?

Math

Read the situation. Then complete the table.

8. Lupita and Sheebah are 5 years apart in age.

Lupita	Sheebah
9	4
11	6
15	10
18	13
21	16
26	21

Reading

Read the paragraphs. Then answer the item.

"When I was your age, 80 years ago," Luke's great-grandmother began, "a wagon pulled by horses picked me up outside our house to take me to school. There wasn't room for us in the schoolhouse, so all of us West End kids went to school in the basement of the library."

Luke was surprised. "That sounds like a fun way to get to school! I ride the school bus. I hope we don't ever have too many kids to fit in my school, because our town library doesn't have a basement!"

9. Paraphrase the dialogue.

✱ They're comparing going to school in different decades. They got to school in different ways, and their buildings were different.

Page 113

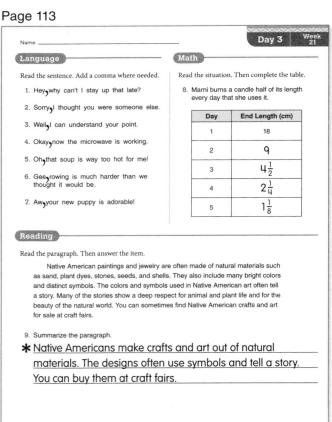

Name _____

Day 3 | **Week 21**

Language

Read the sentence. Add a comma where needed.

1. Hey, why can't I stay up that late?

2. Sorry, I thought you were someone else.

3. Well, I can understand your point.

4. Okay, now the microwave is working.

5. Oh, that soup is way too hot for me!

6. Gee, rowing is much harder than we thought it would be.

7. Aw, your new puppy is adorable!

Math

Read the situation. Then complete the table.

8. Marni burns a candle half of its length every day that she uses it.

Day	End Length (cm)
1	18
2	9
3	$4\frac{1}{2}$
4	$2\frac{1}{4}$
5	$1\frac{1}{8}$

Reading

Read the paragraph. Then answer the item.

Native American paintings and jewelry are often made of natural materials such as sand, plant dyes, stones, seeds, and shells. They also include many bright colors and distinct symbols. The colors and symbols used in Native American art often tell a story. Many of the stories show a deep respect for animal and plant life and for the beauty of the natural world. You can sometimes find Native American crafts and art for sale at craft fairs.

9. Summarize the paragraph.

✱ Native Americans make crafts and art out of natural materials. The designs often use symbols and tell a story. You can buy them at craft fairs.

Page 114

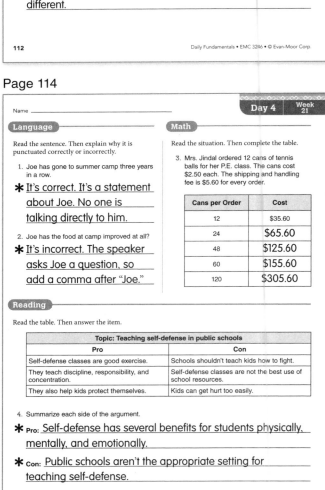

Name _____

Day 4 | **Week 21**

Language

Read the sentence. Then explain why it is punctuated correctly or incorrectly.

1. Joe has gone to summer camp three years in a row.

✱ It's correct. It's a statement about Joe. No one is talking directly to him.

2. Joe has the food at camp improved at all?

✱ It's incorrect. The speaker asks Joe a question, so add a comma after "Joe."

Math

Read the situation. Then complete the table.

3. Mrs. Jindal ordered 12 cans of tennis balls for her P.E. class. The cans cost $2.50 each. The shipping and handling fee is $5.60 for every order.

Cans per Order	Cost
12	$35.60
24	$65.60
48	$125.60
60	$155.60
120	$305.60

Reading

Read the table. Then answer the item.

Topic: Teaching self-defense in public schools	
Pro	**Con**
Self-defense classes are good exercise.	Schools shouldn't teach kids how to fight.
They teach discipline, responsibility, and concentration.	Self-defense classes are not the best use of school resources.
They also help kids protect themselves.	Kids can get hurt too easily.

4. Summarize each side of the argument.

✱ Pro: Self-defense has several benefits for students physically, mentally, and emotionally.

✱ Con: Public schools aren't the appropriate setting for teaching self-defense.

Page 115

Name _____

Day 5 | Week 21

Language

Read the text. Add commas where needed.

1. "Yuri, do you still want to play baseball when you grow up?" Mariah asked.

"No, I'm not a great player," Yuri replied. "I'm thinking about being a historian."

"Wow, that's quite a switch," Mariah remarked. "It's hard to get a job as a historian, isn't it?"

"Well, it depends on where you look," Yuri explained. "Historians are often hired by museums and libraries."

"Hey, I guess you could teach history as well, couldn't you?" Mariah suggested.

"Yes, Mariah, but teaching is harder than baseball!" Yuri responded.

Math

Read the situation. Then complete the table.

2. Thor has 60 apples to give away at the grand opening of his new grocery store.

Customers	Apples for Each
5	12
6	10
10	6
12	5
15	4
20	3

Reading

Read the paragraph. Then answer the items.

Giraffes' towering height is the key to their ability to survive in their often-dry habitat. It allows them to reach the tender leaves at the top of acacia trees. Because these leaves are about three-quarters water, they also provide moisture when there are no watering places nearby. Giraffes didn't just decide to grow longer necks to reach these leaves! Over hundreds of generations, the tallest giraffes, who could reach more leaves, became healthier, lived longer, and had more offspring. Gradually, the average height increased.

3. Paraphrase the first two sentences of the text.

* A giraffe's tall height helps it survive in its habitat.

4. Summarize the paragraph.

* Giraffes eat moist acacia leaves. If they weren't so tall, they couldn't reach them. Over time, the shorter giraffes didn't produce as many offspring as the taller giraffes.

Page 116

Name _____

Day 1 | Week 22

Language

Read the dictionary entry. Use it to answer the items.

> **minute** (MIHN-it) *Noun* 1. a short amount of time; 60 seconds
> **minute** (my-NOOT) *Adj* 1. very tiny

1. How many meanings does *minute* have? __2__

2. What parts of speech can *minute* be? __noun, adjective__

3. Which syllable of *minute* is accented here? "I made a *minute* change." __the second__

Math

Read the problem. Then answer the items.

An elephant's heart beats an average of 30 beats every minute. How many times will it beat in 60 minutes?

4. Describe the relationship between the heart beating and minutes passing. __Multiply the number of heartbeats and the number of minutes.__

5. Circle the correct expression to represent the problem.

a. 30 ÷ 60   (b.) 30 × 60   c. 60 ÷ 30

Reading

Read the timeline. Then answer the items.

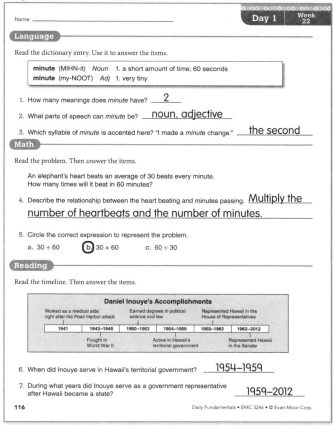

Daniel Inouye's Accomplishments

Worked as a medical aide right after the Pearl Harbor attack	Earned degrees in political science and law		Represented Hawaii in the House of Representatives
1941	1943–1945	1950–1953	1954–1959	1959–1962	1962–2012
	Fought in World War II		Active in Hawaii's territorial government		Represented Hawaii in the Senate

6. When did Inouye serve in Hawaii's territorial government? __1954–1959__

7. During what years did Inouye serve as a government representative after Hawaii became a state? __1959–2012__

Page 117

Name _____

Day 2 | Week 22

Language

Read the dictionary entry and the sentence. Use them to answer the items.

> **sole** (SOHL) *Noun* 1. the bottom of a foot or shoe
> *Adj* 1. only

The *sole* reason I joined the choir was that my best friends had joined.

1. Which meaning is used in the sentence? __only__

2. What part of speech is it? __adjective__

Math

Read the problem. Then answer the items.

Erica is reading a 224-page book. If she reads *r* pages per day, how many days will it take her to finish the book?

3. Describe the relationship between the book length and Erica's reading rate. __Divide the total number of pages by how many she reads daily.__

4. Circle the correct expression to represent the problem.

a. *r* × 224   b. 224 × *r*   (c.) 224 ÷ *r*

Reading

Look at the map and key. Then answer the items.

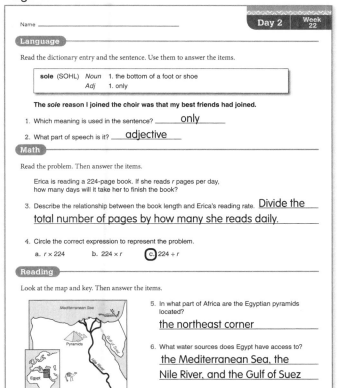

5. In what part of Africa are the Egyptian pyramids located?

__the northeast corner__

6. What water sources does Egypt have access to?

__the Mediterranean Sea, the Nile River, and the Gulf of Suez__

Page 118

Name _____

Day 3 | Week 22

Language

Read the dictionary entry and the sentence. Use them to answer the items.

> **interest** (IN-trest) *Noun* 1. a desire to learn about or be involved in something
> 2. money paid for a loan or earned on a bank account

Ishmael has an *interest* in the finance industry and hopes to work on Wall Street someday.

1. Which meaning is used in the sentence? __a desire to learn__

* 2. How can you tell? __He wants to work, which is a way to be involved.__

Math

Read the problem. Then write and simplify an expression for the problem.

3. In a school fundraiser, students earn 15 points for every calendar they sell and 8 points for every T-shirt they sell. Camille sold 23 calendars and 41 T-shirts. How many points did she earn?

expression: __(15 × 23) + (8 × 41)__   answer: __673 points__

4. Oak Knoll Vista School requires one chaperone for every 12 students on a field trip. If 192 students are visiting a museum, how many tickets will the school buy?

expression: __(192 ÷ 12) + 192__   answer: __208 tickets__

Reading

Read the weather forecast diagram. Then answer the item.

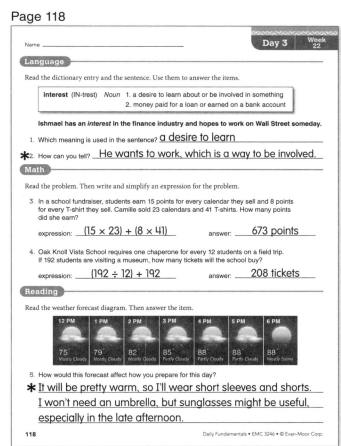

12 PM	1 PM	2 PM	3 PM	4 PM	5 PM	6 PM
75°	79°	82°	85°	88°	88°	88°
Mostly Cloudy	Mostly Cloudy	Mostly Cloudy	Partly Cloudy	Partly Cloudy	Partly Cloudy	Mostly Sunny

5. How would this forecast affect how you prepare for this day?

* It will be pretty warm, so I'll wear short sleeves and shorts. I won't need an umbrella, but sunglasses might be useful, especially in the late afternoon.

✳ These answers will vary. Examples are given.

Page 119

Name _____

Day 4 | Week 22

Language

Read the dictionary entry. Then write a sentence using one of the definitions. Circle the definition.

> **film** (FIHLM) *Verb* 1. to make a movie
> *Noun* 1. material sometimes used to shoot photos or movies
> ②. a thin layer over the surface of something

1. There was a film of algae on the duck pond.
✳ _____

Math

Read the problem. Then write an expression to represent the situation.

2. A frozen yogurt shop charges $2 per ounce of yogurt. Toppings cost $0.25 each. How much did Craig's yogurt cost if he got *y* ounces and *t* toppings?

expression: 2y + 0.25t

3. A movie theater has 302 seats. Tickets cost $8.75. How much did the theater make if there were *u* unsold seats during the last show?

expression: (302 − u) × 8.75

Reading

Look at the diagram. Then answer the item.

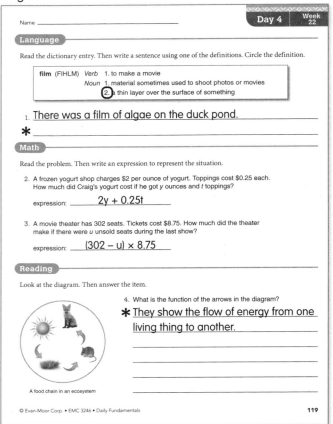

A food chain in an ecosystem

4. What is the function of the arrows in the diagram?
✳ They show the flow of energy from one living thing to another.

Page 120

Name _____

Day 5 | Week 22

Language

Read the dictionary entry. Use it to answer the items.

> **learned** (LURND) *Verb* 1. past tense of *learn*, to gain knowledge or facts
> **learned** (LUR-ned) *Adj* 1. well educated

1. If you heard the phrase "my learned colleague," how would this entry help you find its meaning?
✳ There are two pronunciations, so I'd look at the one I heard. I see that it's an adjective meaning "well educated."

Math

Read the problem. Write an expression to represent the situation. Then simplify the expression using the given values.

2. The animal shelter orders 14 pounds of dog food for every big dog (*b*) and 11 pounds of dog food for every small dog (*s*).

expression: 14b + 11s

3. There are 15 big dogs and 6 small dogs at the shelter. How many pounds of food will the shelter order?

expression: (14 × 15) + (11 × 6)   answer: 276 pounds

Reading

Look at the photo and its caption. Then answer the item.

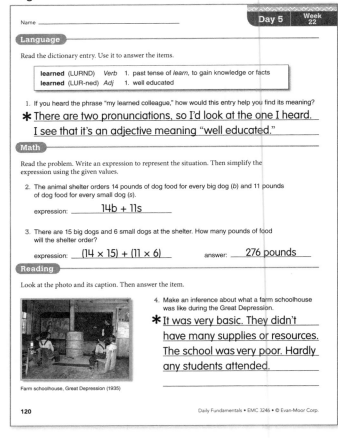

Farm schoolhouse, Great Depression (1935)

4. Make an inference about what a farm schoolhouse was like during the Great Depression.
✳ It was very basic. They didn't have many supplies or resources. The school was very poor. Hardly any students attended.

Page 121

Name _____

Day 1 | Week 23

Language

Read the sentence. Rewrite it using standard English.

1. Ms. Henderson didn't give us no homework today.
✳ Ms. Henderson didn't give us any homework today.

2. Cece never does nothing wrong in the hockey rink.
✳ Cece never does anything wrong in the hockey rink.

Math

Graph the equation on the number line.

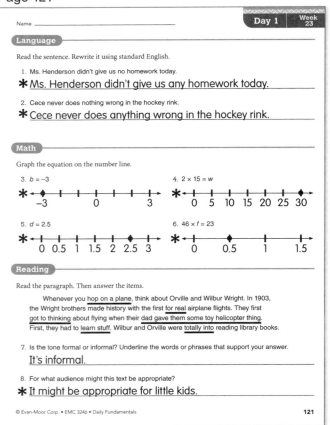

3. *b* = −3

4. 2 × 15 = *w*

5. *d* = 2.5

6. 46 × *f* = 23

Reading

Read the paragraph. Then answer the items.

Whenever you hop on a plane, think about Orville and Wilbur Wright. In 1903, the Wright brothers made history with the first real airplane flights. They first got to thinking about flying when their dad gave them some toy helicopter thing. First, they had to learn stuff. Wilbur and Orville were totally into reading library books.

7. Is the tone formal or informal? Underline the words or phrases that support your answer.
It's informal.

8. For what audience might this text be appropriate?
✳ It might be appropriate for little kids.

Page 122

Name _____

Day 2 | Week 23

Language

Read the sentence. Complete it with a word from the word box.

> a   have   of

1. You should have heard Samji laugh when he read your text!

2. Is Hoda that strong a swimmer that she can miss a week of practice?

3. There are lots of options for our science projects.

Math

Graph the inequality on the number line.

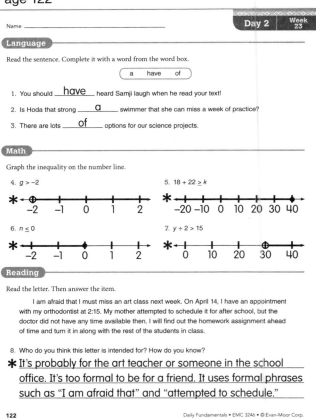

4. *g* > −2

5. 18 + 22 ≥ *k*

6. *n* ≤ 0

7. *y* ÷ 2 > 15

Reading

Read the letter. Then answer the item.

I am afraid that I must miss an art class next week. On April 14, I have an appointment with my orthodontist at 2:15. My mother attempted to schedule it for after school, but the doctor did not have any time available then. I will find out the homework assignment ahead of time and turn it in along with the rest of the students in class.

8. Who do you think this letter is intended for? How do you know?
✳ It's probably for the art teacher or someone in the school office. It's too formal to be for a friend. It uses formal phrases such as "I am afraid that" and "attempted to schedule."

Page 123

Language

Read the sentence. Rewrite it using standard English.

1. I can't hardly wait til y'all come visit us next summer!

✻ I can hardly wait until you come visit us next summer!

2. If it ain't fixing to rain soon, let's all of us go dig for clams.

✻ If it isn't going to rain soon, let's all go dig for clams.

Math

Read the situation. Then graph it on the number line.

3. There were at least 100 people in the parade.

✻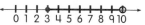
50 100 150 200 250

4. An ad for a clothing store says, "All T-shirts are under $10, some as low as $3!"

0 1 2 3 4 5 6 7 8 9 10

Reading

Read the paragraph. Then answer the item.

Graphic novels are vastly superior to regular books because the pictures are sick, plus, if kids don't comprehend a story, they can look at the pictures and enhance their understanding. Bug your school for more graphic novels!

5. Rewrite the paragraph to be appropriately formal for a newspaper's letter to the editor.

✻ Graphic novels are better than regular books because the pictures are great. If readers don't understand a story, they can use the pictures to figure it out. Ask your school for more graphic novels!

Page 124

Language

Read the sentence. Rewrite it using standard English.

1. That's what I hope is that we'll all get a part in the play.

✻ I hope that we'll all get a part in the play.

2. It's the worst possible decision is to lend Scott more money.

✻ Lending Scott more money is the worst possible decision.

Math

Read the situation. Then complete the table and graph the data.

3. Erino walks her dog 35 minutes every day. The equation below shows this relationship.

$m = 35d$

Day	Min.
1	35
2	70
3	105
4	140

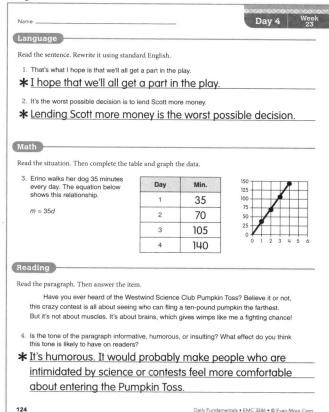

Reading

Read the paragraph. Then answer the item.

Have you ever heard of the Westwind Science Club Pumpkin Toss? Believe it or not, this crazy contest is all about seeing who can fling a ten-pound pumpkin the farthest. But it's not about muscles. It's about brains, which gives wimps like me a fighting chance!

4. Is the tone of the paragraph informative, humorous, or insulting? What effect do you think this tone is likely to have on readers?

✻ It's humorous. It would probably make people who are intimidated by science or contests feel more comfortable about entering the Pumpkin Toss.

Page 125

Language

Read the letter to a school principal. Make the formality appropriate by crossing out and rewriting words as needed.

✻ 1.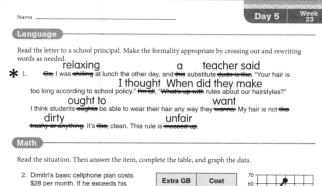
So, I was chilling at lunch the other day, and this substitute dude is like, "Your hair is too long according to school policy." I'm all, "What's up with rules about our hairstyles?" I think students oughta be able to wear their hair any way they wanna. My hair is not like trashy or anything. It's like, clean. This rule is messed up.

Math

Read the situation. Then answer the item, complete the table, and graph the data.

2. Dimitri's basic cellphone plan costs $28 per month. If he exceeds his data limit, he is charged an extra $12 per gigabyte. Write an equation to represent this situation.

c = 28 + 12g

Extra GB	Cost
0	28
1	40
2	52
3	64

Reading

Read the paragraph. Then answer the item.

The North Street railroad crossing has been a problem for years. Why on earth did they build a new ball field next to it? What a lame idea! This crossing has no barriers to prevent someone from being on the track when a train is coming. What were they thinking? The city is just asking for trouble. Either close the ball field or put up a barrier.

3. How would you describe the tone of this text? What kind of tone might be more effective?

✻ It's a complaining tone. It should be more helpful and more factual. It should give suggestions and support for the suggestions, not imply the city is dumb.

Page 126

Language

Read the roots and definitions in the word box. Use them to write a definition of each word.

flex = bend   schola = school

1. flexible: able to bend

✻ _____

2. scholar: someone who
✻ goes to school

Math

Find the area of the quadrilateral using the formula $A = bh$.

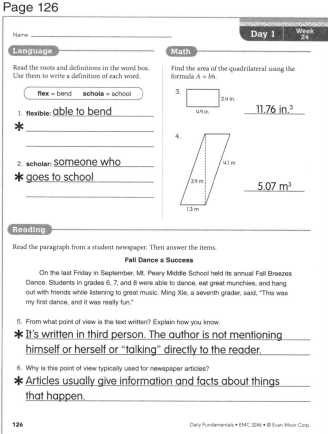

3. 11.76 in.³

4. 5.07 m³

Reading

Read the paragraph from a student newspaper. Then answer the items.

Fall Dance a Success

On the last Friday in September, Mt. Peary Middle School held its annual Fall Breezes Dance. Students in grades 6, 7, and 8 were able to dance, eat great munchies, and hang out with friends while listening to great music. Ming Xie, a seventh grader, said, "This was my first dance, and it was really fun."

5. From what point of view is the text written? Explain how you know.

✻ It's written in third person. The author is not mentioning himself or herself or "talking" directly to the reader.

6. Why is this point of view typically used for newspaper articles?

✻ Articles usually give information and facts about things that happen.

Page 127

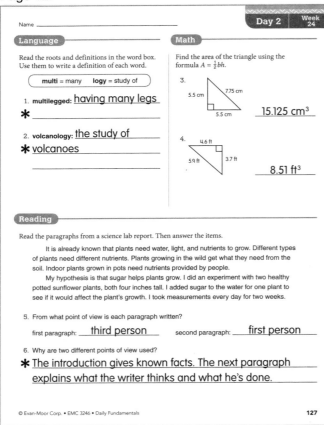

Day 2 — Week 24

Name _____

Language

Read the roots and definitions in the word box. Use them to write a definition of each word.

| multi = many | logy = study of |

1. **multilegged:** having many legs ✳

2. **volcanology:** the study of volcanoes ✳

Math

Find the area of the triangle using the formula $A = \frac{1}{2}bh$.

3. 5.5 cm, 7.75 cm, 5.5 cm → 15.125 cm³

4. 4.6 ft, 5.9 ft, 3.7 ft → 8.51 ft³

Reading

Read the paragraphs from a science lab report. Then answer the items.

It is already known that plants need water, light, and nutrients to grow. Different types of plants need different nutrients. Plants growing in the wild get what they need from the soil. Indoor plants grown in pots need nutrients provided by people.

My hypothesis is that sugar helps plants grow. I did an experiment with two healthy potted sunflower plants, both four inches tall. I added sugar to the water for one plant to see if it would affect the plant's growth. I took measurements every day for two weeks.

5. From what point of view is each paragraph written?

first paragraph: third person   second paragraph: first person

6. Why are two different points of view used?

✳ The introduction gives known facts. The next paragraph explains what the writer thinks and what he's done.

© Evan-Moor Corp. • EMC 3246 • Daily Fundamentals   127

Page 128

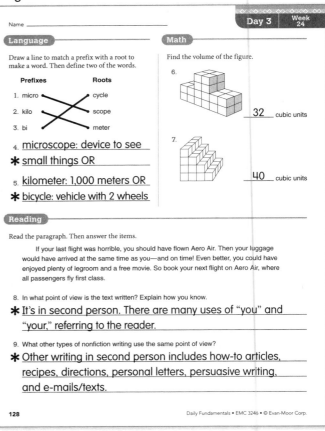

Day 3 — Week 24

Name _____

Language

Draw a line to match a prefix with a root to make a word. Then define two of the words.

Prefixes   Roots
1. micro   cycle
2. kilo   scope
3. bi   meter

4. microscope: device to see small things OR ✳

5. kilometer: 1,000 meters OR ✳

6. bicycle: vehicle with 2 wheels ✳

Math

Find the volume of the figure.

6. 32 cubic units

7. 40 cubic units

Reading

Read the paragraph. Then answer the items.

If your last flight was horrible, you should have flown Aero Air. Then your luggage would have arrived at the same time as you—and on time! Even better, you could have enjoyed plenty of legroom and a free movie. So book your next flight on Aero Air, where all passengers fly first class.

8. In what point of view is the text written? Explain how you know.

✳ It's in second person. There are many uses of "you" and "your," referring to the reader.

9. What other types of nonfiction writing use the same point of view?

✳ Other writing in second person includes how-to articles, recipes, directions, personal letters, persuasive writing, and e-mails/texts.

128   Daily Fundamentals • EMC 3246 • © Evan-Moor Corp.

Page 129

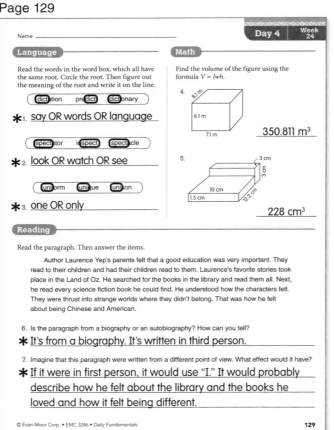

Day 4 — Week 24

Name _____

Language

Read the words in the word box, which all have the same root. Circle the root. Then figure out the meaning of the root and write it on the line.

dictation   predict   dictionary

✳1. say OR words OR language

spectator   inspect   spectacle

✳2. look OR watch OR see

uniform   unique   unison

✳3. one OR only

Math

Find the volume of the figure using the formula $V = lwh$.

4. 8.1 m, 6.1 m, 7.1 m → 350.811 m³

5. 3 cm, 3 cm, 10 cm, 1.5 cm, 12.2 cm → 228 cm³

Reading

Read the paragraph. Then answer the items.

Author Laurence Yep's parents felt that a good education was very important. They read to their children and had their children read to them. Laurence's favorite stories took place in the Land of Oz. He searched for the books in the library and read them all. Next, he read every science fiction book he could find. He understood how the characters felt. They were thrust into strange worlds where they didn't belong. That was how he felt about being Chinese and American.

6. Is the paragraph from a biography or an autobiography? How can you tell?

✳ It's from a biography. It's written in third person.

7. Imagine that this paragraph were written from a different point of view. What effect would it have?

✳ If it were in first person, it would use "I." It would probably describe how he felt about the library and the books he loved and how it felt being different.

© Evan-Moor Corp. • EMC 3246 • Daily Fundamentals   129

Page 130

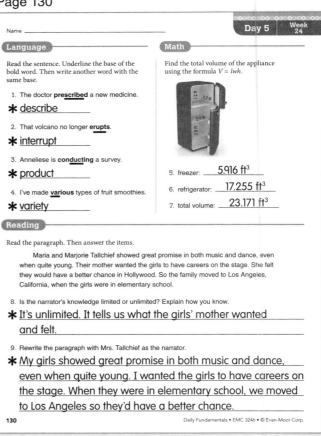

Day 5 — Week 24

Name _____

Language

Read the sentence. Underline the base of the bold word. Then write another word with the same base.

1. The doctor **prescribed** a new medicine.
✳ describe

2. That volcano no longer **erupts**.
✳ interrupt

3. Anneliese is **conducting** a survey.
✳ product

4. I've made **various** types of fruit smoothies.
✳ variety

Math

Find the total volume of the appliance using the formula $V = lwh$.

5. freezer: 5.916 ft³

6. refrigerator: 17.255 ft³

7. total volume: 23.171 ft³

Reading

Read the paragraph. Then answer the items.

Maria and Marjorie Tallchief showed great promise in both music and dance, even when quite young. Their mother wanted the girls to have careers on the stage. She felt they would have a better chance in Hollywood. So the family moved to Los Angeles, California, when the girls were in elementary school.

8. Is the narrator's knowledge limited or unlimited? Explain how you know.

✳ It's unlimited. It tells us what the girls' mother wanted and felt.

9. Rewrite the paragraph with Mrs. Tallchief as the narrator.

✳ My girls showed great promise in both music and dance, even when quite young. I wanted the girls to have careers on the stage. When they were in elementary school, we moved to Los Angeles so they'd have a better chance.

130   Daily Fundamentals • EMC 3246 • © Evan-Moor Corp.

Page 131

Name _____

Day 1 | Week 25

Language

Read the paragraph. Write the name of the type of figurative language above each underlined part.

1. As Stormalong neared the English Channel, he remarked, "It's the size of a
    hyperbole
    personification
    plastic straw!" The ship groaned as it began to squeeze through the narrow passageway.

    "Round up all the soap you can find," Stormalong bellowed. "Soap the sides of the ship.
    simile   *metaphor*
    I want to see suds as thick as whale blubber." After the crew used up every sliver of soap,

    the ship slid right through, leaving a clean channel in its wake.

Math

Plot the points on the coordinate grid and connect them.
Then answer the item.

2. (–3, 5)   (–3, –4)

    (2, 3)   (2, –2)

3. What shape did you draw?

    trapezoid

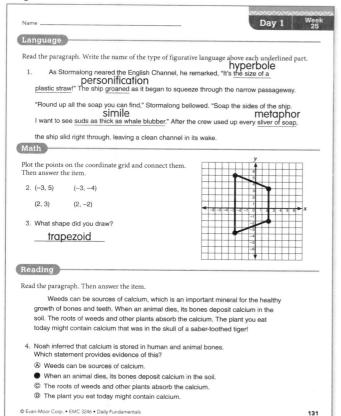

Reading

Read the paragraph. Then answer the item.

Weeds can be sources of calcium, which is an important mineral for the healthy growth of bones and teeth. When an animal dies, its bones deposit calcium in the soil. The roots of weeds and other plants absorb the calcium. The plant you eat today might contain calcium that was in the skull of a saber-toothed tiger!

4. Noah inferred that calcium is stored in human and animal bones. Which statement provides evidence of this?
    Ⓐ Weeds can be sources of calcium.
    ● When an animal dies, its bones deposit calcium in the soil.
    Ⓒ The roots of weeds and other plants absorb the calcium.
    Ⓓ The plant you eat today might contain calcium.

Page 132

Name _____

Day 2 | Week 25

Language

Read the sentence. Then answer the item.

Randy was as scared as a worm in a bird's nest.

1. Why is this simile effective? _It lets the readers visualize how scared_
    ✳ _he is. They can "see" a worm in a bird's nest and imagine._

2. Write a sentence containing a simile.
    ✳ _Meg's hands were as dry as Sahara sand._

Math

Use the coordinate grid to answer the items.

3. Draw a square on the coordinate grid using
    ✳ the point given as one vertex.

4. Write the coordinates of each vertex.
    ✳ _(–5, 3)_   _(–1, 3)_
    _(–5, –1)_   _(–1, –1)_

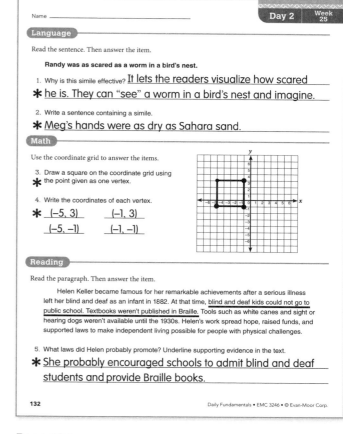

Reading

Read the paragraph. Then answer the item.

Helen Keller became famous for her remarkable achievements after a serious illness left her blind and deaf as an infant in 1882. At that time, blind and deaf kids could not go to public school. Textbooks weren't published in Braille. Tools such as white canes and sight or hearing dogs weren't available until the 1930s. Helen's work spread hope, raised funds, and supported laws to make independent living possible for people with physical challenges.

5. What laws did Helen probably promote? Underline supporting evidence in the text.
    ✳ _She probably encouraged schools to admit blind and deaf_
    students and provide Braille books.

Page 133

Name _____

Day 3 | Week 25

Language

Read the sentence. Then answer the item.

Following the scandal, Mr. Ito's political opponent sailed ahead at the ballot box.

1. Why is this metaphor effective? _It lets the reader compare running for_
    ✳ _office to the image of moving smoothly in a boat race._

2. Write a sentence containing a metaphor.
    ✳ _Mr. Parks is the heart of my school's sports program._

Math

Plot the points on the coordinate grid and connect them.
Then answer the items.

3. (–2, 4)   (–2, 3)   (5, –4)

    (2, 3)   (2, –4)   (5, 4)

4. What is the perimeter of the figure?

    30 units

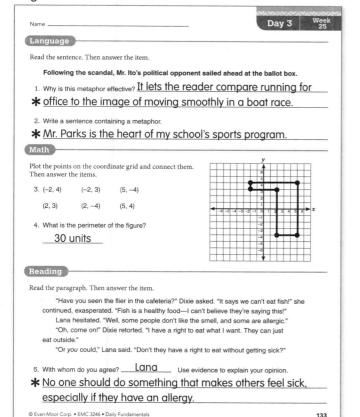

Reading

Read the paragraph. Then answer the item.

"Have you seen the flier in the cafeteria?" Dixie asked. "It says we can't eat fish!" she continued, exasperated. "Fish is a healthy food—I can't believe they're saying this!"
Lana hesitated. "Well, some people don't like the smell, and some are allergic."
"Oh, come on!" Dixie retorted. "I have a right to eat what I want. They can just eat outside."
"Or *you* could," Lana said. "Don't they have a right to eat without getting sick?"

5. With whom do you agree? _Lana_ Use evidence to explain your opinion.
    ✳ _No one should do something that makes others feel sick,_
    especially if they have an allergy.

Page 134

Name _____

Day 4 | Week 25

Language

Read the sentence. Then answer the item.

After I take this test, I want to sleep for five days!

1. Why is the underlined part hyperbole? _It's exaggeration. No one would_
    ✳ _really need to sleep for that long._

2. When can hyperbole be used?
    ✳ _It can be used in a humorous story or informal writing._

Math

Use the coordinate grid to answer the item.

✳ 3. Draw a polygon with a perimeter
    of 38 units.

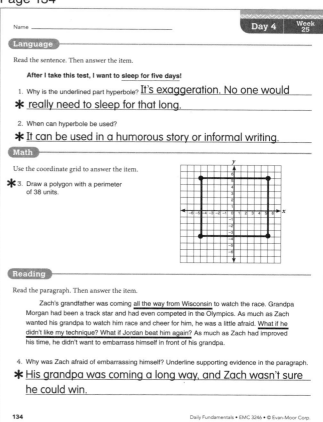

Reading

Read the paragraph. Then answer the item.

Zach's grandfather was coming all the way from Wisconsin to watch the race. Grandpa Morgan had been a track star and had even competed in the Olympics. As much as Zach wanted his grandpa to watch him race and cheer for him, he was a little afraid. What if he didn't like my technique? What if Jordan beat him again? As much as Zach had improved his time, he didn't want to embarrass himself in front of his grandpa.

4. Why was Zach afraid of embarrassing himself? Underline supporting evidence in the paragraph.
    ✳ _His grandpa was coming a long way, and Zach wasn't sure_
    he could win.

✱ These answers will vary. Examples are given.

Page 135

Name _____

Day 5 | Week 25

Language

Read the sentence. Then answer the item.

After record highs, the temperature dove into the mid-forties.

1. Why is this personification effective? ✱ <u>It implies that the temperature went down fast and far, but it's a much simpler way of saying it.</u>

2. Write a sentence using personification.
✱ <u>Nadine painted her room a color that screamed for attention.</u>

Math

Use the coordinate map to answer the items. Each line represents a street, and each square is a block.

3. Melina starts at her apartment (point A) and walks to the bank (point B), to city hall (point C), and to the deli (point D). Draw the shortest route she could take, staying on streets. ✱

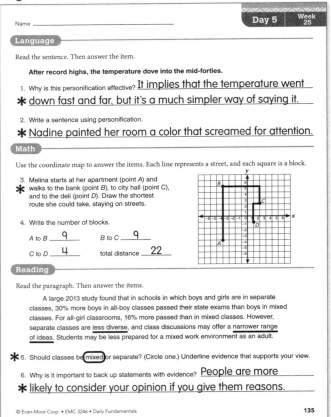

4. Write the number of blocks.

A to B __9__   B to C __9__
C to D __4__   total distance __22__

Reading

Read the paragraph. Then answer the items.

A large 2013 study found that in schools in which boys and girls are in separate classes, 30% more boys in all-boy classes passed their state exams than boys in mixed classes. For all-girl classrooms, 16% more passed than in mixed classes. However, separate classes are <u>less diverse</u>, and class discussions may offer a <u>narrower range of ideas</u>. Students may be less prepared for a mixed work environment as an adult.

✱ 5. Should classes be (mixed) or separate? (Circle one.) Underline evidence that supports your view.

6. Why is it important to back up statements with evidence? <u>People are more</u> ✱ <u>likely to consider your opinion if you give them reasons.</u>

© Evan-Moor Corp. • EMC 3246 • Daily Fundamentals   135

Page 136

Name _____

Day 1 | Week 26

Language

Read the sentence. Then add punctuation to set off the nonrestrictive element.

1. My music teacher, Ms. Crawford, is lending me a bassoon.

2. She introduced me to the other bassoonist, Margie Wilke.

3. I recently found out that my father's only brother, David, played this instrument.

4. It would be wonderful if our family, the Mullers, continued the tradition.

Math

Use the figure to answer the item.

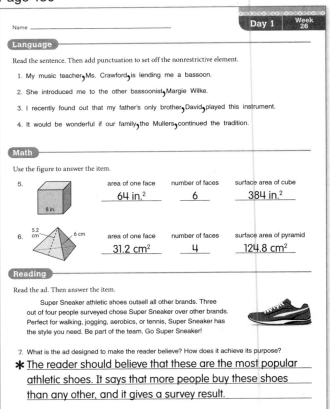

5.
area of one face __64 in.²__   number of faces __6__   surface area of cube __384 in.²__

6.
area of one face __31.2 cm²__   number of faces __4__   surface area of pyramid __124.8 cm²__

Reading

Read the ad. Then answer the item.

Super Sneaker athletic shoes outsell all other brands. Three out of four people surveyed chose Super Sneaker over other brands. Perfect for walking, jogging, aerobics, or tennis, Super Sneaker has the style you need. Be part of the team. Go Super Sneaker!

7. What is the ad designed to make the reader believe? How does it achieve its purpose?
✱ <u>The reader should believe that these are the most popular athletic shoes. It says that more people buy these shoes than any other, and it gives a survey result.</u>

136   Daily Fundamentals • EMC 3246 • © Evan-Moor Corp.

Page 137

Name _____

Day 2 | Week 26

Language

Read the sentence. Then add punctuation to set off the nonrestrictive element.

1. George Washington, the first U.S. president, liked ice cream.

2. He treated Sweet Lips, one of his hunting dogs, like family.

3. Martha, George's wife, had two children from a previous marriage.

4. He was president before Washington, D.C., the nation's capital, was founded.

Math

Use the figure to answer the item.

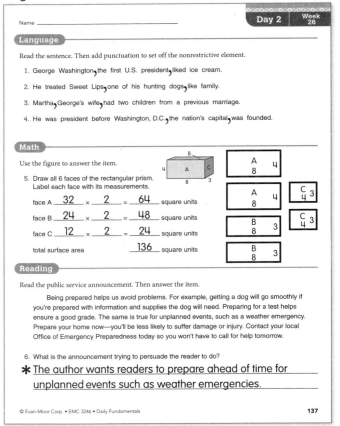

5. Draw all 6 faces of the rectangular prism. Label each face with its measurements.

face A __32__ × __2__ = __64__ square units
face B __24__ × __2__ = __48__ square units
face C __12__ × __2__ = __24__ square units
total surface area __136__ square units

Reading

Read the public service announcement. Then answer the item.

Being prepared helps us avoid problems. For example, getting a dog will go smoothly if you're prepared with information and supplies the dog will need. Preparing for a test helps ensure a good grade. The same is true for unplanned events, such as a weather emergency. Prepare your home now—you'll be less likely to suffer damage or injury. Contact your local Office of Emergency Preparedness today so you won't have to call for help tomorrow.

6. What is the announcement trying to persuade the reader to do?
✱ <u>The author wants readers to prepare ahead of time for unplanned events such as weather emergencies.</u>

© Evan-Moor Corp. • EMC 3246 • Daily Fundamentals   137

Page 138

Name _____

Day 3 | Week 26

Language

Read the sentence. Then add punctuation to set off the nonrestrictive element.

1. The school bus, which usually arrives at 7:55, was late today.

2. After school, I go to the library, which is near my mom's job.

3. I'll stay after school when training starts for my favorite sport, which is baseball.

4. The baseball coach, who lives next door to me, drives me home after practice.

Math

Use the figure to answer the item.

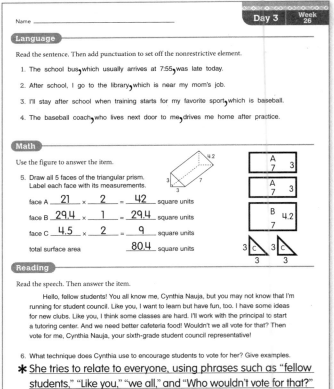

5. Draw all 5 faces of the triangular prism. Label each face with its measurements.

face A __21__ × __2__ = __42__ square units
face B __29.4__ × __1__ = __29.4__ square units
face C __4.5__ × __2__ = __9__ square units
total surface area __80.4__ square units

Reading

Read the speech. Then answer the item.

Hello, fellow students! You all know me, Cynthia Nauja, but you may not know that I'm running for student council. Like you, I want to learn but have fun, too. I have some ideas for new clubs. Like you, I think some classes are hard. I'll work with the principal to start a tutoring center. And we need better cafeteria food! Wouldn't we all vote for that? Then vote for me, Cynthia Nauja, your sixth-grade student council representative!

6. What technique does Cynthia use to encourage students to vote for her? Give examples.
✱ <u>She tries to relate to everyone, using phrases such as "fellow students," "Like you," "we all," and "Who wouldn't vote for that?"</u>

138   Daily Fundamentals • EMC 3246 • © Evan-Moor Corp.

Page 139

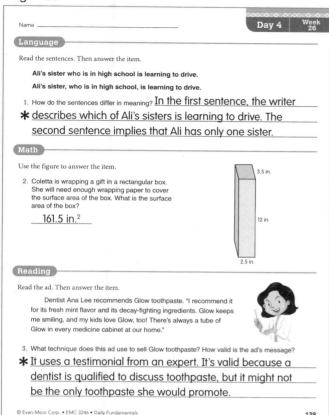

Name _____

Day 4 | Week 26

Language

Read the sentences. Then answer the item.

Ali's sister who is in high school is learning to drive.

Ali's sister, who is in high school, is learning to drive.

1. How do the sentences differ in meaning? In the first sentence, the writer

✳ describes which of Ali's sisters is learning to drive. The

second sentence implies that Ali has only one sister.

Math

Use the figure to answer the item.

2. Coletta is wrapping a gift in a rectangular box. She will need enough wrapping paper to cover the surface area of the box. What is the surface area of the box?

161.5 in.²

3.5 in.
12 in.
2.5 in.

Reading

Read the ad. Then answer the item.

Dentist Ana Lee recommends Glow toothpaste. "I recommend it for its fresh mint flavor and its decay-fighting ingredients. Glow keeps me smiling, and my kids love Glow, too! There's always a tube of Glow in every medicine cabinet at our home."

3. What technique does this ad use to sell Glow toothpaste? How valid is the ad's message?

✳ It uses a testimonial from an expert. It's valid because a

dentist is qualified to discuss toothpaste, but it might not

be the only toothpaste she would promote.

Page 140

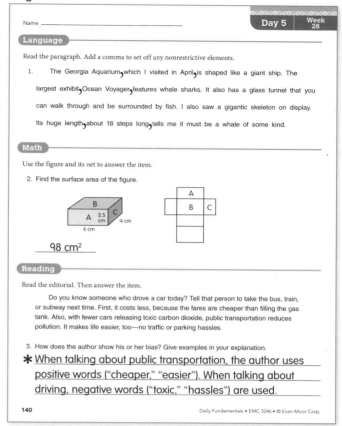

Name _____

Day 5 | Week 26

Language

Read the paragraph. Add a comma to set off any nonrestrictive elements.

1. The Georgia Aquarium, which I visited in April, is shaped like a giant ship. The largest exhibit, Ocean Voyager, features whale sharks. It also has a glass tunnel that you can walk through and be surrounded by fish. I also saw a gigantic skeleton on display. Its huge length, about 18 steps long, tells me it must be a whale of some kind.

Math

Use the figure and its net to answer the item.

2. Find the surface area of the figure.

B
A 2.5 cm C
6 cm   4 cm

A
B C

98 cm²

Reading

Read the editorial. Then answer the item.

Do you know someone who drove a car today? Tell that person to take the bus, train, or subway next time. First, it costs less, because the fares are cheaper than filling the gas tank. Also, with fewer cars releasing toxic carbon dioxide, public transportation reduces pollution. It makes life easier, too—no traffic or parking hassles.

3. How does the author show his or her bias? Give examples in your explanation.

✳ When talking about public transportation, the author uses

positive words ("cheaper," "easier"). When talking about

driving, negative words ("toxic," "hassles") are used.

Page 141

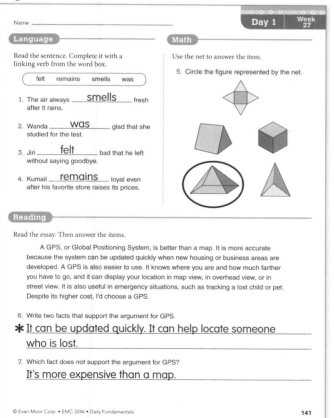

Name _____

Day 1 | Week 27

Language

Read the sentence. Complete it with a linking verb from the word box.

[felt   remains   smells   was]

1. The air always ___smells___ fresh after it rains.

2. Wanda ___was___ glad that she studied for the test.

3. Jiri ___felt___ bad that he left without saying goodbye.

4. Kumail ___remains___ loyal even after his favorite store raises its prices.

Math

Use the net to answer the item.

5. Circle the figure represented by the net.

Reading

Read the essay. Then answer the items.

A GPS, or Global Positioning System, is better than a map. It is more accurate because the system can be updated quickly when new housing or business areas are developed. A GPS is also easier to use. It knows where you are and how much farther you have to go, and it can display your location in map view, in overhead view, or in street view. It is also useful in emergency situations, such as tracking a lost child or pet. Despite its higher cost, I'd choose a GPS.

6. Write two facts that support the argument for GPS.

✳ It can be updated quickly. It can help locate someone

who is lost.

7. Which fact does *not* support the argument for GPS?

It's more expensive than a map.

Page 142

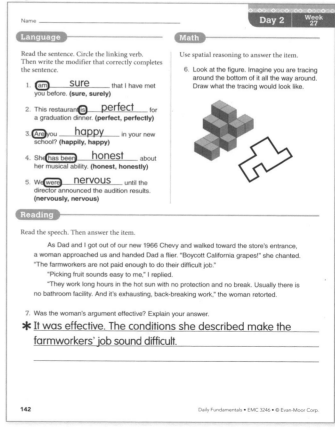

Name _____

Day 2 | Week 27

Language

Read the sentence. Circle the linking verb. Then write the modifier that correctly completes the sentence.

1. (am) ___sure___ that I have met you before. (sure, surely)

2. This restaurant (is) ___perfect___ for a graduation dinner. (perfect, perfectly)

3. (Are) you ___happy___ in your new school? (happily, happy)

4. She (has been) ___honest___ about her musical ability. (honest, honestly)

5. We (were) ___nervous___ until the director announced the audition results. (nervously, nervous)

Math

Use spatial reasoning to answer the item.

6. Look at the figure. Imagine you are tracing around the bottom of it all the way around. Draw what the tracing would look like.

Reading

Read the speech. Then answer the item.

As Dad and I got out of our new 1966 Chevy and walked toward the store's entrance, a woman approached us and handed Dad a flier. "Boycott California grapes!" she chanted. "The farmworkers are not paid enough to do their difficult job."

"Picking fruit sounds easy to me," I replied.

"They work long hours in the hot sun with no protection and no break. Usually there is no bathroom facility. And it's exhausting, back-breaking work," the woman retorted.

7. Was the woman's argument effective? Explain your answer.

✳ It was effective. The conditions she described make the

farmworkers' job sound difficult.

These answers will vary. Examples are given.

Page 143

Name _____

Day 3 | **Week 27**

Language

Read the sentence. Circle the linking verb. Then choose the best modifier from the word box to complete the sentence.

correct	sour	calmly
sickly	wrongly	tired
sweetly	different	similarly

1. The children (felt) __tired__ after school.

2. This lemonade (tastes) too __sour__.

3. Tory's voice (sounded) __different__ on the phone.

4. Does the grammar in this sentence (look) __correct__ to you?

Math

Use spatial reasoning to solve the item.

4. Look at the figure shown. Imagine you are looking at it straight on from the left side. Draw what you would see.

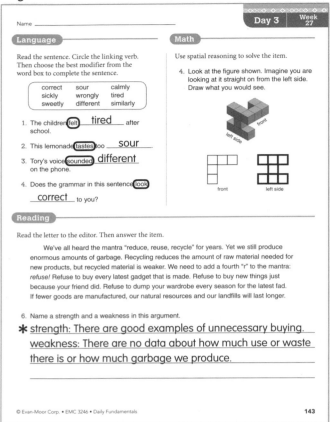

Reading

Read the letter to the editor. Then answer the item.

We've all heard the mantra "reduce, reuse, recycle" for years. Yet we still produce enormous amounts of garbage. Recycling reduces the amount of raw material needed for new products, but recycled material is weaker. We need to add a fourth "r" to the mantra: *refuse!* Refuse to buy every latest gadget that is made. Refuse to buy new things just because your friend did. Refuse to dump your wardrobe every season for the latest fad. If fewer goods are manufactured, our natural resources and our landfills will last longer.

6. Name a strength and a weakness in this argument.

*strength: There are good examples of unnecessary buying. weakness: There are no data about how much use or waste there is or how much garbage we produce.

© Evan-Moor Corp. • EMC 3246 • Daily Fundamentals   143

Page 144

Name _____

Day 4 | **Week 27**

Language

Read the sentence. If a word needs to be changed, cross it out and write the correct word above it.

1. Shani and her cousin from the East Coast became ~~closely~~ **close** last summer.

2. Miguel's cat seemed ~~nicely~~ **nice** until Miguel left the room.

3. The apartment complex appears ~~attractively~~ **attractive** from the outside.

4. The night grew ~~coldly~~ **cold**, with the temperature dropping 40 degrees.

Math

Use spatial reasoning to answer the item.

5. The distance around the whole circle is 24 cm. Estimate the distance from point A to point B.

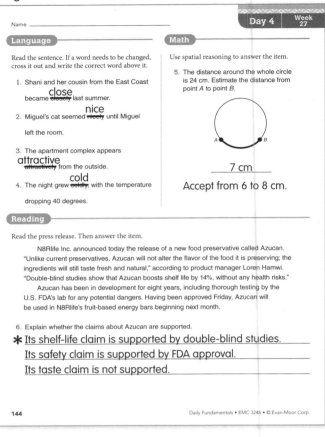

__7 cm__

Accept from 6 to 8 cm.

Reading

Read the press release. Then answer the item.

N8Rlife Inc. announced today the release of a new food preservative called Azucan. "Unlike current preservatives, Azucan will not alter the flavor of the food it is preserving; the ingredients will still taste fresh and natural," according to product manager Loren Hamwi. "Double-blind studies show that Azucan boosts shelf life by 14%, without any health risks."

Azucan has been in development for eight years, including thorough testing by the U.S. FDA's lab for any potential dangers. Having been approved Friday, Azucan will be used in N8Rlife's fruit-based energy bars beginning next month.

6. Explain whether the claims about Azucan are supported.

*Its shelf-life claim is supported by double-blind studies. Its safety claim is supported by FDA approval. Its taste claim is not supported.

144   Daily Fundamentals • EMC 3246 • © Evan-Moor Corp.

Page 145

Name _____

Day 5 | **Week 27**

Language

Write three sentences using a linking verb from the word box and an adjective in each.

| seem | feel | stay | turn |

*1. Jane stayed strong after she heard the bad news.

*2. The weather turned warm for one week in October.

*3. The neighborhood seemed peaceful when we moved in.

Math

Use spatial reasoning to answer the item.

4. The circle graph shows the proportion of students at Northmont Middle School who take a music class. At Southmont, 3 times as many students take a music class. Draw and shade this amount on the second circle graph.

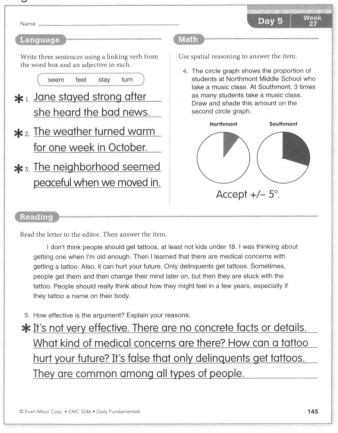

Northmont   Southmont

Accept +/– 5°.

Reading

Read the letter to the editor. Then answer the item.

I don't think people should get tattoos, at least not kids under 18. I was thinking about getting one when I'm old enough. Then I learned that there are medical concerns with getting a tattoo. Also, it can hurt your future. Only delinquents get tattoos. Sometimes, people get them and then change their mind later on, but then they are stuck with the tattoo. People should really think about how they might feel in a few years, especially if they tattoo a name on their body.

5. How effective is the argument? Explain your reasons.

*It's not very effective. There are no concrete facts or details. What kind of medical concerns are there? How can a tattoo hurt your future? It's false that only delinquents get tattoos. They are common among all types of people.

© Evan-Moor Corp. • EMC 3246 • Daily Fundamentals   145

Page 146

Name _____

Day 1 | **Week 28**

Language

Read the sentence. Use context to figure out the meaning of the underlined word. Then match the sentence to the correct word meaning.

1. Ty <u>devotes</u> a lot to his garden, spending hours there daily.

2. Sana attended college, which <u>propelled</u> her career.

3. The two rival teams have been <u>feuding</u> for decades.

4. Dad <u>vetoed</u> my idea, refusing to even listen to my reasons.

to fight for a long time

to commit or give

to reject or prohibit

to push forward

Math

Find the mean of the data set.

5. test scores: 91, 88, 93, 79, 84   __87__

6. ages of parents: 36, 40, 39, 38, 41, 39, 33   __38__

7. books read: 11, 3, 4, 8, 6, 4   __6__

Reading

Read the paragraph. Then answer the item.

Brief exposure to the sun allows our bodies to produce vitamin D. This essential vitamin can help prevent certain diseases and promotes bone growth. Just 10 to 20 minutes of sun each day can protect you. However, the sun can also cause wrinkles, skin cancer, and cataracts in the eyes.

8. Which of the following is a valid conclusion?

Ⓐ The sun affects different people differently.

Ⓑ The sun's benefits outweigh the risks.

Ⓒ People should avoid being in the sun.

● Exposure to the sun should be limited.

146   Daily Fundamentals • EMC 3246 • © Evan-Moor Corp.

These answers will vary. Examples are given.

Page 147

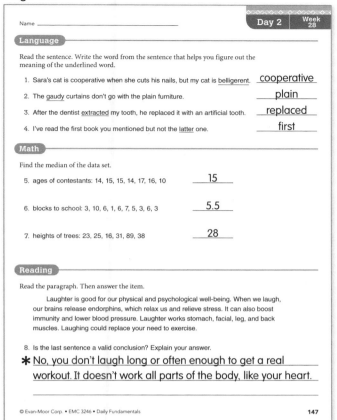

Name _____ Day 2 | Week 28

Language

Read the sentence. Write the word from the sentence that helps you figure out the meaning of the underlined word.

1. Sara's cat is cooperative when she cuts his nails, but my cat is belligerent. *cooperative*

2. The gaudy curtains don't go with the plain furniture. *plain*

3. After the dentist extracted my tooth, he replaced it with an artificial tooth. *replaced*

4. I've read the first book you mentioned but not the latter one. *first*

Math

Find the median of the data set.

5. ages of contestants: 14, 15, 15, 14, 17, 16, 10 *15*

6. blocks to school: 3, 10, 6, 1, 6, 7, 5, 3, 6, 3 *5.5*

7. heights of trees: 23, 25, 16, 31, 89, 38 *28*

Reading

Read the paragraph. Then answer the item.

Laughter is good for our physical and psychological well-being. When we laugh, our brains release endorphins, which relax us and relieve stress. It can also boost immunity and lower blood pressure. Laughter works stomach, facial, leg, and back muscles. Laughing could replace your need to exercise.

8. Is the last sentence a valid conclusion? Explain your answer.

* *No, you don't laugh long or often enough to get a real workout. It doesn't work all parts of the body, like your heart.*

147

Page 148

Name _____ Day 3 | Week 28

Language

Read the sentence. Then answer the item.

A bird's unique anatomy, including its beak, highly flexible neck, and hollow bones, helps it eat, groom itself, and fly.

* 1. Write the meaning of the underlined word. *It means "body" or "structure."*

2. Explain how context in the given sentence helped you figure out the word's meaning.

* *A beak, neck, and bones are all parts of a bird's body.*

Math

Find the mode of the data set.

3. shoe sizes: 3, 5, 4, 4, 7, 5, 6, 4, 5, 2 *4*

4. textbooks used in a year: 5, 7, 5, 4, 5, 6, 6, 4, 5 *5*

5. rooms in a house: 6, 6, 7, 5, 8, 4, 6, 5, 5, 8, 6 *6*

Reading

Read the paragraph. Then answer the item.

Cars need electricity to power headlights and radios, but those things don't make the car run. More importantly, gasoline engines need a constant supply of electric sparks, which ignite tiny controlled explosions that power the cars. When electromagnets spin around in engines, they make electricity. This electricity is used to power many things, including the plugs that create sparks.

6. Write a conclusion based on the information in the text.

* *Traveling would be much more difficult without electricity.*

148

Page 149

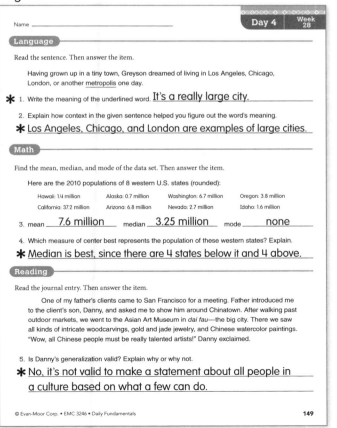

Name _____ Day 4 | Week 28

Language

Read the sentence. Then answer the item.

Having grown up in a tiny town, Greyson dreamed of living in Los Angeles, Chicago, London, or another metropolis one day.

* 1. Write the meaning of the underlined word. *It's a really large city.*

2. Explain how context in the given sentence helped you figure out the word's meaning.

* *Los Angeles, Chicago, and London are examples of large cities.*

Math

Find the mean, median, and mode of the data set. Then answer the item.

Here are the 2010 populations of 8 western U.S. states (rounded):

Hawaii: 1.4 million   Alaska: 0.7 million   Washington: 6.7 million   Oregon: 3.8 million
California: 37.2 million   Arizona: 6.8 million   Nevada: 2.7 million   Idaho: 1.6 million

3. mean *7.6 million*   median *3.25 million*   mode *none*

4. Which measure of center best represents the population of these western states? Explain.

* *Median is best, since there are 4 states below it and 4 above.*

Reading

Read the journal entry. Then answer the item.

One of my father's clients came to San Francisco for a meeting. Father introduced me to the client's son, Danny, and asked me to show him around Chinatown. After walking past outdoor markets, we went to the Asian Art Museum in dai fau—the big city. There we saw all kinds of intricate woodcarvings, gold and jade jewelry, and Chinese watercolor paintings. "Wow, all Chinese people must be really talented artists!" Danny exclaimed.

5. Is Danny's generalization valid? Explain why or why not.

* *No, it's not valid to make a statement about all people in a culture based on what a few can do.*

149

Page 150

Name _____ Day 5 | Week 28

Language

Read the sentence. Use context to figure out what the underlined word means. Then write a new sentence using the underlined word.

1. The judges made a unanimous decision about who won the science fair.

* *Everyone chose the same person, so the vote was unanimous.*

2. Henry doesn't seem to react to poison oak, poison ivy, or any other allergens.

* *Pollen is a common allergen in springtime.*

Math

Read the problem. Then answer the item.

Pierre recorded the weights in pounds of each animal examined by a veterinarian on one day. His data are shown in the table.

Dogs	Cats
18	11
18	8
107	10
55	8
34	9
98	17

3. Find the mean, median, and mode for each type of animal.

dogs: mean *55*   median *44.5*   mode *18*

cats: mean *10.5*   median *9.5*   mode *8*

Reading

Read the paragraph. Then answer the item.

Imagine being locked in a crowded, sweltering room for a 12-hour shift, six days a week. In New York factories in the early 1900s, factory owners gave employees only one 30-minute break. If employees took too long in the bathroom, they were sent home without pay. They could be fired just for talking to each other or singing to themselves. At this time in history, most factory owners treated employees like equipment.

4. Which statement from the text is a generalization? Is it valid? Explain.

* *The last sentence is a valid generalization. The text gives five examples that support the generalization.*

150

© Evan-Moor Corp. • EMC 3246 • Daily Fundamentals

195

Page 151

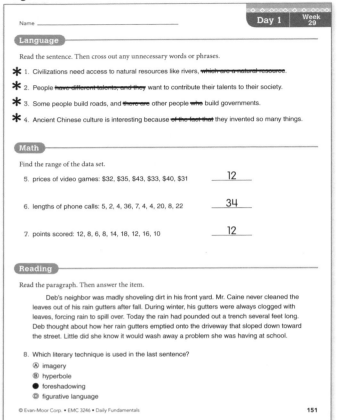

Name _____

Day 1 | Week 29

Language

Read the sentence. Then cross out any unnecessary words or phrases.

* 1. Civilizations need access to natural resources like rivers, ~~which are a natural resource~~.

* 2. People ~~have different talents, and they~~ want to contribute their talents to their society.

* 3. Some people build roads, and ~~there are~~ other people ~~who~~ build governments.

* 4. Ancient Chinese culture is interesting because ~~of the fact that~~ they invented so many things.

Math

Find the range of the data set.

5. prices of video games: $32, $35, $43, $33, $40, $31 ___12___

6. lengths of phone calls: 5, 2, 4, 36, 7, 4, 4, 20, 8, 22 ___34___

7. points scored: 12, 8, 6, 8, 14, 18, 12, 16, 10 ___12___

Reading

Read the paragraph. Then answer the item.

Deb's neighbor was madly shoveling dirt in his front yard. Mr. Caine never cleaned the leaves out of his rain gutters after fall. During winter, his gutters were always clogged with leaves, forcing rain to spill over. Today the rain had pounded out a trench several feet long. Deb thought about how her rain gutters emptied onto the driveway that sloped down toward the street. Little did she know it would wash away a problem she was having at school.

8. Which literary technique is used in the last sentence?

Ⓐ imagery
Ⓑ hyperbole
● foreshadowing
Ⓓ figurative language

© Evan-Moor Corp. • EMC 3246 • Daily Fundamentals — 151

Page 152

Name _____

Day 2 | Week 29

Language

Read the sentence. Rewrite it as a single sentence without duplicating any information.

1. Mesopotamia was an ancient culture. Mesopotamia was where Iraq is now.

* Mesopotamia, an ancient culture, was where Iraq is now.

2. The region is very fertile. The region has two large rivers. The rivers provide irrigation.

* The fertile region has two large rivers that provide irrigation.

Math

Look at the data set. Then answer the items.

high temperatures this week: 72°, 78°, 82°, 77°, 85°, 77°, 81°

3. Write the values in order from least to greatest. Circle the lowest, median, and highest values.

⑦② 77, 77,⑦⑧ 81, 82,⑧⑥

4. Find the distance from the bottom of the range to the median. ___6___

5. Find the distance from the median to the top of the range. ___8___

Reading

Read the paragraph. Then answer the item.

Everyone in Laurence's family worked in the grocery store. Laurence and his brother stocked shelves, sorted bottles, and flattened boxes. Prices needed to be marked on groceries. When the family could leave the store, they enjoyed picnics and other outdoor activities. Laurence built a sandbox on the roof of their apartment building. It was there that he first created imaginary kingdoms that would later influence his life's work.

6. What part of the text shows foreshadowing? Explain how you know.

* The last sentence contains foreshadowing. It uses "would later" and "life's work," which hint at being an adult.

152 — Daily Fundamentals • EMC 3246 • © Evan-Moor Corp.

Page 153

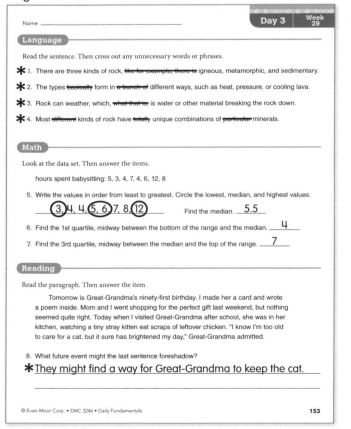

Name _____

Day 3 | Week 29

Language

Read the sentence. Then cross out any unnecessary words or phrases.

* 1. There are three kinds of rock, ~~like for example, there is~~ igneous, metamorphic, and sedimentary.

* 2. The types ~~basically~~ form in ~~a bunch of~~ different ways, such as heat, pressure, or cooling lava.

* 3. Rock can weather, which, ~~what that is,~~ is water or other material breaking the rock down.

* 4. Most ~~different~~ kinds of rock have ~~totally~~ unique combinations of ~~particular~~ minerals.

Math

Look at the data set. Then answer the items.

hours spent babysitting: 5, 3, 4, 7, 4, 6, 12, 8

5. Write the values in order from least to greatest. Circle the lowest, median, and highest values.

③ 4, 4,⑤ ⑥ 7, 8,⑫   Find the median. ___5.5___

6. Find the 1st quartile, midway between the bottom of the range and the median. ___4___

7. Find the 3rd quartile, midway between the median and the top of the range. ___7___

Reading

Read the paragraph. Then answer the item.

Tomorrow is Great-Grandma's ninety-first birthday. I made her a card and wrote a poem inside. Mom and I went shopping for the perfect gift last weekend, but nothing seemed quite right. Today when I visited Great-Grandma after school, she was in her kitchen, watching a tiny stray kitten eat scraps of leftover chicken. "I know I'm too old to care for a cat, but it sure has brightened my day," Great-Grandma admitted.

8. What future event might the last sentence foreshadow?

* They might find a way for Great-Grandma to keep the cat.

© Evan-Moor Corp. • EMC 3246 • Daily Fundamentals — 153

Page 154

Name _____

Day 4 | Week 29

Language

Read the sentence. Rewrite it, eliminating wordiness and making it concise.

1. Every single living thing has its own individual pattern that is a pattern of DNA.

* Every living thing has its own DNA pattern.

2. What DNA is, is like programming for each and every cell in your body.

* DNA is like programming for every cell in your body.

Math

Look at the data set. Then answer the items.

lengths of different whale species: 20, 110, 12, 15, 48, 59, 27, 45

3. Write the values in order from least to greatest. Circle the lowest, median, and highest values.

⑫ 15, 20,㉗ 45,⑷⑻ 59,⑴⑽   Find the median. ___36___

4. Find the 1st and 3rd quartiles: 1st quartile ___20___   3rd quartile ___48___

5. Find the interquartile range, the range between the 1st and 3rd quartiles. ___28___

Reading

Read the paragraph. Then answer the item.

The kingdom knew that King Alexander's unreasonable demands would someday make him topple from the throne; they just didn't know how literally it would happen. King Alexander wanted the moon, which he believed was filled with gold. "Bring me the wisest person in the kingdom," the king demanded of his advisor. "I'll need help if I am to reach the moon."

6. Which sentence contains foreshadowing? What future event might that sentence foreshadow?

* The first sentence contains foreshadowing. It suggests that the king will fall.

154 — Daily Fundamentals • EMC 3246 • © Evan-Moor Corp.

These answers will vary. Examples are given.

Page 155

Day 5 | Week 29

Language

Read the paragraph. Edit it, eliminating wordiness and making it concise.

✻ 1. Everyone ~~in the world~~ cries, and there are ~~quite a lot of~~ reasons ~~why~~.
many
The most obvious ~~reason is that~~ people cry if they are hurt. People also cry if they are ~~becoming~~ frustrated. ~~Maybe they're frustrated~~ with having too much work ~~to do,~~ or ~~they might be frustrated~~ if they are having an argument with ~~like,~~ a friend. Experts who study crying believe that ~~crying~~ relieves stress.
it

Math

Read the problem. Then find the values.

In Chevauton, a haircut at eight hair salons costs $35, $43, $38, $52, $47, $49, $41, and $47.

2. range __17__

3. median __45__

4. 1st and 3rd quartiles: 1st quartile __41__   3rd quartile __47__

5. interquartile range __6__

Reading

Read the paragraph. Then answer the item.

It started as an assigned research paper about the value of clean water for science class. Diego gathered a water sample from his own backyard and gave it to his cousin Sofia for testing. Sofia was taking a chemistry course at the local community college, and she gave the sample to her professor. Little did Diego know what a can of worms the results would open.

6. Which sentence contains foreshadowing? Why do you think the author used this technique?

✻ The last sentence contains foreshadowing. It creates a mystery and motivates the reader to find out more.

Page 156

Day 1 | Week 30

Language

Complete each row of the table to show different connotations of the same idea.

✻ 1.

Connotations		
Positive	Neutral	Negative
modest	quiet	**timid**
reliable	predictable	boring
innocent	inexperienced	**clueless**
economical	**thrifty**	stingy
certain	secure	egotistical

Math

Read the problem and the dot plot. Then answer the item.

A class survey asked how many bones each student had broken.

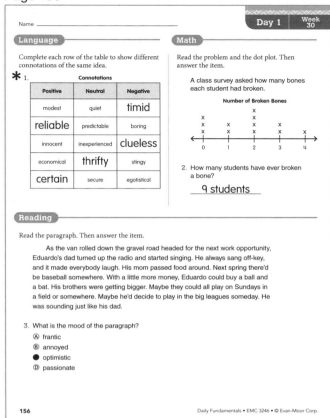

2. How many students have ever broken a bone?

__9 students__

Reading

Read the paragraph. Then answer the item.

As the van rolled down the gravel road headed for the next work opportunity, Eduardo's dad turned up the radio and started singing. He always sang off-key, and it made everybody laugh. His mom passed food around. Next spring there'd be baseball somewhere. With a little more money, Eduardo could buy a ball and a bat. His brothers were getting bigger. Maybe they could all play on Sundays in a field or somewhere. Maybe he'd decide to play in the big leagues someday. He was sounding just like his dad.

3. What is the mood of the paragraph?
Ⓐ frantic
Ⓑ annoyed
● optimistic
Ⓓ passionate

Page 157

Day 2 | Week 30

Language

Read the sentence. Complete it with a word from the word box that has the appropriate connotation.

> observed   spied   watched

1. Bryan __spied__ on his older sister as she talked on the phone, and then he repeated the conversation to their father.

2. As the moon rose, Calista __observed__ its shape and described it in her notebook.

3. The audience __watched__ the brilliant actors bring the play to life.

Math

Read the problem and the circle graph. Then answer the item.

A class survey asked favorite book genres.

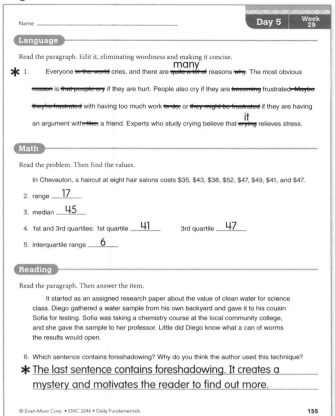

4. Write the genres in order from most to least popular.

__graphic novels, mystery, drama, humor, poetry__

Reading

Read the paragraph. Then answer the item.

As the Great Depression deepened, its effects were stamped on the faces of almost everyone; only the very young and the rich were spared. After my dad finished a government road repair project, we continued chasing the cotton harvest around Texas, as we had for the past three years. This time, however, we found that work opportunities had dried up with the land. A drought had struck with devastating results, and there were no crops to harvest.

5. What is the mood of the paragraph? What helped you figure it out?

✻ The mood is desperation. It's the Depression. Work had dried up. There was a drought, so there were no crops, no food, and no work. It was devastating.

Page 158

Day 3 | Week 30

Language

Answer the item.

1. What is the difference between these two words? When would you use *ambitious*?

pushy, ambitious

✻ "Pushy" has a negative connotation, and "ambitious" is positive. I'd use it to talk about someone I admire.

Math

Read the problem. Then answer the item.

Each week, Shineda spends 3 hours on language arts homework, 2 hours on math, 2 hours on Chinese, 2 hours on social studies, and 1 hour on science.

2. Make a circle graph to show how much time Shineda spends on each subject.

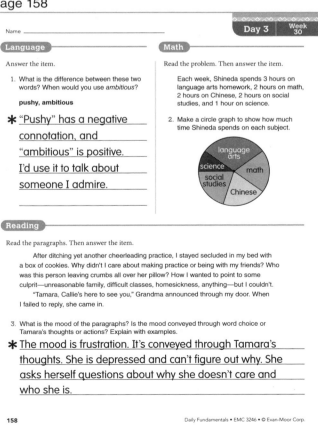

Reading

Read the paragraphs. Then answer the item.

After ditching yet another cheerleading practice, I stayed secluded in my bed with a box of cookies. Why didn't I care about making practice or being with my friends? Who was this person leaving crumbs all over her pillow? How I wanted to point to some culprit—unreasonable family, difficult classes, homesickness, anything—but I couldn't.

"Tamara, Callie's here to see you," Grandma announced through my door. When I failed to reply, she came in.

3. What is the mood of the paragraphs? Is the mood conveyed through word choice or Tamara's thoughts or actions? Explain with examples.

✻ The mood is frustration. It's conveyed through Tamara's thoughts. She is depressed and can't figure out why. She asks herself questions about why she doesn't care and who she is.

Page 159

Language

Read the sentence. Choose the best word to complete it. Then explain your choice.

1. It was ___reckless___ of you to race across the train tracks after you heard the train whistle. **(daring, gutsy, reckless)**

✱ It was careless and dangerous, all negative.

2. The fans cheered the ___stealthy___ winning play right at the end of the game. **(stealthy, devious, deceitful)**

✱ The fans had a positive impression of the play.

Math

Read the problem and the histogram. Then answer the item.

A weather report showed daily snowfall.

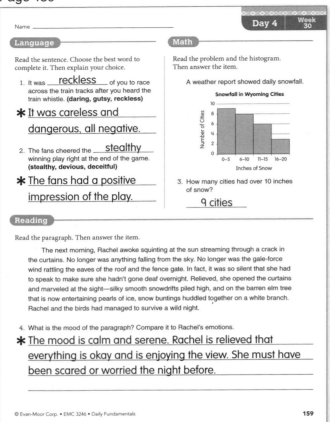

Snowfall in Wyoming Cities

3. How many cities had over 10 inches of snow?

___9 cities___

Reading

Read the paragraph. Then answer the item.

The next morning, Rachel awoke squinting at the sun streaming through a crack in the curtains. No longer was anything falling from the sky. No longer was the gale-force wind rattling the eaves of the roof and the fence gate. In fact, it was so silent that she had to speak to make sure she hadn't gone deaf overnight. Relieved, she opened the curtains and marveled at the sight—silky smooth snowdrifts piled high, and on the barren elm tree that is now entertaining pearls of ice, snow buntings huddled together on a white branch. Rachel and the birds had managed to survive a wild night.

4. What is the mood of the paragraph? Compare it to Rachel's emotions.

✱ The mood is calm and serene. Rachel is relieved that everything is okay and is enjoying the view. She must have been scared or worried the night before.

Page 160

Language

Write a sentence with the given word. Make sure the word's connotation is clear.

1. **unusual**

✱ "What an unusual gate you built," I commented, walking past the pink steel door.

2. **crazy**

✱ Friday was crazy, with 60° heat in the morning and a snowstorm in the afternoon!

Math

Read the problem. Then answer the item.

Students spent the following number of minutes exercising in one week:

| 23 | 55 | 60 | 45 | 38 | 45 | 95 |
| 110 | 90 | 120 | 48 | 60 | 75 | 82 |

3. Use the data to complete the histogram.

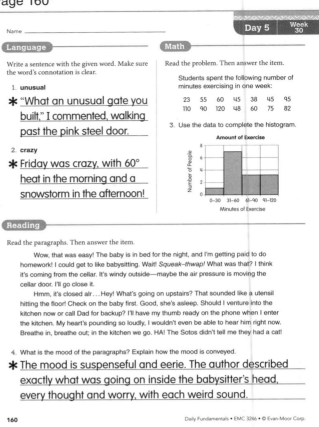

Amount of Exercise

Reading

Read the paragraphs. Then answer the item.

Wow, that was easy! The baby is in bed for the night, and I'm getting paid to do homework! I could get to like babysitting. Wait! *Squeak–thwap!* What was that? I think it's coming from the cellar. It's windy outside—maybe the air pressure is moving the cellar door. I'll go close it.

Hmm, it's closed alr . . . Hey! What's going on upstairs? That sounded like a utensil hitting the floor! Check on the baby first. Good, she's asleep. Should I venture into the kitchen now or call Dad for backup? I'll have my thumb ready on the phone when I enter the kitchen. My heart's pounding so loudly, I wouldn't even be able to hear him right now. Breathe in, breathe out; in the kitchen we go. HA! The Sotos didn't tell me they had a cat!

4. What is the mood of the paragraphs? Explain how the mood is conveyed.

✱ The mood is suspenseful and eerie. The author described exactly what was going on inside the babysitter's head, every thought and worry, with each weird sound.

Take It to Your Seat Centers

Math

Grades K–6

Independent practice, perfect for students at all levels.

Take It to Your Seat Centers: Math

Hands-on practice of core math skills! Each of the 12 centers focuses on key math concepts and presents skill practice in engaging visual and tactile activities. The easy-to-assemble centers include full-color cards and mats, directions, answer keys, and student record forms. Ideal for any classroom and to support RTI or ELLs. 160 full-color pages. Correlated to state standards and Common Core State Standards.

www.evan-moor.com/tmcent

Teacher's Edition Print		Teacher's Edition E-book	
GRADE	EMC	GRADE	EMC
K	3070	K	3070i
1	3071	1	3071i
2	3072	2	3072i
3	3073	3	3073i
4	3074	4	3074i
5	3075	5	3075i
6	3076	6	3076i

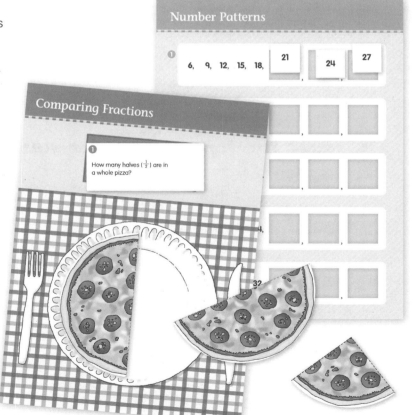

Daily Word Problems

Students' problem-solving skills improve day by day as they take part in meaningful, real-life math practice!

Grades 1–6

- Students learn to persevere in solving 180 word problems through engaging practice of meaningful, theme-based problems.

- The 36 weeks of practice activities address grade-level math concepts such as addition, fractions, logic, algebra, and more.

- Monday through Thursday activities present students with a one- or two-step word problem, while Friday's format is more extensive and requires multiple steps.

Correlated to state standards and Common Core State Standards.

www.evan-moor.com/dwp

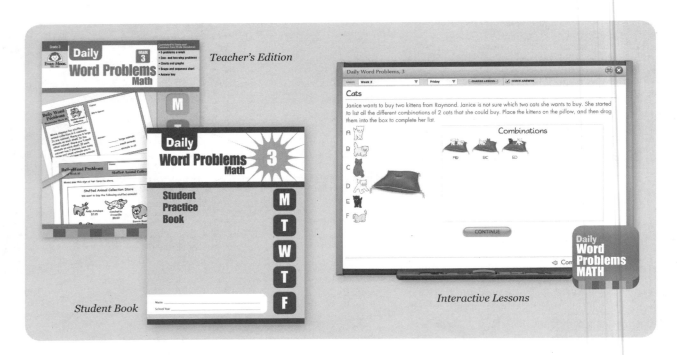

Teacher's Edition

Student Book

Interactive Lessons

Order the format right for you

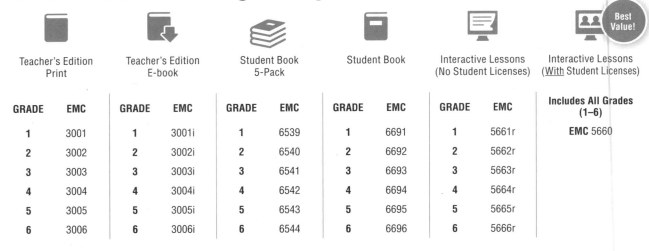

Teacher's Edition Print		Teacher's Edition E-book		Student Book 5-Pack		Student Book		Interactive Lessons (No Student Licenses)		Interactive Lessons (With Student Licenses)
GRADE	EMC	GRADE	EMC	GRADE	EMC	GRADE	EMC	GRADE	EMC	**Includes All Grades (1–6)**
1	3001	1	3001i	1	6539	1	6691	1	5661r	**EMC 5660**
2	3002	2	3002i	2	6540	2	6692	2	5662r	
3	3003	3	3003i	3	6541	3	6693	3	5663r	
4	3004	4	3004i	4	6542	4	6694	4	5664r	
5	3005	5	3005i	5	6543	5	6695	5	5665r	
6	3006	6	3006i	6	6544	6	6696	6	5666r	

Best Value!